ARDATH

KELLY'S
TOURIST & TRAVEL
BUREAU
ETAP
BEIRUT-LEBANON, HEAD OFFICE : FAKHRY BEY STREET.
ADRESSE TELEG. : KELLY'S Beirut.
PHONE : Office 20697 Home 23608

EUROPE → THE MIDDLE EAST
MEA Souvenir Route Map

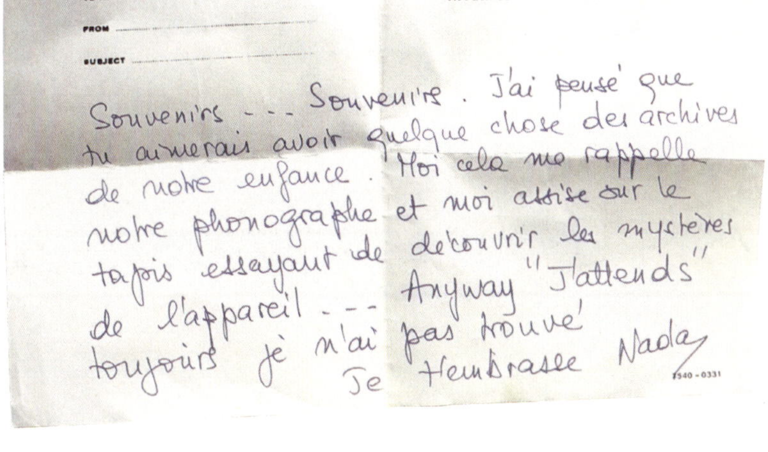

AMERICAN UNIVERSITY OF BEIRUT
INTER-OFFICE CORRESPONDENCE

TO
FROM
SUBJECT

Souvenirs --- Souvenirs. J'ai pensé que
tu aimerais avoir quelque chose des archives
de notre enfance. Moi cela me rappelle
notre phonographe et moi assise sur le
tapis essayant de découvrir les mystères
de l'appareil --- Anyway "J'attends"
toujours je n'ai pas trouvé
Je t'embrasse Nada

7540-0331

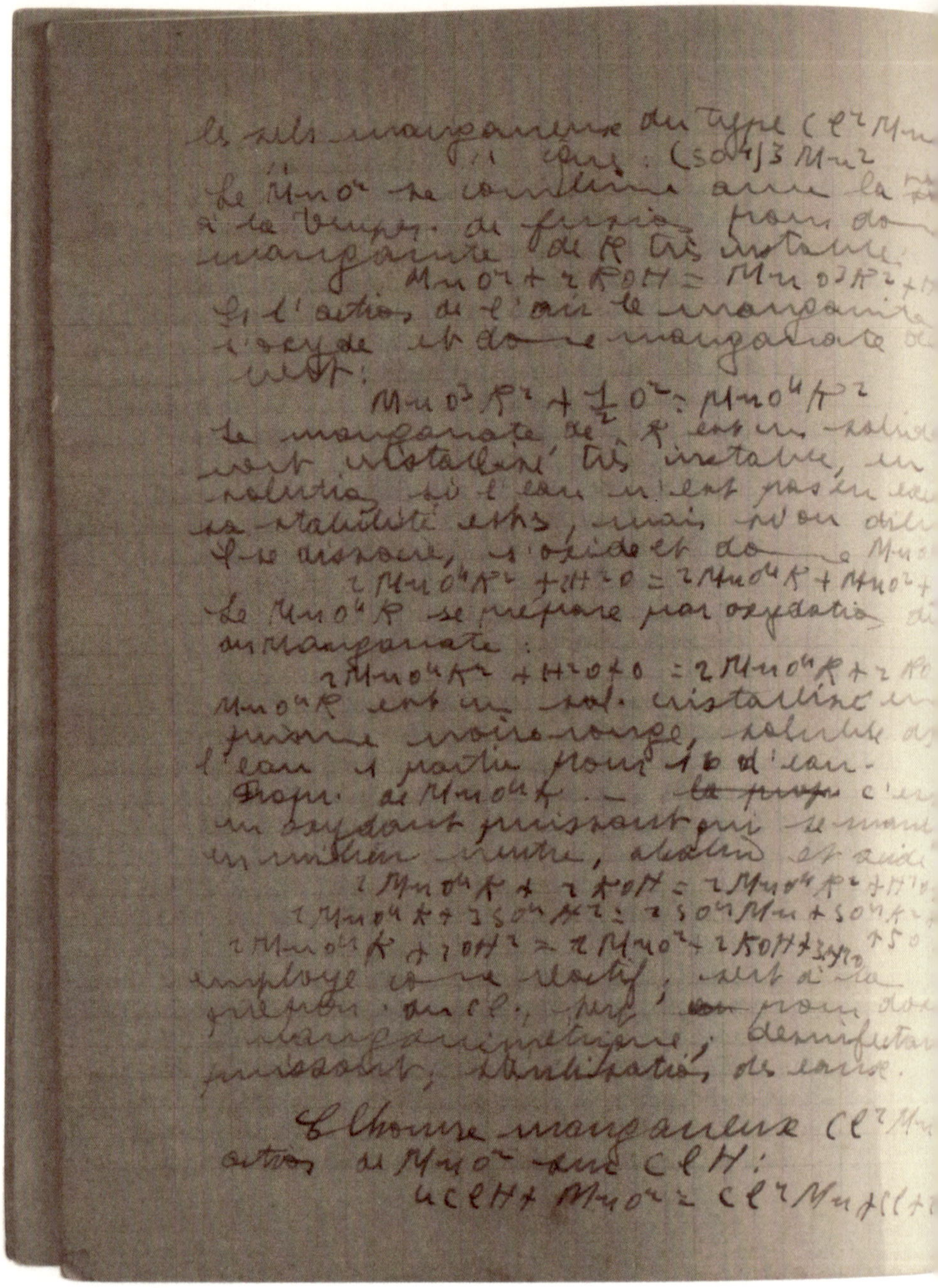

les sels manganeux du type Cl^2Mn
ou : $(SO^4)^3Mn^2$
Le MnO^2 se combine avec la potasse à la tempér. de fusion pour donner manganite de K très instable.

$$MnO^2 + 2KOH = MnO^3K^2 + H^2O$$

Si l'action de l'air le manganite s'oxyde et donne manganate vert :

$$MnO^3K^2 + \frac{1}{2}O^2 = MnO^4K^2$$

Le manganate de K est un solide vert cristallisé très instable, en solution si l'eau n'est pas en excès sa stabilité existe, mais si on dilue il se dissocie, s'oxide et donne MnO^4K

$$2MnO^4K^2 + 2H^2O = 2MnO^4K + MnO^2 + \ldots$$

Le MnO^4K se prépare par oxydation du manganate :

$$2MnO^4K^2 + H^2O + O = 2MnO^4K + 2KOH$$

MnO^4K est un sel cristallisé en prisme noire-rouge, soluble dans l'eau 1 partie pour 16 d'eau.
Propr. de MnO^4K. — ~~la propr.~~ c'est un oxydant puissant qui se manifeste en milieu neutre, alcalin et acide

$$2MnO^4K + 2KOH = 2MnO^4K^2 + H^2O + O$$

$$2MnO^4K + 3SO^4H^2 = 2SO^4Mn + SO^4K^2 + \ldots$$

$$2MnO^4K + 2OH^2 = 2MnO^2 + 2KOH + 3H^2O + 3O$$

employé comme réactif, sert à la préparation du Cl., prép. pour dosage manganimétrique, désinfectant puissant, stérilisation des eaux.

Chlorure manganeux Cl^2Mn
action de MnO^2 sur ClH :

$$4ClH + MnO^2 = Cl^2Mn + Cl^2 + \ldots$$

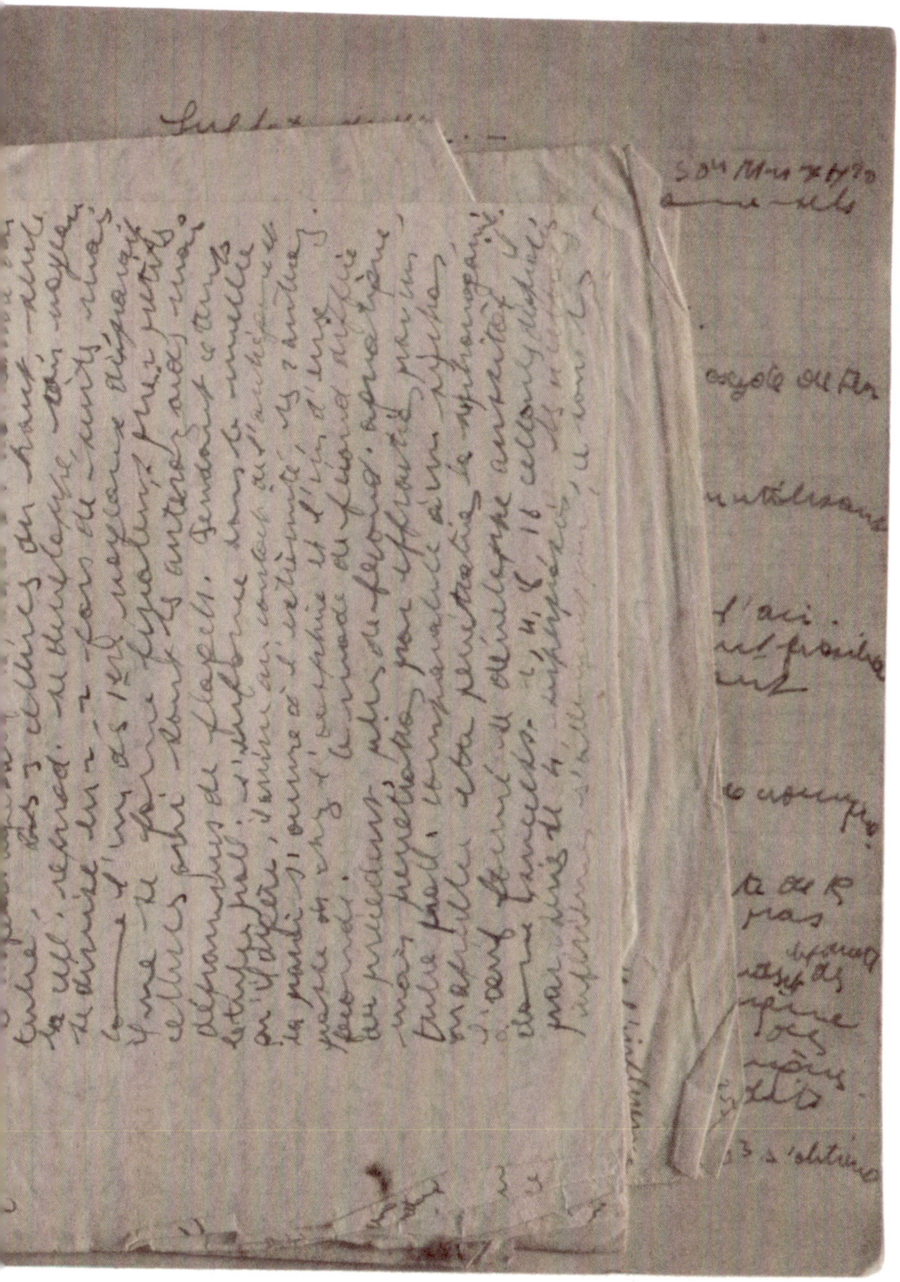

ramassage

GREGORY BUCHAKJIAN

ABANDONED DWELLINGS

A HISTORY OF BEIRUT

To Annie

"So it told us that our city was dying – dying if not already dead – but also that we had even forgotten it ever existed, even forgotten that we had forgotten, lost as we were in our struggle with meaningless words, like Nostalgia, Memory, Future, Centre, or Reconstruction."

Pierre Hage-Boutros

TABLE OF CONTENTS

Above and following pages: Gregory Buchakjian and Valérie Cachard, Abandoned Dwellings – Archives, 2017. Performance filmed by Malek Hosni.

FOREWORD

They are still standing in spite of everything. And their dignity moves us. Imbued with stories, they hold us in thrall. While they weave their web, we absorb what has gone before us and what remains to be lived in order to be able to approach them, place them and make them ours, in the space of what we call a visit.

Gregory and I wandered through Beirut for months. We measured it against our dreams. Vast, pungent and generous, it seemed nevertheless to be receding and fading from sight. Before it disappears, we had to cross the frontier. Make its calcified buildings quiver and then come back to life, nuance their silence. Create a cartography dedicated solely to them.

One autumn afternoon, in one of these buildings, Gregory asked me to walk in front of his camera lens. He doesn't like the word "pose." That day, he had forgotten his tripod. That felicitous lapse allowed me to lose myself among the various floors, to absorb the increasingly blue and vast horizon afforded me by all the paneless windows. This lapse allowed for strolling, contamination, gnawing emotions. This place had given up. That is what would continually bring us back to it and others like it. Now, it was nothing but itself. It did not lie, we could not pretend. When Gregory came back, I already knew that I had become an integral part of this story. That I also wanted to fall into a hole. Of memory. That I wanted to disinter. With my hands.

For six years, we crouched and kneeled between the walls of those buildings to excavate, sometimes collect, clean up and classify unlikely treasures. Gregory often contorted himself, making himself small in order to get to them. Which is hard to imagine, given how tall he is. He paid homage to them through a thesis, photographic projects, articles and now this book.

These houses, apartments and gardens are open-air archives. Exploring them has made us more human, more alive, more aware of our state of semi-darkness. We are film–beings covered in a fine layer of dust.

Valérie Cachard

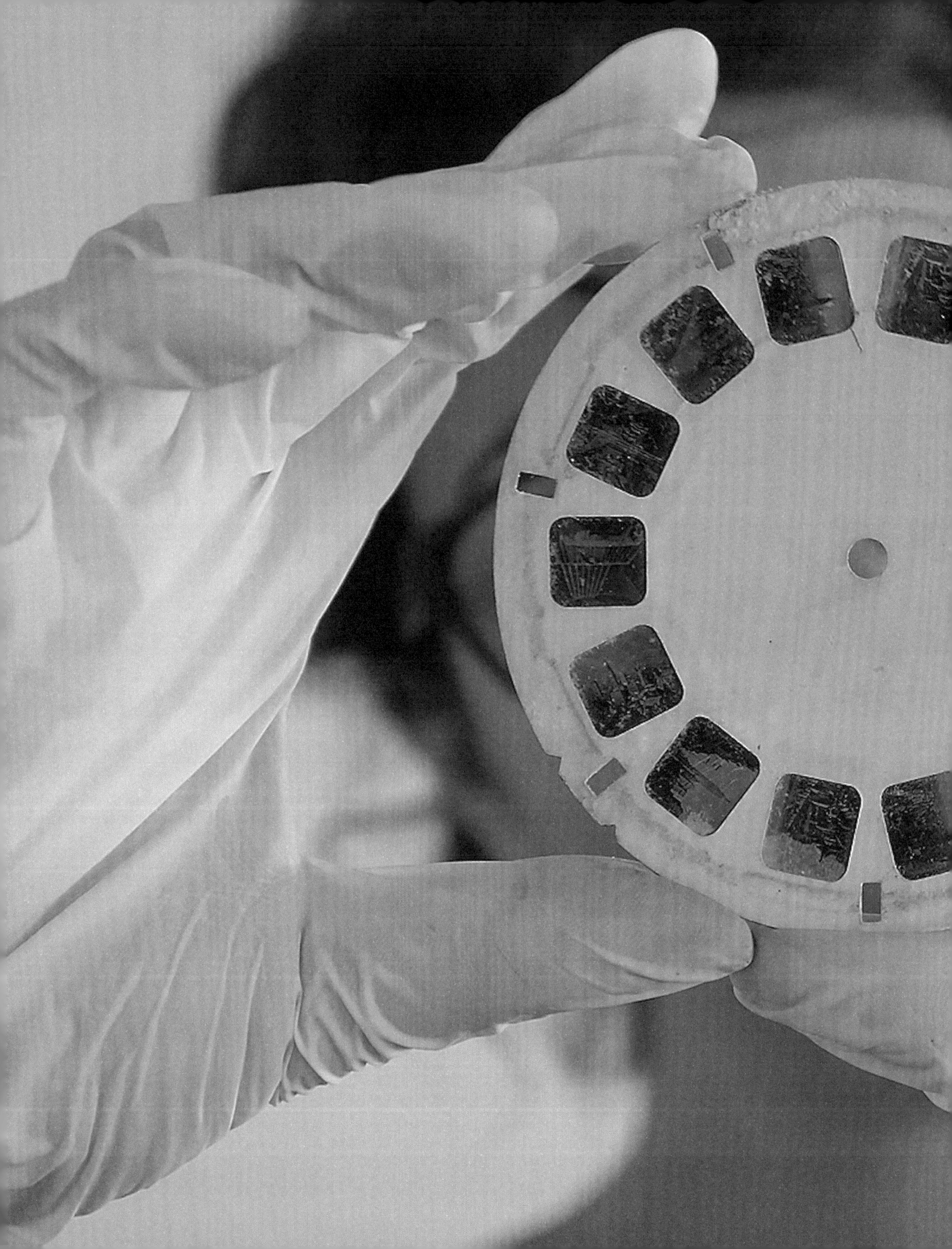

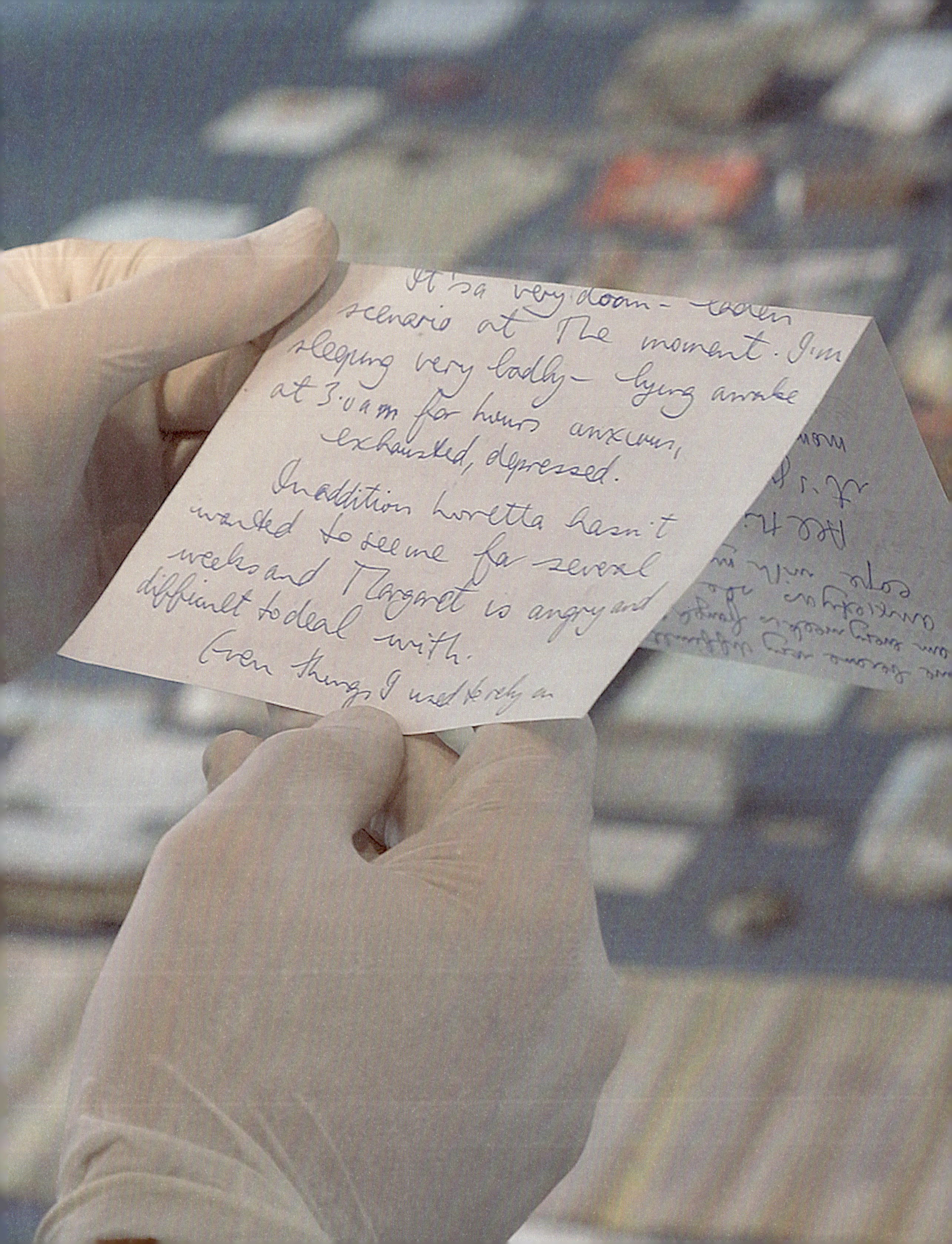
It's a very doom-laden
scenario at the moment. I'm
sleeping very badly – lying awake
at 3.00am for hours anxious,
exhausted, depressed.
In addition Loretta hasn't
wanted to see me for several
weeks and Margaret is angry and
difficult to deal with.

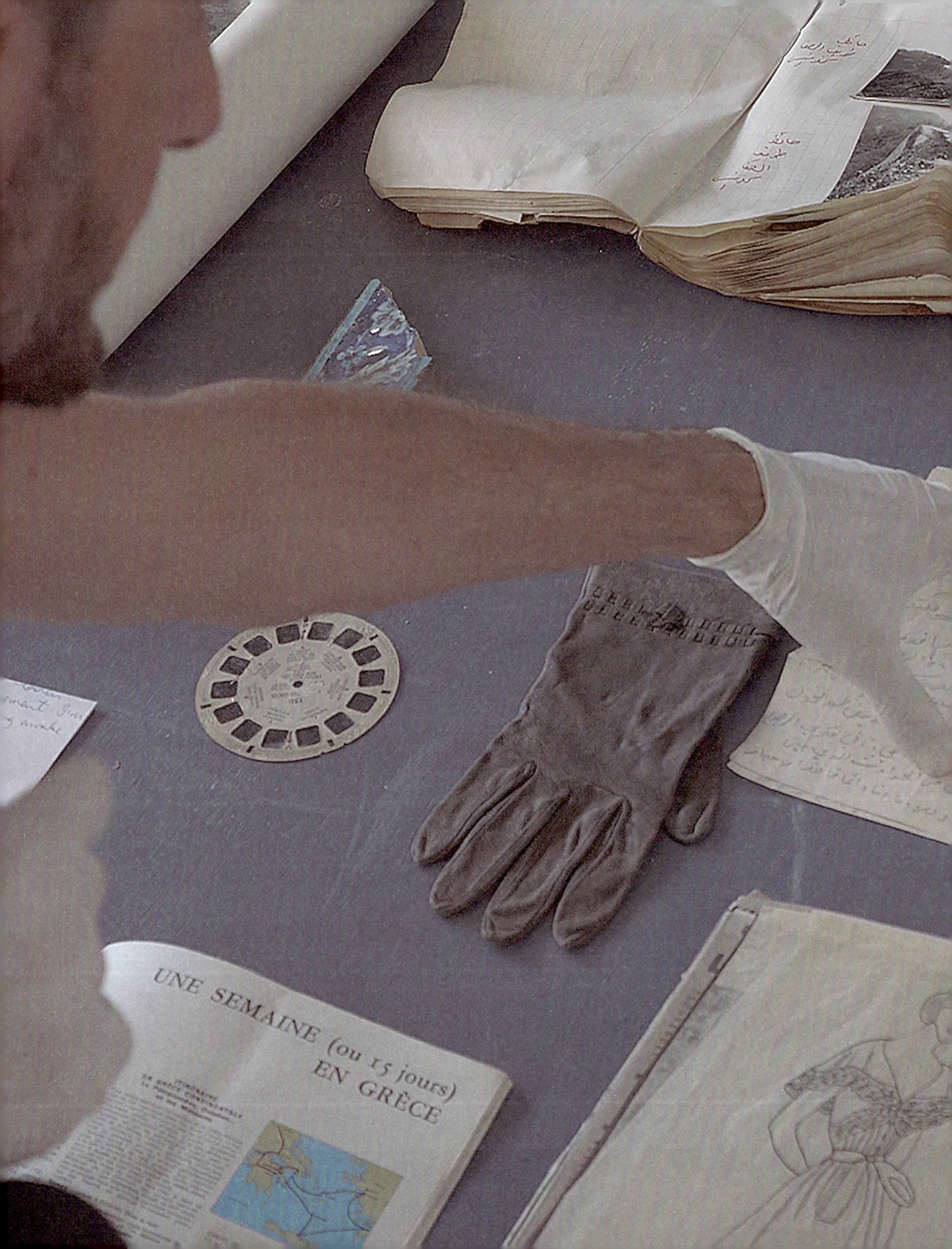
UNE SEMAINE (ou 15 jours)
EN GRÈCE

hôtels
votre horoscope
1980

En exclusivité:

is Buchakjian

Contre vos douleurs
IONOPLAST
الحياة
الحواجز الليلية

TOURING
LIBAN
UNE NOUVELLE PRÉSIDENTE
MEA

UNDERSTANDING DEVASTATION AND ABANDONMENT IN AN EARLY 21st CENTURY CITY

Over the past 150 years, Beirut has witnessed a cycle of unbridled growth, war, economic and social crises and migratory movements. It is in this city with a constantly growing population, this city ceaselessly destroyed and rebuilt, broken and regenerated, that, in 2009, I began taking photographs – creating tableaux of abandoned interiors with the subjects surrounded by sagging furniture and mounds of rubbish. In the months that followed, I began to make a provisional inventory of these crumbling edifices, as well as to gather documents found in situ, following Michel Foucault's principle that archaeology speaks of "discontinuities, ruptures, gaps and entirely new forms of positivity and of sudden redistributions."[1]

1 Foucault, Michel, *The Archaeology of Knowledge and The Discourse on Language*, translated by A. M. Sheridan Smith, New York, Pantheon Books, 1972, p. 169.

In 2012, this mass of documents provided the framework for an Art History doctoral thesis under the supervision of Jean-Yves Andrieux, an expert on heritage and its identity. The dissertation sets out to examine the use to which these places have been put and the transformations they have undergone. Three chapters are devoted to appropriations for the purposes of war. Chapter One deals with the Battle of the Hotels and how fighting forces exploited the architectural advantages of luxury establishments to convert them into strongholds. Chapter Two explores the demarcation line that divided the city in two for fifteen years, while Chapter Three focuses on barracks and places where people were imprisoned and tortured. And finally, Chapter Four addresses the many other re-appropriations, including the informal developments that are often the result of the migratory movements resulting from hostilities.

Both the thesis and the artistic project are based on descriptions and storytelling. As well as considering the evidence offered by these *lieux de mémoire* (sites of memory), conflict and history, we go on to examine the testimonies of people from different sectors of society – residents, refugees, war veterans, journalists, researchers and artists. This miscellany of indicators – vestiges, recollections and testimonies – together form a rhizome. They have no hierarchy, nor are they in any predetermined order. The permutations are infinite and can activate every possible or imaginable cross-fertilisation. The model for this multiplicity of representations is Aby Warburg's *Mnemosyne Atlas*. This consists of wooden panels covered in black cloth on which the art historian made constantly changing associations between reproductions of works of art. Like a kaleidoscope, this device of many parts enabled spectators to experience for themselves the polarities that riddle culture and thought. Its very form can be seen as a refutation of any attempt to constitute an overview or to search for definitive meaning.[2]

The following pages set out to unravel the knots in the process by which this project developed.

FIG.1 *Antoine-Alphonse Montfort, Khan near Beirut, 1837. Watercolor on paper, 27 × 38 cm.*

2 Didi-Huberman, Georges, *L'image survivante. Histoire de l'art et temps des fantômes selon Aby Warburg*, Paris, Éditions de Minuit, 2002, pp. 452–505 (Paradoxe).

THE PROCESS, THE ENCOUNTERS

When war broke out in 1975, I was four years old. I had never known the Lebanon "of before" the subject of nostalgic stories and richly coloured postcards. One of my earliest memories is of seeing the blackened shell of the Holiday Inn. When there was a lull, my family would go to Saint George's Beach, from where we had an uninterrupted view of the burned-out hotels. Not far from there, in the little bay near the Normandy Hotel, there was an ever-growing garbage dump, but this did not deter bathers from jumping into the water. In a film, which has since disappeared, my sister, Karina, could be seen water-skiing amid the debris. We could also see the harbour "on the other side." The harbour was my favourite crossing point from West to East Beirut, because it took you through the ghost town that the city centre had become (FIG.62). There was also the Ring, on which you drove like a bat out of hell to avoid being mowed down by snipers, and the National Museum, whose Egyptian temple-style façade was so riddled with bullet holes that, in my mother's words, it had "turned into a museum piece."

In 1993, while studying art history in Paris, I visited the exhibition *Beyrouth Centre-Ville* (*Beirut City Centre*) at the Palais de Tokyo. It was a revelation; all the more so because in the early 1990s, I was incapable of taking even the simplest shot of those awe-inspiring scenes of destruction. Ten years earlier, the kid that I was back then had taken photos of my neighbourhood, devastated by the Israeli invasion of 1982, and the city centre where my cousin Ariane Delacampagne used to take me (FIG.2).

FIG.2 *Gregory Buchakjian, Beirut City Centre, 1983. Photograph.*

In 1997, Pierre Hage-Boutros and Rana Haddad invited me to co-found a research workshop within the Lebanese Academy of fine Arts (ALBA), "a centre for research, experimentation and design, focusing on urban reality."[3] In 2000, the Barakat Building – a derelict apartment block that became a blockhouse – inspired the research workshop to devise an installation entitled *Machines Célibataires*, a title borrowed from a term coined by Marcel Duchamp (FIG.66). Also around that time, Patrick Kassardjian suggested we create Baron & Baron, a community of travellers.[4] Ruins were the chief feature of our tours, especially Palmyra, which can be appreciated at any time of day or night, as Volnay once did, having "advanced to the Valley of Sepulchres [. . .] from whence the eye commands the whole group of ruins and the immensity of the desert", he delighted in the clear sky, "the air calm and serene", and in the "profound silence."[5] One morning, just as the sun was rising, my companion fainted and fell into my arms at the foot of a tetrapylon. It was an excruciating but sublime moment, straight out of a painting from the Romantic period. That visit to the city of Zenobia would be the last (FIG.3).

During that same period, houses with red tiles, art deco villas and modernist apartment buildings were razed to the ground to make way for ostentatious tower blocks, creating a state of urban chaos and confirming Nadia Tueni's observation that "Beirut is to architecture what automatic

3 "Atelier de Recherche ALBA. Démarche et Intervenants", Atelier de Recherche ALBA website, 2004.
4 NICOLAZZI, ANTHONY, "Les voyages improbables de Baron et Baron", *Grands Reportages*, February 2005, p. 104.
5 VOLNEY, CONSTANTIN-FRANÇOIS, *A New Translation of Volney's Ruins*, New York, Garland Publishing, 1979, p. 3.

FIG.3 *Théodore Frère, Ruins of Palmyra, 1880. Oil on canvas, 104 × 174 cm.*

writing was to literature."[6] Confronted by such carnage, internet users shared images of a very loosely determined "past", extending from 1800 to 1975. With Facebook groups ranging from Pure Nostalgia, instigated by Imad Kozem, to Save Beirut Heritage, an organisation attempting to safeguard whatever was possible, social networks became both history book and living geography. Added to the visual documents were expert commentaries from people trying to find the exact location of a particular palm tree, or a specific section of the city wall. The historian May Davie and her geographer husband, Michael Davie, Gabriel Daher, a banker turned art connoisseur, Lea Pavlikevitch, descended from a family of hoteliers and Camille Tarazi, custodian of the memory of a family famous for producing oriental furniture and interiors, came together to form a community passionate about the city. Each member pursued their own particular interest: for Antoine Atallah, it was cartography, for Marc Chelhot, postcards and for Lyna Yared, the city seen through the lens of the cine camera. Kheireddine el-Ahdab focused on television coverage of the war, and Lina Ezzedine on street names. For Fadi Ghazzaoui, it was the Ras el-Nabeh neighbourhood and for Naji Assi, the Badaro district, while Georges Boustany published on Facebook each day excerpts from newspaper articles from the same date forty years earlier.

At the end of 2009, Philippe Acar took me to see the ruins of his grandparents' house. He told me how, as the bombs fell, his uncle "threw carpets and silverware out of the window, straight onto a truck." A few days later, I met Karen Klink, an illustrator based in Barcelona where she lived in an illegal squat. Her experience inspired me to invite her to go with me to the ruined building. On a freezing-cold New Year's Eve, she wandered in front of my camera lens, clad in a red dress that a fallen princess might have worn. (PL.1). From that day on, the house and others like it haunted me. To enter derelict spaces and take photographs became a need which nothing else could assuage.

A HISTORY OF DEVASTATION AND THE DEVASTATION OF HISTORY

This obsession that had not yet become a project had encountered a sizeable problem. The sheer quantity of films, writings, articles and conference papers whose titles or content included the words "Beirut" and "ruin(s)" was dizzying. Fifteen years earlier, François Cheval had already pointed out that "Beirut is no longer a subject. The litany of photographers who have 'shot it' embraces 'heroic photojournalists' and 'committed artists' – it is more than unbearable."[7] Whatever direction my work might take, if it was to be consistent and make sense, it had to take into account what had already been and continued to be done.

Ruins appear in one of the first photographic images of Lebanon, namely Joseph Philibert Girault de Prangey's

FIG4 *Joseph Philibert Girault de Prangey, "Baalbec. P. temple. Int. Porte", 1842-1844. Photograph directly laid on silver-plated copper [daguerreotype], 8 × 9.5 cm.*

6 Tuéni, Nadia, "Au-delà du regard", in *La Prose, œuvres complètes*, Beirut, Dar an-Nahar, 1986, p. 243.
7 Cheval, François, "Les Heures Immobiles - Saida - Bab El-Saray - Photographies Anciennes du Moyen-Orient + Documents de Jean-Luc Moulène", Musée Nicéphore Niepce, Chalon-sur-Saône, 2002.

FIG.5 *Dr Eugène Cottard, Remains of the fountain at the bazaar, 1919. Stereograph transparency, 10.5 × 4.5 cm.*

portico of the Temple of Bacchus at Baalbek, taken between 1842 and 1844 (FIG.4). A few years earlier, on 17 April 1837, Antoine-Alphonse Montfort (FIG.1), who was spending two months in Beirut,[8] executed two watercolours of a "tall ruined structure surrounding a large tree."[9] From then onwards, the majority of paintings, lithographs, watercolours and photographs of Beirut's ruins would represent two scenarios: war, in particular bombardments by the British and Italian fleets, in 1840 and 1912 respectively, and the demolition of old Beirut in readiness for modernisation at the beginning of the 20th century. In 1911, Eugène Cottard, a doctor who also practised amateur glass-plate stereography, roamed the city and photographed Sahat al-Khoubz – Bread Square "recognisable by the fountain surmounted by a wrought-iron gazebo standing in the centre."[10] In 1919, he was back on the scene, leaving behind him the image of "souks ripped apart and the fountain and a few other fragments still standing, but which would in their turn succumb, so as to make way for the French scheme for the Étoile quarter"[11] (FIG.5). More than half a century later, Maroun Bagdadi filmed *Bayrout ya Bayrout* (*Beirut oh Beirut*) in a city where tensions were about to explode: it was 1975, and we were on the eve of war. In a shot taken during the construction of Boulevard Salim Salam, Bagdadi shows a cross-section of a building stripped of its façade, which Kamal, played by Ezzat al-Alayli, dressed in a beige suit has the temerity to explore (FIG.6). *Beirut oh Beirut* condemns the violence of a liberal economy as it destroys the urban and social fabric, as did Gordon Matta Clark's *Anarchitecture* project of that same period.

After the "two-year war" of 1975–6, Beirut's citizens contemplated their ravaged city. Volker Schlöndorff came to film *Circle of Deceit* – a work of fiction set against the backdrop of a real war, with real militiamen and real explosives. Fouad Elkoury, then a stills photographer, spoke of his indignation at the way the film-maker had sought out scenes of devastation to fulfil the needs of cinema. Subsequently, film-makers such as Bagdadi, Borhane Alaouieh and Jocelyne Saab followed the

FIG.6 Bayrout ya Bayrout, *film by Maroun Bagdadi, 1975. [Ezzat el-Alayli in a building being demolished for the construction of Selim Salam avenue].*

8 DUCHARD, RENÉ, "Le peintre Montfort en Syrie (1837–1838)", *Syria* I, 1920, pp. 58–71.
9 AGÉMIAN, SYLVIA, et AL., *Regards sur Beyrouth. 160 ans d'images 1800–1960*, Beirut, Sursock Museum, 2013, p. 378 (Cat. no. 290–1).
10 DAVIE, MAY, "Une vieille ville en métamorphose" in *Traversées photographiques. Le journal du Docteur Cottard*, Beirut, Arab Image Foundation, 2017, pp. 104–48.
11 *Ibid.*

FIG.7 *Martin Giesen, Temporel, 1977. Etching, 1st state, 48 × 54 cm.*

FIG.8 *Fouad Elkoury, The Ganges, Civil War series, 1977. Photograph. [The shore in Ain el-Mreisseh]*

pattern set by Roberto Rossellini's *Germany Year Zero* in depicting the horrors of war, in accordance with which their "traumatic cartography of the city of Beirut creates a precarious filmic and geographic space, strewn with 'suspended spaces' or 'ruins in waiting'."[12] Also in the late 1970s, Martin Giesen attracted attention with his lithographs and watercolours, depicting a landscape torn between disaster and normality (FIG.7).[13] In 1977, he made an etching of a derelict house on the Ain el-Mreisseh waterfront. The building was to have been pulled down to clear the way for the extension of the seafront promenade. The works were interrupted by the war and the house gained a two-year reprieve before it was demolished. Soon afterwards, Fouad Elkoury took a photo of bathers at the same spot, framed by railings resting on the ground, the final remains of the building (FIG.8). In autumn 2016, as the photographer and I were going through his archive of images of Lebanon, I came across this previously unpublished slide, but did not recognise the location. In the ensuing book, entitled *Passing Time*, I point out that "in an other-worldly atmosphere, two groups of people are busying themselves around two metal structures, resembling balcony railings, whose function remains mysterious."[14] It was only when I hung a print of this next to the Giesen etching on my sitting-room wall, that my mother, Annie, who grew up in Ain el-Mreisseh, identified both images as being shot in the same location.

The years went by and Elkoury observed that "each battle left destruction in its wake, the life of many neighbourhoods, progressively emptied of their inhabitants, was dying before my eyes and all that remained were buildings, looted and eaten away by shell and bullet holes, bearing witness to a time almost impossible to remember."[15] He continued to photograph these relics of the past. At the end of 1982, Giesen took advantage of the lull to go to the city centre and draw "buildings that look as though they are suffering from smallpox, having withstood the worst of the violence" (FIG.9).[16] There, he might have bumped into Sophie Ristelhueber who had come to work on *Beirut: Photographs*. For her, this was not only about "making an inventory of the ruins, but rather to attempt to use them as a means of grasping the events that caused them."[17] At the same time, as David Campany stresses, she stripped the shots "of almost all information that makes it possible to contextualise them"[18] (FIG.56).

12 Sayegh, Ghada, "Images d'après : l'espace-temps de la guerre dans le cinéma au Liban, du 'nouveau cinéma libanais' (1975) aux pratiques artistiques contemporaines (de 1990 à nos jours)", doctoral thesis, Paris Ouest Nanterre la Défense, 2013, p. 31.
13 Munro, John, *Giesen's Lebanon*, Beirut, The Rihani House, 1984, p. 13.
14 Buchakjian, Gregory, "Selecting, sorting, looking: an archaeology of Fouad Elkoury's photographic career", in *Passing Time*, Beirut, Kaph Books, 2017, p. 230.
15 Elkoury, Fouad, *La Sagesse du Photographe*, Sagesse d'un métier, Le Vesinet, L'œil neuf éditions, 2004, p. 26.
16 Khoury, Hala, "Pour Martin Giesen, le centre-ville est le paradis des peintres", *L'Orient-Le Jour*, 4 November 1982, p. 4.
17 Polledri, Claudia, "Photographier la ville, penser l'histoire : Beyrouth dans la représentation photographique artistique contemporaine", doctoral thesis, University of Montreal, 2015, pp. 179-83.
18 Campany, David, *Dust. Histoires de poussière d'après Man Ray et Marcel Duchamp*, Paris, Le Bal, MACK Books, 2015, p. 53.

FIG.9 *Martin Giesen, Les Divorcés : Cinema Rivoli, 1982. Watercolor on paper, 61 × 44 cm.*

FIG.10 *Paola Yacoub, Summer 88, 1988. Photograph.*

Five years later, along the Green Line, Paola Yacoub, accomplished "an implicit deviation from documentary photographic practice." Her seemingly dispassionate views of ruins and vegetation, in which sometimes people could be seen "were the result of fear and of the way in which fear clings on to these places" (FIG.10).[19] It is hard to imagine that during this same period, these ruins also provided the setting for action and sci-fi films, local versions of *Mad Max* and *Rambo* – Z-movies, whose locations would be mapped by Vartan Avakian.

In November 1991, Dominique Eddé set up *Beyrouth Centre-Ville/Beirut City Centre.* This photographic mission brought together Gabriele Basilico, René Burri, Raymond Depardon, Fouad Elkoury, Robert Frank and Josef Koudelka (FIG.11). It followed the initiatives organised in France by the Delegation for Planning and Regional Action (DATAR) in 1983 and 1989, the aim of which was to chart the transformation of the French landscape.[20] At the 1993

FIG.11 *Beyrouth Centre Ville / Beirut City Centre, book published by Dominique Eddé, 1991.*

19 Yacoub, Paola and Lasserre, Michel, "A Brief Journey towards Scepticism", in *Out of Beirut*, Oxford, JRP|Ringier, Modern Art Oxford, 2007, pp. 9–10.
20 Polledri, *op. cit.*, p. 209.

exhibition at the Palais de Tokyo, and in the book of the same name, edited by Robert Delpire, *Beyrouth Centre-Ville* revealed a land where time had stood still and, apart from the few rare appearances of human beings, the only signs of life were vegetation and water gushing forth. *Beyrouth Centre-Ville* took place one year after the end of hostilities and shortly before the beginning of the demolition and reconstruction of the city centre. This survey is comparable to the photographic coverage of the demolition of Paris in the 19th century when "the ruins revealed by the photographic image appeared to herald a glorious restoration" and were seen as "the search for a bygone age", as well as "evidence of the calamity and the symbol of a diachronic and historic link." [21]

Following on from *Beyrouth Centre-Ville*, artists and researchers turned their attention to the city, memory and history. From 1993 to 1995, Elkoury went every day to the vast construction site that the city centre had become. For *Traces of War*, he photographed the "crazy city", now home to a multitude of down-and-outs, and then the arrival of the excavators that destroyed the entire neighbourhood, transforming it into a wasteland. Joana Hadjithomas and Khalil Joreige compiled a body of photographs in *Fictions Urbaines*,[22] a book–object as misaligned and lopsided as the scenes it depicted. The spiral-bound pages were postcards held together by a strip which the reader was invited to cut, thereby dismantling and destroying this boxful of pictures of ruins and debris (FIG.12). Well aware that the annihilation of the city was inevitable, Bernard Khoury created *Evolving Scars*, a device that might have enabled the process to be rescheduled, thus avoiding "an instant shift of grave malady to an immediate recuperation"[23] (FIG.13). Through his writings and films, Jalal Toufic sought to "create a labyrinthine space in time where ghosts might appear. These beings are just as likely to be captured by the human memory – ruins stir up the past – as they are to emerge under psychoanalysis as returning figures, representing the reappearance of the repressed and of the person who has come back to haunt because they are not dead."[24] Beginning with *Phantom Beirut*, Ghassan Salhab "filmed solitary, disembodied, absent, amnesiac figures, with no past or future, moving in a transitional space, the threat of disaster past or still to come providing a precarious geographic and filmic setting, the texture of which hinges on disconnectedness."[25]

FIG.12 *Joana Hadjithomas and Khalil Joreige, Beyrouth : Fictions urbaines. Book, 1997.*

FIG.13 *Bernard Khoury, Evolving Scars, 1991. Design Studies.*

21 De Font-Réaulx, Dominique, "Photographier la catastrophe : enregistrement et mise en scène au XIXe siècle", in *Villes en ruine : images, mémoires, métamorphoses*, Paris, Hazan, Musée du Louvre, 2015, p. 268.

22 Hadjithomas, Joana and Joreige, Khalil, *Beyrouth: Fictions Urbaines*, Karl Bassil (ed.), Beirut, Mind the Gap Éditions, 1997.

23 Khoury, Bernard, *Bernard Khoury: Local Heroes*, Milan, Skira, 2015, pp. 42–3.

24 Tamraz, Nayla, "Pour une lecture de la ruine : Berytus de Rabee Jaber et Attempt 137 to Map the Drive de Jalal Toufic et Graziella Rizkallah Toufic", in *Littérature, art et monde contemporain. Récits, histoire, mémoire*, Beirut, Presses de l'Université Saint-Joseph, 2015, pp. 201–21.

25 Sayegh, Ghada, "Devant Les Ruines", *Hors Champ*, November 2017.

FIG.14 *Ziad Antar, Côte d'Azur Hotel, Jnah, built in 1973, Beirut Bereft series, 2007. Photograph.*

FIG.15 *Chaghig Arzoumanian, Asfurieh, Webster House, 2017. Photograph from On Fools and Lands.*

FIG.16 *Abed Al-Kadiri, The Story of the Rubber Tree, 2018. Painting in progress.*

In the 2000s, images of abandoned buildings are an occasional or constantly recurring theme in the photographs of Randa Mirza, Dalia Khamissy and Houda Kassatly, as well as in Maha Nasrallah's watercolours. Ziad Antar's *Beirut Bereft* created a series of half-finished concrete skeletons, which he saw as sculptural forms[26] (FIG.14). The new generation of artists set out not to eradicate the subject but to give it a new slant. When, in late 2010, Chaghig Arzoumanian heard that the Asfurieh – Beirut's psychiatric hospital closed down in 1975 – was to be demolished, she decided to appropriate it in her own imagination, a domain to which she alone would hold the key.[27] Like so many derelict sites, the Asfurieh, once a garden, had become a jungle (FIG.15). Rubber trees, which had survived and continued to flourish in deserted houses, are at the heart of Abed al-Kadiri's work. Starting at the home of his grandfather, he cast the rubber trees in the role of witnesses that remembered the families who had left (FIG.16).

In *Un Cercle Autour du Soleil* (A Circle Around the Sun), made one year before the war of 2006, Ali Cherri presents "the outward appearance of buildings, overpasses and main roads [that have] become the skeleton, the arteries and the skin of an organism that retains memories, musings and disembodied associations."[28] The film marked the beginning of an approach where the artist introduces a relationship between the human body and ruins and a parallel between the city and physical violence against people[29] (FIG.17).

FIG.17 *Ali Cherri, Un cercle autour du soleil, 2005. Video.*

26 ELDERTON, LOUISA, "Beirut // Magnifying the Imagination: An Interview with Ziad Antar", *Berlin Art Link*, 5 December 2016.
27 ARZOUMANIAN, CHAGHIG, *On Fools and Lands*, Beirut, 2017, p. xiii.
28 COTTER, SUZANNE, "Beirut Unbound", in *Out of Beirut*, Oxford, JRP|Ringier, Modern Art Oxford, 2007, p. 27.
29 *Un cercle autour du soleil by Ali Cherri*, Words on Works, Saradar Collection website, 2017.

Around the same time, Joanna Andraos and Caroline Tabet immortalised the last days of the house at 290 Rue du Liban, where the Tabet family once lived. As the two photographers see it, this is a case of "using a relatively structured scenic process to leave the ghosts of memory free to choose and record on film whatever they are willing to reveal about themselves"[30] (FIG.18). Karine Wehbe returns to the beach resorts built on Beirut's north shore between the 1960s and 80s, where she spent some of her teenage years. She poses next to an empty swimming pool or at the door of a closed-down nightclub. Following on from shots referring to the presence in the public imagination of bathers – especially women – among the ruins, specifically by the pool at St George's Beach,[31] she made with Nadim Tabet *Summer 91*, a film which juxtaposes memories of young love with "the blood of that man found dead on the beach" (FIG.19).

FIG.19 *Karine Wehbé, Tabarja Beach 1 / The pool, 2009. Photograph.*

FIG.18 *Engram (Caroline Tabet and Joanna Andraos), 290 Rue du Liban 09, 2006. Photograph.*

Having acknowledged this rich history of ruins, I travelled around the country in search of abandoned spots. Like Martí Llorens, I was in a frantic race against the demolition workers. Armed with a pinhole camera, Llorens documented the disappearance of neighbourhoods on the site of which Barcelona's Olympic village was to be built. So assiduous was he that the demolition crews "noticed the photographer and even waited until he had found the ideal spot for his tripod and camera."[32] I never encountered such support but was constantly in fear of ending up like Richard Nickel, whose "death in 1972, crushed in the bricks and dust of the demolished Stock Exchange Building, has given him a martyr's mantle and given his powerful architectural photography a sorrowful shadow."[33] His Piranesian images of the proscenium of Louis Sullivan's Garrick Theater as it was razed to the ground was a major contribution to the campaign for the preservation of Chicago.[34] Here, people who became aware of my work urged me to "save what can be saved." I told them there was nothing I could do in the face of property developers and corruption, but, by taking photographs, I was at least contributing to keeping a memory alive. Photography would serve on two levels – as documentation and to create tableaux.

30 Medawar, Alexandre, "290 rue du Liban", in *290 rue du Liban*, Beirut, Engram, 2010, pp. 6–7.

31 Parry-Davies, Ella, "Towards Theatricality", in *Stop Here for Happy Holidays. An Investigation into the Beach Resorts of the North Littoral in Lebanon*, Beirut, 2017, pp. 22–3.

32 Fontcuberta, Joan, *Le baiser de Judas. Photographie et vérité*, Arles, Actes Sud, 2005, p. 96.

33 Kogan, Rick, "A Poet's Lens", *Chicago Tribune*, 15 October 2006.

34 Hild, Theodore W., "The Demolition of the Garrick Theater and the Birth of the Preservation Movement in Chicago", *Illinois Historical Journal* 88, no. 2, summer 1995, pp. 79–100.

THE UTOPIAN INVENTORY

Between 2009 and 2016 I took tens of thousands of reconnaissance photographs documenting each edifice and its particularities. These were classified by district, sector and location. A second, thematic classification made it possible to categorise them based on their typology, architectural features, décor and furniture. There were 180 headings, including "Courtyard", "Crenellations", "Façade with three arches" and "Façade with gallery." It was essential to visit the inside of a building and I was prepared to do whatever it took – legal or otherwise – to achieve this end. This might mean asking permission, stepping through an open door, scaling a wall, scrambling up a tree, slithering through a hole or finding a secret passage. In the space of six years, I surveyed 744 Beirut properties and visited 138 of them.

The approach was intended to be systematic, the objective being to catalogue all, or at least most, of the samples collected. The first restriction was to limit the geographical scope to Beirut municipality, although this was not an obvious choice, the city having once consisted of "both the heart and suburbs" and "Greater Beirut", and "divided in half."[35] The second restriction concerned the type of structures. All sorts of edifices had been left abandoned: offices, industrial and leisure facilities, as well as public amenities and administrative buildings. Here, the focus was on residential properties – individual houses, apartment blocks and hotels – places that most represented human life. The third restriction concerned the timeframe, between the 19th century, when the transformation of Beirut began, and the 21st, which witnessed the 2006 war and the Syrian conflict, and was also the period during which I was studying the area. Here, it should be pointed out that as opposed to ruins resulting from war damage, many more were casualties of recent activity – for example, plots kept on hold while investors await "the right moment" for demolition. This speculative practice was already commonplace in pre-war Beirut, dating back to Augustus's Rome where, amid concern about downward slides in the property market,[36] "new buyers pulled down houses they had purchased, one after the other, in order to build others in their place."[37]

The buildings investigated and photographed were entered into a database. Each entry included the following information: address (district, street and number of the property, names of owners, tenants and occupants, when known); description (number of storeys, construction date); state of preservation; dates of first and most recent visit. However well structured records might be, there is something unrealistic about the desire to categorise. How to study 32,599 plots occupying 67 km^2 of Beirut? The catalogue would be as quixotic as Borges' imaginary cartographic exercise, in which "the map of a single Province occupied the entirety of a City, and the map of the Empire, the entirety of a Province."[38] Far from being frozen in time, the built environment is in a constant state of flux.

The database in no way professes to be a *catalogue raisonné*, but a survey conducted within a specific timeframe. The 744 buildings listed did not all exist in their dilapidated state at the same time. Hence the need to raise a second point concerning the date of the most recent visit and the state of preservation recorded on that day. These indications lend intellectual integrity to a database that makes no secret of its limitations. Another restriction relates to buildings that no longer existed when the project began. If the idea of listing *what was there* was not unrealistic enough, any attempt to create a retrospective record would be utter madness. Even if it had been possible to find traces of all the missing buildings, how far back would the search have to go? As far as the post-1990 reconstruction? To the outbreak of war in 1975? Or the turn of the 20th century? Faced with such a dilemma, how to incorporate important buildings that could no longer be investigated because they had been renovated (such as the Résidence des Pins or the Phoenicia Hotel) or demolished (such as the Hilton or the Normandy hotels)? Another crazy idea would be to create a system capable of measuring the age of a building and showing periods of use and disuse.

35 Davie, Michael F., "Quelles limites géographiques pour Beyrouth ?" in *Beyrouth : Construire l'avenir, reconstruire le passé ? Proceedings of the colloquium organised by the 'Urban Research Institute in April 1992*, Beirut, Urban Research Institute reports, 1995, p. 31.

36 Papini, Massimiliano, "Construire du neuf, conserver l'ancien : les destructions dans la Rome antique", in *Villes en ruine : images, mémoires, métamorphoses*, Paris, Hazan, Musée du Louvre, 2015, pp. 150–67.

37 Strabo, quoted by Papini, op. cit. p. 156.

38 Borges, Jorge-Luis, *Collected Fictions*, translated by Andrew Hurley, London/New York, Penguin Publishing Group, 1999 p. 326.

Examples

	Use	Disuse
Dimitri Tarazi house	90 years	70 years
Résidence des Pins	67 + 15 years	15 years
Holiday Inn Hotel	2 years	40 years

The information on the database is supported by two image libraries. The first contains my reconnaissance photos. The second consists of photographs, paintings, drawings, prints and screenshots of television programmes and films. These visuals, gleaned from a variety of places, are filed geographically, so that it is possible to visualise a particular neighbourhood or building at different moments in its history. To date, this library holds nearly six thousand documents.

ORAL STORIES, WRITTEN STORIES

From the outset, walking around the city led to some unexpected encounters – with residents, passers-by, partisans, police officers and security guards, each with subjective and unverifiable stories, which together amounted to a fascinating collection of tales of the city. When Camille Tarazi and I strolled through a working-class neighbourhood looking as if we had stepped out of the pages of Proust, it was not surprising that people directed us to the most spectacular ruins, which, according to Raed Charaf, "the bourgeois would appreciate" where an *abadaye* – tough guy – broke down the door blocking the entrance to allow these visitors to satisfy their curiosity. To quote Guy Debord, "In the 'possible rendezvous'. . . the element of exploration is minimal in comparison with that of behavioural disorientation."[39] We could have been redirected by advice such as, "Don't look here, look there," and continued our quest following instructions like, "Turn right, then turn left until you get to the police station. Then turn right and keep going for 200 metres." These often vague instructions were more likely to make us lose our bearings than help us find our way; our exploration drifted off course, making precise mapping even more impossible.

As the doctoral thesis progressed, more people were directly approached to give their testimony. War veterans, squatters and residents of sensitive areas told their stories. At the risk of being misleading, as they spoke to an ashen Buchakjian, the veterans emphasised the savagery of their deeds – executing one of their own men for insubordination or beheading enemies as they slept. Their statements were supplemented by others published in newspapers, books and television broadcasts. Going back as far as the 19th century and mostly covering wars and the post-war periods, all these material sources were as precious as they were contradictory. The process of "finding out what happened" ran up against an array of setbacks and variations. One such example is the history of the Battle of the Hotels. Motivated by a desire to describe how these lavish icons of the hospitality industry were put to military use, the investigation took all sorts of twists and turns. I found myself unravelling accounts, the variations in which were often down to journalists, and even combatants, being ill-informed about events. Press reports, liberally cited in my thesis, are a valuable source of information and personal experience.

With all these different witnesses, I was not only the researcher but also the subject, as were all the artists and scholars who had lived in Beirut. I was just as subjective and just as fallible. One day, I was telling friends how, as a child, I had seen Julio Iglesias singing "*Une nuit de carnaval*" at St George's Beach. He was standing on the prow of a yacht, surrounded by swimsuit beauties, with an audience of bathers and a backdrop of bombed-out hotels. My friends thought I was imagining it, influenced by the never-ending media presence of bathers and the incongruous glamour they provided during the most dramatic period in our nation's history (FIG.30). One month later, completely by chance, Alfred Tarazi published on social media proof that my story was true – a photo from *Monday-Morning* magazine, showing Iglesias with my sister, Karina Buchakjian. As we shall see later, archives uncovered amid the ruins produce equally outlandish

39 DEBORD, GUY, "Theory of the Dérive", *Les Lèvres nues*, no. 9 (December 1956), pp. 10-13, translated by Ken Knabb.

stories. Furthermore, although they are classified as fiction, the novels of Charif Majdalani and Oliver Rohe, and the films of Maroun Bagdadi, Jocelyne Saab and Borhane Alaouieh, constitute a mine of information about the history of the city and its inhabitants. As Nayla Tamraz writes of Elias Khoury: "It [the novel] focuses on deconstructing the prevailing discourses so as to rely more heavily on fragmented storytelling."[40]

TABLEAUX AND PERFORMATIVE RE-ENACTMENTS

FIG.20 *Hamasat, film by Maroun Bagdadi, 1980. [Nadia Tueni in the ruins of Beirut city center].*

At the same time as I was taking reconnaissance photos and following my visit to the Acar family home with Karen Klink, another kind of exercise was taking shape, the aim of which would be to create tableaux, rather than produce purely documentary evidence. It was all about scenes in which a human, female presence appeared in a ruined interior. This was the only part of the project focusing on abandoned homes that would continue on a regular basis during the six years' research and would go on to raise the greatest number of questions. This intuitive approach, which owed much to that adopted by Joana Andraos and Caroline Tabet – although they were simultaneously photographers and models – was inspired by scenes from Lebanese cinema. Characters wandering through the streets of the ghost city centre was a recurring theme in many films made during the war, revealing to what extent "the body of Beirut mirrors the bodies of its inhabitants."[41] A presence that has never ceased to haunt me is that of the poet Nadia Tueni in *Hamasat* (*Whispers*). Maroun Bagdadi's documentary, filmed in 1980, tells of the lives and records the testimonies of people living in a country torn between war and hope. The film opens with Tueni who, accompanied by a photographer, picks her way through the ruins of the city towards the seashore, reciting a litany: (FIG.20)

> *Beirut has been reduced to ruins. With time, ruins become beautiful. But I will never get used to it. Maybe Beirut was ugly. But it was my city. Maybe it was a bad place. But it was my city. In the course of history, many cities have been destroyed. That makes me sad, but not as sad as I am about my city.*[42]

Hamasat was not released until the 2000s, although Nadia Tueni died in 1983. Her image on film and her recorded voice echo Rebecca Schneider's theory that performance can centre on what is left, rather than what has been lost. Despite the fact that the body is doomed to die, from this point of view it can still be considered as "an archive and host to a collective memory."[43] It was with this idea in mind that I created photographic tableaux in abandoned houses where each human presence was a re-enactment of Nadia Tueni's performance. It was not a matter of reproducing or imitating, but of letting each person perform as dictated by their body, their sensibility, their feelings and their interaction with space.

Throughout the history of art, there have been numerous examples of the human presence in ruins, from Hubert Robert's Roman washerwomen to Francesca Woodman's fleeting images of nude figures against peeling walls. In his analysis of Renaissance painting, Aby Warburg identified *Ninfa* as "sylphlike but essentially incarnate, elusive but essentially tactile."[44] Warburg perceived this

40 TAMRAZ, NAYLA, "Le Roman Contemporain Libanais et la Guerre : Récit, Histoire, Mémoire", *Contemporary French and Francophone Studies* 18, no. 5, 20 October 2014, p. 467.
41 KHATIB, LINA, *Lebanese Cinema. Imagining the Civil War and Beyond*, Tauris World Cinema Series, London, I. B. Tauris, 2008, p. 61.
42 TUENI, NADIA, in BAGHDADI, MAROUN, *Hamasat* (*Whispers*), 1980.
43 SCHNEIDER, REBECCA, "Performance Remains", *Performance Research* 6, no. 2, 2001, pp. 100–8.
44 DIDI-HUBERMAN, GEORGES, "Aby Warburg et l'archive des intensités", *Études photographiques*, no. 10: La ressemblance du visible/Mémoire de l'art, November 2001, pp. 144–68.

"heroine" with the "ephemeral movement of her hair and her garments. . . as the misplaced indicator of the pathos of the images."[45] In our case, pathos refers to catastrophes past or yet to come. Writing in the early 2000s, Samir Kassir states: "The Arab world is the region where men, and to an even greater extent, women, have the least chance of thriving."[46] One year after the photographic series began, the region was plunged into a spiral of violence and horror, causing devastation and mass exodus. In the midst of this descent into hell, the presence of *Ninfa* in spaces previously used as barracks (PL.3, 9, 10, 13, 25, 34-36), military headquarters (PL.2), bunkers (PL.17), sniper positions (PL.14-16) and places where people were imprisoned and tortured (PL.7, 22, 39, 47-48), injected a dialectic between life, death and survival.

Between 2009 and 2016, forty women agreed to take part (ten having refused), five of whom undressed, two of them completely. This was significant, bearing in mind the risks involved, including harassment, accidents, bugs and filth. In November 2010, I asked Valérie Cachard to move inside an apartment block previously occupied by the Syrian army (PL.3). A few months earlier, she had written and performed *Matriochka*, about femininity and memory. Clad in her stage costume, she made her way across the dreary modernist spaces typical of Karol Schayer's architecture. She then went on to express her wish to write about photographs and arranged to discuss ideas with me. Ranging between art history and psychoanalysis, our conversations unearthed buried memories, fears and fantasies. She concluded that my obsession with persuading beautiful women to wander among the ruins was like the syndrome of the young archaeologist in Wilhelm Jensen's novella *Gradiva*, in which "the figure of the woman he loves unknowingly, is perceived as a real person: that is his delirium."[47] On 27 December 2013, Valérie Cachard created an installation of these pictures in the ghost town of Kolmanskop in Namibia. Built by diamond prospectors at the end of the 19th century, Kolmanskop slowly died and was overrun by the desert sand. Shot by Yannick Clément, arranging the prints in the dunes, she created a story within a story, a kind of *mise en abyme* – a forerunner of the performance we would create together with the archives in 2017 (FIG.21).

FIG.21 *Valérie Cachard, installation of photographs taken by Gregory Buchakjian in the Abandoned Dwellings of Beirut, Kolmanskop, Namibia, 2013.*

45 *Ibid.*
46 KASSIR, SAMIR, *Being Arab*, translated by Will Hobson, London and New York, Verso Books, 2013, p. xi.
47 BARTHES, ROLAND, *A Lover's Discourse: Fragments*, translated by Richard Howard, London, Vintage Publishing, 2002, p. 126.

THE ARCHIVES – STORIES WITHIN STORIES

In addition to the two purposes of photography (documentation and creating tableaux), the databases and personal statements, Valérie Cachard's arrival awakened the desire to explore spaces and shed light on their mysteries, particularly by examining objects and other clues left behind by residents, squatters or nature. These clues bore witness to what had been a home where furniture is "arranged around an axis which ensures a regular chronology of actions. . . the family is always present to itself."[48] There, the pieces of furniture were mismatched, dismantled, squeezed together, crushed, piled up or totally wrecked, in some cases inadvertently forming sculptures.

In summer 2012, Valérie Cachard and I began conducting archaeological excavations in abandoned apartment buildings. The first stage was to photograph artefacts in situ. The second was to retrieve the objects and documents which provided the most information about the lives of those who had owned or lived in the property, for, as Jacques Derrida reminds us, it is "in this domiciliation, in this house arrest, that archives take place."[49] Official documents – such as contracts, identity papers, water and electricity bills and rent receipts – and personal papers – including letters, photographs, journals and diaries – were cleaned up, photographed and filed, with the idea of returning them to their rightful owners or their heirs or to the city via a public institution.

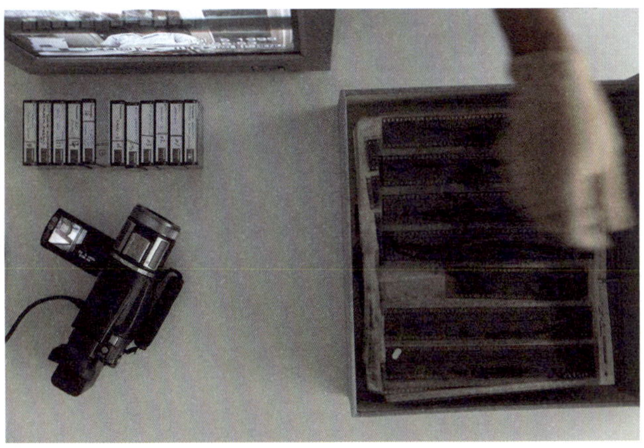

FIG.22 *Akram Zaatari, On Photography People and Modern Times, 2010. 2-channel video. Still from left channel*

FIG.23 *Gregory Buchakjian, Office Dada, 2008. Installation.*

The archive compiled in abandoned places joined another which I had at home. This one documented Fontana, a department store and an architecture and design practice active between the 1960s and the 1990s. In 2008, I moved into what had once been Fontana's headquarters. The keyring I was presented with bore the words "Office Dada", which became the name of the studio, where one of the rooms was piled high with Fontana company paperwork. I had been ordered by Leonardo Matossian, son of Jack Matossian who headed the organisation until his death, not to throw any of these files away, although he suggested they might be destroyed. One month after my arrival, I decided to tear up all the accounts by hand. It took me three days and three nights. The room was filled with a pile of paper one metre high (FIG.23). Having got rid of all those sheets, I was then able to extricate the "real" Fontana archives – drawings, furniture, photo albums, press cuttings and advertising campaigns.

Once brought together at Office Dada, the Fontana archives and those of the abandoned buildings did not fail to generate a "nervousness about the archive following a fascination, a promise."[50] In the 20th and 21st centuries, "the paranoid dimension of archival art is the other side of its utopian ambition – its desire to turn belatedness into becomingness, to recoup failed visions in art, literature, philosophy and everyday life into possible scenarios of alternative kinds of social relations, to transform the

48 BAUDRILLARD, JEAN, *The System of Objects*, translated by James Benedict, London and New York, Verso Books, 2005, p. 68.
49 DERRIDA, JACQUES, *Archive Fever: A Freudian Impression*, translated by Eric Prenowitz, Chicago, University of Chicago Press, 1998, p. 2.
50 CHÉROUX, CLÉMENT, paper given at the symposium, *History of the Last Things Before the Last: Art as Writing History*, organised by the Arab Image Foundation and the Centre Pompidou at Ashkal Alwan Home Workspace, Beirut, 30 November–1 December 2012.

no-place of the archive into the no-place of a utopia."[51] The uses to which the archive was put by the various users took it beyond its intended function of preserving historical data, while also making it lose its neutral character.[52] In 1990s' Lebanon, in the face of the government's policy of amnesia, the archive was one of the "formal strategies" adopted by artists "to confront the historical specificities of the Civil War."[53] Dossiers of all kinds amassed by Jayce Salloum in the 1980s and 90s constituted a multifaceted installation entitled *There Was and There Was Not*. In 1997, Akram Zaatari became a co-founder of the Arab Image Foundation, whose mission was to gather and study the photographic heritage. For years, he focused his attention on the photographic studio of Hashem el-Madani, in an approach that blurred the line between researcher and artist (FIG.22). Around the same time, Walid Raad created The Atlas Group, an organisation whose stated aim was to create and conserve historical archives. However, the artist made no secret of the fact that the group, of which he was the sole member, was as much pure invention as the archive it contained (FIG.102). In 2010, Said Baalbaki put together a fictitious archaeological exhibition based on the purported discovery of a bone of al-Buraq, the Prophet Muhammad's mythical horse (FIG.24).[54] Conversely, Walid Sadek's *Love Is Blind* is an installation consisting of information panels describing works by the landscape painter Mustapha Farroukh (1901–57), displayed on the stark white walls of a gallery in such a way that the "absence of paintings reinforces the wartime destruction of these geographical sites. . . Sadek's act of negation also implicitly questions the ability of visual language to convey loss."[55]

Archives, whether real, invented or missing, are part of the same sensory system.[56] The Fontana archive had the distinctive feature of being alive. I used the pieces of furniture that belonged in the flat and willingly invited my guests to rummage through it. Then it was their turn to be photographed and joined onto a video loop which was constantly being added to, thereby helping to turn *Office Dada* into an archive which, born out of its own destruction, would perpetually self-generate. This could not have happened to the archive of abandoned spaces.

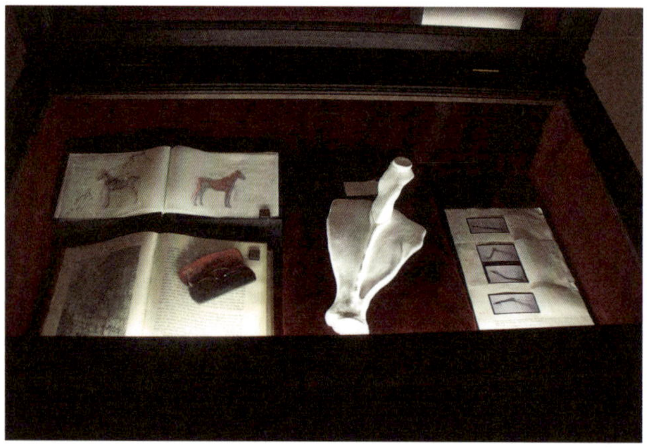

FIG.24 *Saïd Baalbaki, Al-Burak I, 2007-2009. Installation.*

Of all the people whose lives the archives brought forth from abandoned houses, the one who fascinated us most was Victoria, a teacher at the French Protestant College, whose home we began to explore in November 2011. Among her personal possessions, jewellery and clothes, we recovered documents relating to her career, as well as private papers, like letters exchanged with the widow of a Lebanese painter who had retired to Alsace, naive poems, diaries and journals, especially one dating from 1958, in which she records a visit to Jerusalem and the war that shook Lebanon that same year. These writings led Valérie Cachard into a process of re-appropriation and, with the passage of time, the apartment became the focal point of the many links that she had forged with the city. Victoria's archive also contained an undertaker's invoice for her funeral in December 1997, as well as records of medical examinations she appeared to have undergone in 2001 and 2002. The contradictions posed by these unquestionably valid artefacts, uncovered in an archaeological excavation, highlighted Jacques le Goff's views on the primacy of documents as a historical source.[57] This, in turn, confirmed Rancière's thinking that "the real must be fictionalised in order to be thought" and "writing history and writing stories come under the same regime of truth."[58] In 2017, Victoria's enigmatic death was the Gordian knot in a contribution on the subject of "validity" to the second edition of the Oxford Artistic and Practice Based Research Platform.[59]

51 Foster, Hal, "An Archival Impulse", *October*, no. 110, autumn 2004, pp. 3–22.
52 Marks, Laura, U., *Hanan al-Cinema. Affections for the Moving Image*, Cambridge, MA, MIT Press, 2015, p. 171.
53 Rogers, Sarah, "Culture '45 and the Rise of Beirut's Contemporary Art Scene", in *Six Lines of Flight: Shifting Geographies in Contemporary Art*, San Francisco, University of California Press, SFMOMA, 2012, pp. 34–43.
54 Wilson-Goldie, Kaelen, "Always Struggle with the Object, Always Rewrite the World", *South Magazine*, documenta 14 #1, 2015.
55 Demos, T.J., *The Migrant Image: The Art and Politics of Documentary during Global Crisis*, Durham, N.C., Duke University Press, 2013, p. 185.
56 Wright, Stephen, "Tel un espion dans l'époque qui naît : la situation de l'artiste à Beyrouth aujourd'hui", *Parachute*, no. 108 (2002), p. 28.
57 Le Goff, Jacques, *History and Memory*, translated by Steven Rendall and Elizabeth Claman, New York, Columbia University Press, 1996, xvii.
58 Rancière, Jacques, *The Politics of Aesthetics: The Distribution of the Sensible*, translated by Gabriel Rockhill, London and New York, Continuum, 2007, p. 38.
59 Buchakjian, Gregory, "The Lives and Deaths of Inhabitants in Abandoned Houses", *OAR: The Oxford Artistic and Practice Based Research Platform*, no. 2, "Validity", 2017.

The question of the future of these archives remained unanswered until 8 October 2017. That day, Valérie Cachard and I transferred them to a studio, a neutral space in which to spread them out. We took it in turns to remove an item from the pile, carry it across the room and place it on the floor. On the way, we described each piece or, if it was a text, read aloud an extract in its original language. Filmed by Malek Hosni, the performance that became a video did not try literally to repeat the traumatic events for fear, as Susan Little emphasises, of triggering distorted memories, or even departing from what was ethically acceptable.[60] It was also nothing like a dreary, even funereal, museum display. We handled the archive in such a way that the performance brought it back to life just as, in the years between 2009 and 2016, human bodies had breathed a little more life into abandoned spaces.

The photographic tableaux, reconnaissance photos, databases and witness statements, as well as the doctoral thesis and the filmed performance of the archive all served to confirm that what counted in the end was not the initial subject, namely how war had impacted on Beirut's residential properties, nor the ambition of writing a history of Lebanon or the art in Lebanon. What mattered was that abandoned homes and the stories they told created an instrument for reclaiming cities confronted with various forms of violence, ethnic segregation, state surveillance and neoliberal policies.

Beirut will never again be "what it used to be" and most of the ruined buildings photographed will ultimately disappear. One is reminded of the words of Roland Barthes: "Photography does not necessarily say *what is no longer,* but only and for certain, *what has been.*"[61] Thus, depending on a person's point of view, rather like the question of the glass being half full or half empty, they will see the research and artistic project either as a memorial, or quite the opposite, a sign of life.

For Michel de Certeau, "writing speaks of the past only to inter it. . . But unlike other artistic or social 'tombs', here taking the dead or the past back to a symbolic place is connected to the labour aimed at creating in the present a place (past or present) to be filled, a 'something that must be done'." [62] It is with such thoughts in mind that we are prompted to revisit the Super 8 scene in *Paris, Texas,* in which, according to Serge Yared, we "see onscreen, with this inexpressible feeling of loss, an idyllic past that in reality never was"[63] and the closing sequence of *My Architect,* when the director–narrator succeeds in his quest to follow in the footsteps of his father, Louis I. Kahn, in front of the National Assembly Building in Dacca, his final masterpiece. A voice-off speaks these words:

> *What was has always been.*
> *What is has always been.*
> *What will be has always been.*[64]

60 Little, Susan, "Repeating Repetition", *Performance Research,* 20, no. 5, 2015, pp. 44–50.
61 Barthes, Roland, *Camera Lucida: Notes on Photography,* translated by Richard Howard, London, Vintage Classics, 1993, p. 85.
62 De Certeau, Michel, *The Writing of History,* translated by Tom Conleyn, New York, Columbia University Press, 1993, p.101.
63 Serge Yared, email to the author, 18 February 2016.
64 In Tyng, Alexandra, *Beginnings: Louis I. Kahn's Philosophy of Architecture,* Hoboken, NJ, Wiley-Interscience, 1984, p. 127.

GREGORY BUCHAKJIAN

ABANDONED DWELLINGS TABLEAUX, 2009–2016

PHOTOGRAPHS

1 _ BF1824-Mousseitbé _ 29'12'2009

2 _ BF4229-Achrafieh _ 14'11'2010

3 _ BF212-Aïn el-Mreïssé _ 28'11'2010

5 _ BF191-Minet Hosn _ 05'08'2011

6 _ BF191-Minet Hosn _ 15'06'2011

7 _ BF142-Medawar _ 07'11'2011

9 _ BF1281-Bachoura _ 15'08'2011

14 _ BF1237-Achrafieh _ 22'11'2011

15 _ BF1237-Achrafieh _ 22'11'2011

16 _ BF1237-Achrafieh _ 07'12'2011

17 _ BF1237-Achrafieh _ 21'12'2011

18 _ BF1237-Achrafieh _ 21'04'2012

19 _ BF1237-Achrafieh _ 13'04'2012

21 _ BF335-Aïn el-Mreïssé _ 17'06'2012

23 _ BF702-Achrafieh _ 08'10'2013

24 _ BF702-Achrafieh _ 08'10'2013

25 _ BF2413-Ras Beyrouth _ 05'09'2014

26 _ BF585-Ras Beyrouth _ 06'12'2014

27 _ BF1083-Achrafieh _ 09'09'2012

31 _ BF671,-Remeil _ 09'11'2014

32 _ BF482/681-Saifi _ 20'06'2015

33 _ BF11-Medawar _ 20'06'2015

34 _ BF1351-Achrafieh _ 19'07'2014

35 _ BF1351-Achrafieh _ 19'07'2014

36 _ BF1351-Achrafieh _ 19'07'2014

37 _ BF630-Mazraa _ 28'12'2013

39 _ BF4025-Mousseitbé _ 06'10'2014

40 _ BF363/372/753-Minet Hosn _ 16'01'2016

41 _ BF622-Zokak el-Blat _ 02'09'2015

42 _ BF622-Zokak el-Blat _ 02'09'2015

43 _ BF585-Ras Beyrouth _ 11'10'2015

46 _ BF1083-Achrafieh _ 04'10'2015

47 _ BF787-Minet Hosn _ 04'06'2016

48 _ BF787-Minet Hosn _ 04'06'2016

49 _ BF585-Ras Beyrouth _ 04'06'2016

50 _ BF585-Ras Beyrouth _ 04'06'2016

51 _ BF562-Achrafieh _ 14'05'2016

52 _ BF562-Achrafieh _ 14'05'2016

CHAPTER 1

DISPUTED TERRITORY: THE BATTLE OF THE HOTELS

FIG.25 *Lamia Ziadé, Phoenicia Hotel in fire, 2010. Illustration from Bye Bye Babylone.*

HOW THE "RIVIERA OF THE MIDDLE EAST" BECAME A BATTLEFIELD

What became known as the Battle of the Hotels was a succession of armed combats that marked the beginning of the war in the heart of the city. Taking place intermittently between the autumn of 1975 and the spring of 1976, they set the two warring camps head-to-head at the outbreak of the conflict. On the one side were the Joint Forces, also known as the Palestinian-Progressive Forces, Leftist-Muslim Forces or Forces of the Left, among whom were the Independent Nasserists or *Murabitun*, the Communist Party, the Communist Action Organisation in Lebanon (CAOL) and the Palestine Liberation Organisation (PLO). On the other side stood the conservative Christian forces, principally the Kataeb or Phalangist Party and the "Tigers" of the National Liberal Party (NLP).[1]

The battle was widely discussed and also portrayed on film and in the visual arts. Even so, at the time this research project got under way, it had never been the subject of any extensive study and the only attempt to produce a summary of events was a single page on Wikipedia.[2] The battle's very nature as an act of war was called into question by a federal court in New York following a trial during which the Holiday Inn chain claimed US$11 million from its insurers, to compensate for damage suffered by its hotel in Beirut.[3]

AN ARCHITECTURE OF VIOLENCE

FIG.26 *Camille Tarazi, Minet Hosn, Phoenicia and Hilton Hotels seen from Alcazar Hotel, 1997. Photograph.*

1 See Appendix, "Forces Involved in the Lebanese Civil War (1975–90)", p. 207.
2 While our research was under way, Mayssa Jallad completed a Master's degree thesis entitled "Beirut's Civil War Hotel District: Preserving the World's first High-Rise Urban Battlefield" at Columbia University, New York, 2017.
3 Lewin, Tamar, "Beirut Insurance Ruling Favours Holiday Inn", *New York Times*, 21 September 1983.

Given the spectacular nature of the destruction, the battle had a traumatic effect on the collective imagination (FIG.26). In a global context, it belongs to series of events dating back to the early 20th century, where violence invaded hotel establishments. In his *Journal d'un attaché d'ambassade* (*Diary of an Embassy Attaché*), Paul Morand reported from Russia:

> *The [Astoria] hotel had been requisitioned by the military in 1915, with two generals as managers, soldiers as housekeeping staff and, according to Beaumont, an admiral as bathroom attendant! The chief of staff was reading out an order by candlelight, saying that the hotel might be attacked the following day. And indeed, from first thing the next morning there arose a great wave of noise; then came room inspection, followed by total silence. All at once came the groans and screams of officers whose throats were being slit as they lay in their beds.*[4]

On 26 September 1976, four commandos from the pro-Iraqi Arab Liberation Front stormed the Hotel Semiramis in Damascus, taking guests hostage and killing five.[5] On 26 November 2008, Mumbai was devastated by attacks on several targets, including the Hotel Taj Mahal, one of the world's most legendary establishments. On 26 June 2015, at Sousse in Tunisia, one man massacred 38 people on the beach of the Hotel Riu Imperial Marhaba.[6] Five months later, a Jihadist group attacked the Radisson Blu in Bamako, Mali, taking 150 hostages.[7] On 24 June 2014, at Beirut's Duroy Hotel, Lebanese General Security personnel seized several Saudi nationals linked to terrorist activity. One suspect blew himself up.[8]

In a paper devoted to hotels where acts of violence had been staged, Paola Yacoub writes of a "cycle" which is not yet "at an end", but will continue to expand, embracing "new buildings in the course of new events."[9] Born at the time of the industrial revolution and developments in modes of transport, hotel architecture grew up alongside the democratisation of tourism and business travel. An essential feature of the urban landscape, the hotel is a symbolic structure and an easy target. On 22 July 1946, a wing of the King David in Jerusalem collapsed after explosives were detonated by the Zionist organisation, Irgun. It was one of the first large-scale bombings. On 20 July 1983, three terrorists detonated a car bomb in the car park of the Summerland Hotel in Beirut.[10] On 20 September 2008, the Islamabad Marriott "a symbolic place in the capital of the country" was completely destroyed by a truck bomb.[11]

Tenuous it may be, but there is a difference between a terrorist attack and militarisation, such as that which occurred at the Astoria or during the Battle of the Hotels. Following the latter, the journalists who had evacuated the Saint Georges chose the Commodore Hotel in the Hamra district as their headquarters (FIG.27). In 1987, the Commodore was itself embroiled in a confrontation,[12] falling prey to wholesale looting, during which raiders seized "liquor, television sets, typewriters, vacuum cleaners, linen and cutlery", and the last remaining guests, two Americans negotiating the release of Western hostages, were brutalised: "We felt we were violated," they told the press.[13] Could the Commodore's fate be described as "collateral damage"? And what about the incident on 8 April 2003, when an American tank shelled Baghdad's Hotel Palestine where press representatives were based?[14]

The hotel can, in turn, become a source of violence. During demonstrations in Cairo against the regime of Hosni Mubarak, snipers reportedly shot at the crowd from the Ramses Hilton, situated close to Tahir Square.[15] In Sarajevo, on 6 April 1992, tens of thousands of civilians marched to demand an end to inter-ethnic violence. Men from Radovan Karadzic's Serb Democratic Party (SDS), stationed at the Holiday Inn, opened fire on demonstrators.

4 Morand, Paul, *Journal d'un attaché d'ambassade (1916–1917)*, new edition with additional text and annotations by Michel Collomb, Paris, Gallimard, 1948, 1997, p. 227.
5 El-Khazen, Farid, *The Breakdown of the State in Lebanon*, Cambridge, MA, Harvard University Press, 2000, p. 348.
6 Stephen, Chris, "Tourists desert Tunisia after June terror attack", *Guardian*, 25 September 2015.
7 Le Monde and AFP, "Mali : 21 morts dans la prise d'otages dans un hôtel de Bamako", *Le Monde*, 21 November 2015.
8 Khraiche, Dana and Shaheen, Kareem, "Beirut bomber blows himself up to evade arrest", *Daily Star*, 25 June 2014.
9 Yacoub, Paola, "Holiday Inn Cycle" in *Conflict and Memory: Bridging Past and Future in [South East] Europe*, Baden Baden, Nomos, 2010.
10 Zaide, Mona,"Six killed in terrorist attack on Beirut Hotel", *Times News*, 20 July 1983.
11 Gall, Carlotta, "Bombing at Hotel in Pakistan Kills at Least 40", *New York Times*, 21 September 2008, International/Asia Pacific sect.
12 Hijazi, Ihsan, "Unrivalled clashes raging in streets of Western Beirut", *New York Times*, 19 March 1987.
13 Associated Press, "Druze Militia Gains Control of Most of W. Beirut", *Los Angeles Times*, 20 February 1987.
14 Abend, Lisa, "Spanish Court Seeks Arrest of U.S. Soldiers in Hotel Attack", *Time*, 29 July 2010.
15 "Police snipers shot protesters in Cairo, government inquiry finds", *New York Post*, 4 March 2011.

In the weeks that followed, the Serbs were driven out of the hotel and its surroundings. In the besieged city, the Holiday Inn, located on the sadly notorious "Sniper Alley", was the last operational hotel and headquarters of the foreign press.[16] Hotel staff had to be vigilant against incursions, such as when "a Bosnian fighter burst onto the tenth floor firing his weapon at a Serb gunman in a building some 300 yards away. Hotel employees coaxed him out. That same week, a mortar round landed on the eighth floor, turning much of it into plaster rubble."[17] Day by day, the hotel was falling apart:

> *I turned the doorknob on the first door I came to; it swung open smoothly. On the other side of the door, perhaps 10 feet away, the floor gave way to twisted steel rods and smashed concrete and then nothing. The outside wall was gone, open to the light rain and intermittent sunshine that washed through what had once been a hotel room.*[18]

At the Holiday Inn in Sarajevo, the paradigms of ruin, military occupation and normality converged. Neither the guests nor the staff acknowledged the city's chaos. "To do so would bring its misery inside the hotel to fester. And then there would be nowhere to go."[19]

FIG.27 *Eli Reed, During rocket attacks on West Beirut, photojournalist Françoise Demulder makes a phone call at the front desk the Commodore Hotel, 1984. Photograph.*

THE BACKDROP

The Battle of the Hotels was so called because it was played out in an area known as the "hotel district", on the seafront at Ain el-Mreisseh and Minet Hosn, northwest of the city centre.[20] In the mid-19th century, this part of the coast became established as a tourist destination, with the opening of cafés built on stilts, like the Hajj Daoud, and hotels including the Bellevue and the Bassoul, also known as the Grand Hôtel d'Orient.[21] Herman Melville stayed there during his trip to Jerusalem in 1857. The author of *Moby Dick* thought it did not provide all the comforts a British traveller might demand, but was still the best hotel in Syria.[22] The mandate period saw the inauguration of the Saint Georges in 1932 and the Normandy in 1940. Designed by disciples of Auguste Perret,[23] the Saint Georges was characterised by the stark simplicity of its architecture. Cantilevered balconies ran across each façade, accentuated by the awnings above the French windows. These compact openings gave guests the choice of opening up and sitting on the balcony or retreating into the quiet privacy of their suite. Behind its "extreme rationalism"[24] this oasis of luxury and refinement was, as its advertising slogan claimed, the "rendezvous of the international élite."

Following independence, Phoenicia Street became famous as a leisure hotspot where many establishments bore the trademark of Jean-Prosper Gay-Para. These included the Grenier des Artistes and the Palm Beach and Excelsior Hotels (PL.40). The Excelsior was famous for its nightclub, Les Caves du Roy, a favourite jet-set haunt.[25] Opposite the Saint Georges, the Alcazar Hotel offered its guests a view across the bay, as might be seen from a ship, while the vast Phoenicia, "ultramodern with its oriental-style décor",[26] opened its doors in 1961. As the first luxury hotel of an international chain, InterContinental, it was unprecedented

16 Demick, Barbara, "Life and death on my street in Sarajevo", *Guardian*, 3 April 2012.
17 Kenny, Timothy, "The Siege of Sarajevo, July 1992", *The Kenyon Review* XXXIV, no. 3, summer 2012.
18 *Ibid.*
19 *Ibid.*
20 Minet Hosn (which translates literally as "the harbour by the ramparts") was one of the fishing ports surrounding the mediaeval city walls, pulled down at the end of the 19th century.
21 Kassir, Samir, *Histoire de Beyrouth*, Paris, Fayard, 2004, p. 256.
22 Fitchett, Joseph, "From Khans To Khiltons", *Saudi Aramco World*, 24, no. 6, November 1973, pp. 16–29.
23 Jacques Poirier, André Lotte, Georges Bordes and Antoine Tabet, and not Auguste Perret himself as is often said or written. For example, Ching, Francis D., Jarzombek, Mark M. and Prakash, Vikramaditya, *A Global History of Architecture*, London, John Wiley & Sons, 2007, p. 712.
24 Yacoub, Gebran, *Dictionnaire de l'Architecture au Liban au XXe siècle*, Beirut, Alphamedia, 2003, p. 983.
25 Buchakjian, Gregory, "Beirut by Night. A Century of Nightlife Photography", *Middle East Journal for Culture and Communication*, 8, no. 2–3, 2015, pp. 256–81.
26 B. Ed., "Le Phoenicia, géant des palaces du Liban, ouvrira ses portes le 23 décembre", *La Revue du Liban*, 30 September 1961, pp. 12–13.

in terms of scale, especially when a twenty-two-floor extension, added in 1968, increased its capacity to 600 guest rooms. The late 1960s also witnessed the construction of the Saint Charles City Center behind the Phoenicia. Designed by André Wogenscky, a disciple of Le Corbusier, this "city within a city"[27] boasted a twenty-five-floor tower and a triangular building set on a platform embedded in sloping ground. Initially intended as a residential block, the use of the tower changed following market fluctuations[28] and the building was divided between offices and a hotel. This was to become the Holiday Inn, a mass of concrete reminiscent of a blockhouse, with balconies affording each room a stunning view. At the beginning of the 1970s on the Avenue des Français, the Normandy was dwarfed by the no less massive Hilton, which would never open its doors.

As well as the hotels, there was another protagonist located uphill from the neighbourhood. Murr Tower could be described as off-camera, and also off-topic, in the context of research devoted to living spaces. The thirty-six-storey skyscraper was still under construction, but its carcass would become emblematic. The battle would set "two of the capital's tallest buildings" against one another – Murr Tower in the hands of the Palestinian-Progressive Forces, and the Holiday Inn, held by the Phalangists. At first, the fight was dubbed "Battle of the Towers",[29] before earning the name "Battle of the Hotels",[30] or even "Battle of Holiday Inn"[31] (FIG.28). From a human perspective, the conflict was a confrontation in a confined space involving different groups:

- Hotel guests
- Hotel staff and other leisure industry employees
- Local residents
- Construction workers
- Militiamen
- Internal Security Forces and the Lebanese Army
- Firefighters and first-aid workers, in particular members of the Red Cross
- Journalists and press photographers (some of them hotel guests)
- Looters (possibly members of one or more of the groups mentioned above)

FIG.28 *Raed Yassin, China / War of the Hotels, 2012. Porcelain, 96 × 33 cm.*

27 "Le Saint-Charles City Center, nouveau centre urbain de Beyrouth", *La Revue du Liban*, 9 November 1963, p. 15.
28 "Lebanon a Year Later: The Crisis Deepens", *Middle East Research and Information Project (MERIP) Reports*, no. 30, August 1974, pp. 26–8.
29 Saab, Édouard, "La bataille des tours", *Le Monde*, 29 October 1975.
30 United Press International, "All Yanks Told to Flee Beirut", the *Milwaukee Sentinel*, 3 November 1975, p. 2.
31 Saab, Édouard, "Tandis que l'État se désagrège : de violents combats se poursuivent dans plusieurs régions", *Le Monde*, 15 December 1975.

HISTORICAL OVERVIEW: THE BATTLE OF THE HOTELS UNFOLDS

In October 1975, following an abortive attempt to advance to Hamra, to the west of the capital, Phalange forces withdrew to the residential neighbourhood of Kantari,[32] moving from there to the hotel district. On 26 October, armed men entered the Holiday Inn and the Phoenicia.[33] The following day, "Tiger" militiamen aboard three launches came ashore at the Saint Georges,[34] where they stayed for two days before being relieved by Phalangists. An armed duel took place between the latter and the Joint Forces positioned in the Murr Tower and at Ain el Mreisseh. After ten days or so, a ceasefire was negotiated and the militia on both sides abandoned their barricades.[35]

The lull lasted a month. On 6 December, following the discovery of the bodies of four Phalangists, Christian militias kidnapped and executed hundreds of civilians, purely on the basis of their religious faith. That was "Black Saturday." To appease the wrath of his comrades, George Hawi suggested "liberating" the hotel district.[36] The Joint Forces seized the Saint Georges, Alcazar and Excelsior Hotels and, on 9 December, they launched their attack on the Phoenicia, where fire broke out.[37] The following day, it was the turn of the Saint Georges to burn. With the loss of the Saint Georges and the Phoenicia, the Phalangists were surrounded at the Holiday Inn, their only escape being in the direction of Wadi Abu Jamil and the city centre. On 17 December, a ceasefire was declared.[38]

During the night of 9 January 1976, Phalangist troops returned to the Holiday Inn while the Joint Forces, who had found their way into Phoenicia via a "secret passage",[39] attempted to storm the Holiday Inn car park, but were encircled by the defenders.[40] During the night of 12 January, the *Murabitun* launched an unsuccessful second attack, "placing explosives in a pick-up truck, which they pushed from Georges Picot Street towards the hotel entrance."[41] With the city ablaze, a ceasefire came into force on 23 January.[42] This was the only phase of the battle where there were no changes in position.

On 14 March 1976, the shooting resumed.[43] On 21 March, shelling by heavy artillery enabled the Joint Forces to enter the Holiday Inn.[44] The fighting was fierce and the chaos total.[45] On 22 March, the Phalangists failed in a

FIG.29 *Camille Tarazi, Minet Hosn, Hilton (in the background) and Monroe Hotels (on right) seen from Alcazar Hotel, 1997. Photomontage.*

32 Chahine Fayad, interview with the author, 24 July 2013: "At the start of the battle of Kantari, we advanced as far as the Banque du Liban and Wardieh. I held the UAP building, from 2 pm to 6 pm. There were four of us. We received a very warm welcome there. Many Christian families lived around Justinian Street and Trad Hospital. But no one came to relieve us."

33 "La ligne de feu Kantari-Georges Picot en vedette", *L'Orient-Le Jour*, 28 October 1975.

34 Aburish, Said K., *The St. George Hotel Bar*, London, Bloomsbury, 1989, pp. 204–5.

35 Boutros, Antoine (ed.), *Wathiqat Harb Lubnân – Documentation of the Lebanese War. Vol. 1.*, Beirut, Dar Assayad, 1977, p. 137.

36 Hawi, Georges in Issaoui, Omar, "Harb Lubnan (The Lebanese War), 3", Al Jazeera, 2001.

37 "Army commandos establish a demarcation line between Karantina and the corniche", *An-Nahar*, 10 December 1975, p.1.

38 "Tours et grands hôtels évacués hier", *L'Orient-Le Jour*, 16 December 1975, pp. 1, 4.

39 "Further clashes in the hotel district", *As-Safir*, 11 January 1976, p. 1.

40 *Ibid.*

41 "The tower blocks and hotels again", *An-Nahar*, 14 January 1976, p. 1.

42 "Successful first-day attempt and calm restored on the fronts: four committees to ensure safety agreement", *As-Safir*, 24 January 1976, p. 1.

43 *An-Nahar*, 15 March 1976.

44 "The Joint Forces occupied the Holiday Inn after clashes that began at dawn and lasted 10 hours", *An-Nahar*, 22 March 1976, p. 1.

45 "Who is in control of the Holiday Inn?" *An-Nahar*, 23 March 1976, p. 4.

counteroffensive designed to recapture the hotel and were forced to retreat to the Normandy and the Hilton, where they waged a desperate struggle. On 28 March, the fighting moved to the interior of the Hilton.[46] On 29 March, at 01.00 hours, the Joint Forces proclaimed the fall of the two hotels[47] and, on 30 March, *An-Nahar* announced that, after six months, the Battle of the Hotels was over.[48]

BURNED-OUT TOWERS, A BEACH AND A GARBAGE DUMP

FIG.30 *Unidentified photographer, Saint-Georges Hotel and Swimming Club, c. 1977-1980. Photograph.*

After the battle, the district was left in ruins, a continuation of the scene of devastation in the city centre. In the spring of 1977, the Saint Georges Yacht Motor Club opened its doors to bathers (FIG.30). Behind the bar, the manager Serge Nader, preserved a wall riddled with bullet holes, "so that people will remember and talk about the madness that was the Civil War."[49] At the beginning of the same year, "the little bay below the Avenue des Français became a giant garbage dump where, every day, dozens of municipal trucks came to deposit the city's household waste."[50] During the 80s and 90s, many abandoned hotels and apartment blocks were occupied by refugees. Then reconstruction got under way (FIG.29). The Bassoul and Normandy hotels were razed to the ground by Solidere, the redevelopment company operating in the city centre. The firm then decided to destroy the Hilton by controlled implosion. The Alcazar became a bank, while the Palm Beach, Vendôme and Phoenicia Hotels were renovated. In 2002, the latter hosted the summits of the Arab League and the International Organisation of La Francophonie. From the top floor, in front of a bay window, Catherine Deneuve spoke the words "Je veux voir" (I want to see) in the opening sequence of the eponymous film, made after the war in July 2006.

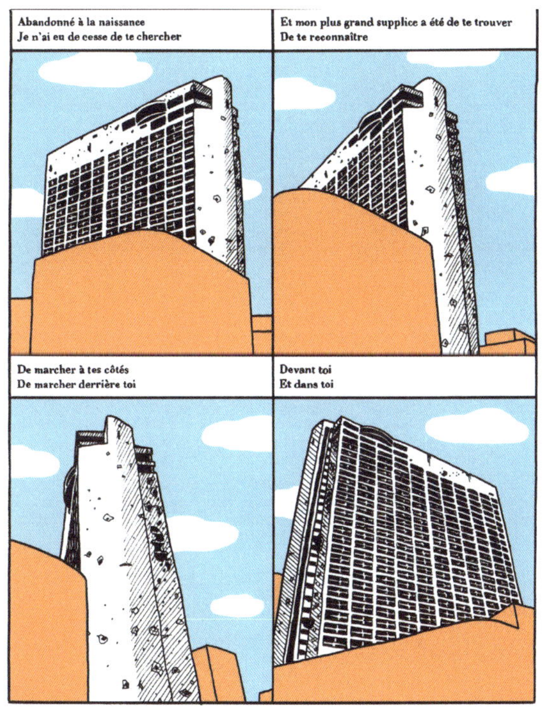

FIG.31 *Mazen Kerbaj, Lettre à la mère (page 2/10), 2010. Ink on paper, 23 × 28,5 cm.*

The Murr Tower, the Holiday Inn, Saint Georges and the Excelsior are still no more than empty shells. In the 1990s, renovations of the Saint Georges were interrupted

46 "At 1 am: the Hilton and the Normandy fall", *An-Nahar*, 29 March 1976, p. 1.
47 *Ibid.*
48 "The Battle of the Hotels ends and that of the stock exchange begins", *An-Nahar*, 30 March 1976, p. 4.
49 PRAGER, KARSTEN, "Beirut: Better, But Not Yet Well", *Time* 110, no. 20, 14 November 1977, p. 46.
50 "Ordures aujourd'hui, jardin public demain", *L'Orient-Le Jour*, 9 April 1977, p. 3.

due to a conflict between its owners and Solidere.[51] The company had extended its control over the waterfront, thereby depriving the hotel access to the sea. From then onwards, there was a giant banner on the façade of this luxury establishment saying "Stop Solidere."[52] It was there that, on 14 February 2005, a devastating attack ended the life of the former Prime Minister, Rafic Hariri, the prime mover behind Solidere, and some twenty others. As for the Saint Charles City Center of which the Holiday Inn formed a part – the chain had ended its lease agreement in 1977[53] – it was the subject of litigation between its shareholders, the Kuwaiti group represented by Fadia al-Sabbah, and the land and real-estate developers, Compagnie Immobilière Libanaise (CIL). The former wanted to demolish the centre, the latter wished to restore it (FIG.31). As for the Murr Tower, whose structure failed to match the specifications required at the time, but whose demolition would be too costly, the building was condemned to remain a reluctant monument commemorating the war. Since the 2000s, the building of new skyscrapers and leisure complexes on the seafront has completed the transformation of the hotel district.

OCCUPYING AND ABANDONING THE GRAND HOTELS

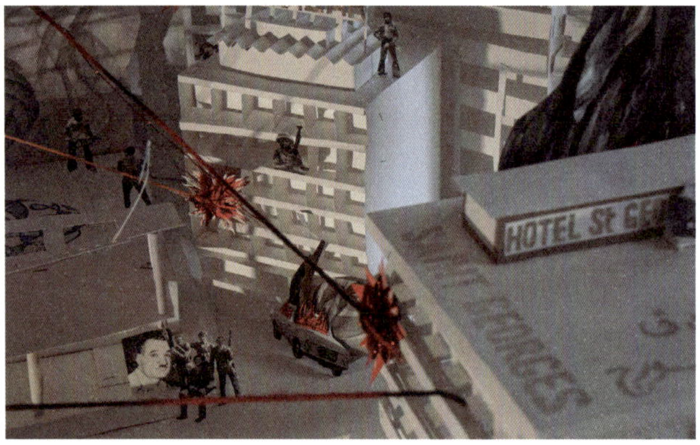

FIG.32 *Lamia Ziadé, Battle of the Hotels, 2009. Installation.*

In 1975, as the security situation deteriorated, the hotel occupation rate declined, dropping from 98 per cent at the Holiday Inn on 13 April,[54] for example, to 30 per cent in May at the Alcazar. In early June, Kamel el-Assaad, Speaker of the Lebanese parliament, took up residence at the Holiday Inn. Prime Minister Rashid Karami asked him why he had moved. "We were frightened, for God's sake," he replied. "What could we do? Our house was hit by two shells, which did some damage."[55] July saw the occupation rate at the Alcazar rise to 45 per cent, before sinking to 20 per cent in September.[56] On 26 October, eleven rooms were occupied, while at the Saint-Georges there remained two businessmen, five journalists and the Dutch ambassador.[57] Against all expectations, the Holiday Inn had, in the meantime, seen an influx of some two hundred guests – American, British, Canadian and Swiss – who had fled a city centre in flames.[58]

The staff did their utmost to keep up a sense of normality amid the growing chaos.[59] At the Saint-Georges, "the porter, maintaining his customary calm and style, continued to solicitously open taxi doors for fleeing guests, bidding them a formal goodbye. He disappeared a while, when the shooting was at its height, before returning to his post to utter an endless succession of '*Bon voyage*', interspersed with the odd 'Welcome to Beirut' addressed to new arrivals."[60] The hotel was operating with an exhausted staff of 12 out of 225,[61] and offered for lunch no more than a ham-and-cheese sandwich.[62] A few guests still slept in their allotted quarters, while others took refuge in rooms at the back of the building, in corridors or even in the laundry)[63] – scenes that would be repeated throughout the war.

51 *Nida' al Watan*, 18 October 1995.
52 LARKIN, CRAIG, "Remaking Beirut: Contesting Memory, Space, and the Urban Imaginary of Lebanese Youth", *City & Community* 9, no. 4, 2010.
53 "L'hôtel Holiday Inn rompt son contrat de bail", *L'Orient-Le Jour*, 20 December 1977.
54 HADDAD, VIVIANE, "Les dégâts des grands hôtels. Le Holiday Inn : 3 millions de L.L. de pertes rien qu'en équipement hôtelier", *L'Orient Le Jour*, 3 April 1976.
55 "Karamé: J'espère former le gouvernement avant la semaine", *L'Orient-Le Jour*, 4 June 1975, p. 1.
56 Register of the Hôtel Alcazar (1975), Archives Maison Tarazi.
57 RANDAL, JONATHAN C. and FITCHETT, JOSEPH, "A Suddenly Neutral Hotel: Once Posh Beirut Hotel Becomes a Battleground", *Washington Post*, 30 October 1975, p. A1.
58 UNITED PRESS INTERNATIONAL, "Beirut Shelling Traps Yanks", *Milwaukee Sentinel*, 29 October 1975, p. 1.
59 RANDAL, JONATHAN C., "War Invades Old Elegant Beirut Hotel", *Washington Post*, 29 October 1975, p. A10.
60 UNITED PRESS INTERNATIONAL, cited in "Seconde journée de violents combats sur tous les fronts", *L'Orient-Le Jour*, 27 October 1975, pp. 1 and 4.
61 RANDAL, "War Invades Old Elegant Beirut Hotel", op. cit.
62 RANDAL and FITCHETT, "A Suddenly Neutral Hotel", op. cit.
63 ZIADÉ, LAMIA, *Bye Bye Babylone. Beyrouth 1975–1979* (graphic novel), Paris, Denoël, 2010.

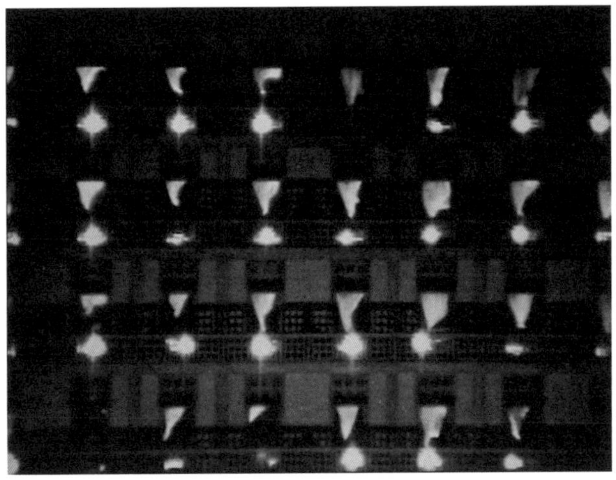

FIGS.33-34 *Hale Tenger, Beirut, 2005-2007. Vidéo.*

At the Palm Beach, the staff managed to negotiate a ceasefire to enable their guests to leave in safety.[64] At the Saint-Georges, after Chamoun's men had departed, they hung white sheets from the front to proclaim the hotel's non-alignment, in the hope of being spared by the warring parties.[65] This neutrality lasted less than two hours, but the sheets would make a ghostly but incidental reappearance in the video that Hale Tenger made thirty years later (FIGS.33-34). On 29 October, the Dutch ambassador and his wife finally resigned themselves to leaving the Saint-Georges in their red BMW coupé, whose diplomatic plates saw it through the barricades and out of the combat zone.[66] That same day, the hotel manager, too, succeeded in getting out, taking a taxi to the airport.[67] The journalists who remained in the abandoned luxury establishments found a bottle of whisky and settled in at the bar as the artillery was fired all about them.[68] The next day, following a request by the *Washington Post* to secretary of state Henry Kissinger, an armoured sedan from the American embassy arrived to extricate them. Unable to call on such support, the other guests[69] and the remaining staff decided to leave on foot, alone and with no escort, holding white flags.[70]

After the first phase of the fighting, the Alcazar was the only hotel in the neighbourhood to reopen its door to guests, essentially friends of the proprietors, the Tarazis. Every evening they listened to records from different parts of the world and the chef prepared a dish from that country.[71] In other establishments, a certain limited activity returned, as when the Pan Am office opened at the Phoenicia. There were cleaning and repairs to be done, and each time the fighting flared up the workers sent to clear the rubble would find themselves pinned down again. When the Phoenicia was besieged by the Joint Forces and fire broke out as a result, sixty people were trapped in the burning building:

> *At 8.30 in the morning an attempt was made to bring out those trapped in the hotel by helicopter, but the aircraft was unable to land on account of the intensity of the conflagration and the sustained fire it came under. It was then decided to send in army commandos to assist in the evacuation. After an exchange of fire, the helicopter returned and rescued those on the upper floors while those below were taken out in army armoured personnel carriers.*[72]

Many lost their lives, among them the chef, Nasri Harouni,[73] and the hotel manager, Hans Teufl, who "like a captain at the helm of a ship in distress, had been unwilling to abandon his post."[74]

64 Randal and Fitchett, "A Suddenly Neutral Hotel", op. cit.
65 *Ibid.*
66 *Ibid.*
67 *Ibid.*
68 Aburish, *The St. Georges Hotel Bar*, op. cit., p. 205.
69 *Ibid.*, p. 206.
70 Associated Press, "Third American Kidnapped", *Milwaukee Sentinel*, 31 October 1975, p. 2.
71 Alfred Tarazi, interview with the author, 13 October 2013.
72 "Army commandos establish a demarcation line between Karantina and the corniche", *An-Nahar*, 10 December 1975, p. 1.
73 "Calm in Beirut threatened by the spate of kidnappings. Corpse at the Phoenicia", *An-Nahar*, 18 December 1975, p. 4.
74 Diab, Jean, "La lente agonie d'un des plus grands ensembles hôteliers et touristiques du Proche-Orient", *La Revue du Liban*, no. 878, 2 July 1976, pp. 48–51.

INTRUSIONS AND COHABITATIONS

FIG.35 *"Fleeing automobile in the lobby of the Holiday Inn Hotel, hit by a shell", 1975. Photograph published in An-Nahar, November 5, 1975.*

Militia incursions into the hotels made only too real the intrusion of war upon the world of luxury – the bubble the porter at the Saint-Georges had sought to preserve at all costs. "Seeing the militiamen arrive with arms and ammunition, the few hotel staff who remained conscientiously rolled up the carpets to prevent them from getting dirty."[75] That same impulse was shared by residents of the neighbourhood. In her apartment next door to the Normandy Hotel, Madame Ghandour had dust covers put on the two great crystal chandeliers in the drawing room. Forty years on, those chandeliers still hang there amid the peeling white panelling, enveloped in veils that no one has dared remove (PL.6). On 5 November, *An-Nahar* printed a photograph taken at the Holiday Inn: a driver caught in sniper fire had ended his journey under the imposing chandeliers of the hotel lobby. The least one could say is that the battered vehicle took something off the shine of the opulent interior (FIG.35).

There are many accounts by civilians indicating that militiamen of either side were not always aggressive towards them. At the Alcazar, "we received an unexpected visit from a group of men, hooded and dressed in black, [who] behaved with the greatest propriety."[76] At the Saint-Georges, the Tigers came in without a shot fired and fraternised with the Muslim security guards employed by the hotel.[77] The Phalangists who came after proved to be less sympathetic and locked them in the basement. When the Joint Forces arrived, they acted likewise, keeping the Christian employees in irons in the laundry. The latter would owe their lives to an appeal to the PLO from journalists who had stayed at the hotel.[78] The Ghandours, too, found themselves obliged to accommodate fighters. When the sector was captured by the Joint Forces, "the house was a battlefield, we were holed up like rats, death was everywhere around us."[79] Sparrows had flown in through the broken panes of glass in the lobby – a solitary gleam of hope for Joumana Ghandour, who found the spirit of their presence recalled by one of our photographs of abandoned residential buildings (PL.5).[80]

"I'm going to sleep at the Holiday Inn tonight," declared a Joint Forces militiaman,[81] while inside the hotel the Phalangist Elie Hobeika would quip to his comrade-in-arms Jocelyne Khoueiry: "Tonight, mademoiselle, we can offer you our finest suite."[82] Fighters' accounts abound in anecdotes of the luxury of the then still intact grand hotels, of sumptuous meals washed down with vintage wines from their cellars. During the November ceasefire, "the refrigerators were full of food and a gendarme was doing the cooking: great platters wheeled in on trolleys."[83] When the fresh food ran out or went off, they fell back on tinned foods or such things as the "packet soups unearthed in the dusty cupboards of the kitchens",[84] sandwiches or even dry bread.[85]

75 Ziadé, *Bye Bye Babylone. Beyrouth 1975-1979*, op. cit.
76 Tarazi, Emile, typewritten memoir, 1975–87, Archives Maison Tarazi.
77 Randal, "War Invades Old Elegant Beirut Hotel", op. cit.
78 Aburish, *The St. George Hotel Bar*, op. cit., pp. 207–8.
79 Nayla Ghandour de Coster, interviewed by the author, 16 January 2014.
80 Joumana Ghandour, interviewed by the author, 20 May 2011.
81 Prager, Karsten, "Last Rites for a Mortally Wounded City", *Time*, vol. 106, no. 19, 10 November 1975, p. 43.
82 Duplan, Nathalie and Raulin, Valérie, *Le cèdre et la croix : Jocelyne Khoueiry, une femme de combats*, Paris, Presses de la Renaissance, 2005, p. 81.
83 Former Phalangist party official who asked to remain anonymous, interviewed by the author, 23 October 2013.
84 Duplan and Raulin, *Le cèdre et la croix*, op. cit., p. 363.
85 Former Phalangist party official, interview of 23 October 2013.

On 12 December, *An-Nahar* published a report from the bar at the Saint-Georges, before it went up in flames. It shows men in keffiehs making Vs for victory and others seated at a piano. A month earlier, another soldier at the piano had made the front page, at the Holiday Inn. Yet he can't have played very much, for the sound would have been heard outside and given away his position (FIG.36).[86] Schlöndorff would use his picture in *Circle of Deceit*. In the film, as in the photographs, the pianists are hooded and masked, like many of those engaged in the fighting. At that point, the front lines were still porous, and these men could well find themselves on the opposite side.

FIG.36 *Lamia Ziadé, Warrior playing piano. Illustration from Ma très grande mélancolie arabe, 2017.*
[Based on a photograph taken by Harry Koundakjian at the Holiday Inn Hotel on November 3, 1975].

THE CITADELS BESIEGED

Reporting on the Battle of the Hotels made much use of the words "citadel", "fortress" and "bunker" to describe the hotels – the Holiday Inn, above all – and the Murr Tower. And in 2011, Mona Hatoum gave the name *Bunker* to an installation of stacks of rectangular metal tubing, cut and burned,[87] denuded carcasses that allude to the hotels of Beirut (FIG.37).

FIG.37 *Mona Hatoum, Bunker, 2011. Twenty-two mild steel tubing structures, dimensions variable. Installation view at White Cube, London.*

While the advantages these offered in terms of firing positions and combat posts were evident, fighters faced a number of challenges in making use of them, the most important being the risk of fire occasioned by the presence of flammable materials, such as textiles and panelling. Whereas the Saint-Georges and the Phoenicia burned out in one, the Holiday Inn saw a succession of fires on different floors (FIG.38). Preventive measures were taken: "That's why internal walls were knocked down. In the most highly exposed rooms, the floors were kept running with water, and in many places you'd be walking on thick, soaking-wet carpet."[88]

A problem facing the Phalangists, who were surrounded and cut off from their base, was replenishment. In October, they were able to make use of the Saint-Georges' direct access to the sea to run boats back and forth from the port of Jounieh.[89] There are stories, too, of militiamen who abandoned their posts and made their way to Christian areas in stolen craft.[90] After the fall of the Saint-Georges and the Phoenicia, it became much trickier to relieve the men at the Holiday Inn. "You had to race across this avenue that lay in the line of fire from the Murr Tower and the Phoenicia, before getting into the hotel through the basement."[91] One day, a Joint Forces fighter "succeeded in hitting two Phalangists who were crossing the road from

86 *Ibid.*
87 BARIAA MOURAD, "Memory and Identity in Beirut: The (Im)possibilities of Artistic Historiography", in *Arts and Culture in Times of Conflict: Contemporary Reflections*, Leuven, 2014, p. 48.
88 "La bataille du Holiday Inn rapportée par les agences internationales", *L'Orient Le Jour*, 16 December 1975.
89 FAYAD, interview of 24 July 2013.
90 Former Phalangist party official, interview of 23 October 2013.
91 "La bataille du Holiday Inn rapportée par les agences internationales", op. cit.

their barricades to the hotel entrance."[92] The Phalange would thus wait for the cover of night to get their people in and out (FIG.39).[93]

> *One evening, a youth posted on the sixteenth floor of the Holiday Inn suffered an epileptic fit. R. and I, who were in Sector 4,[94] had to get there by car, crossing the avenue in full sight of the snipers, climb sixteen floors on foot, carry the patient down, get him into the car, get past the snipers again and drive to party headquarters in Saifi.*[95]

There was speculation about underground passages linking the Holiday Inn to the Phoenicia or the city centre, a suggestion denied by the military.[96] There was also vague talk of an armoured metal cylinder that protected militiamen inside,[97] even of a wall of sheet steel "built in a workshop, installed with wooden supports, and reinforced."[98]

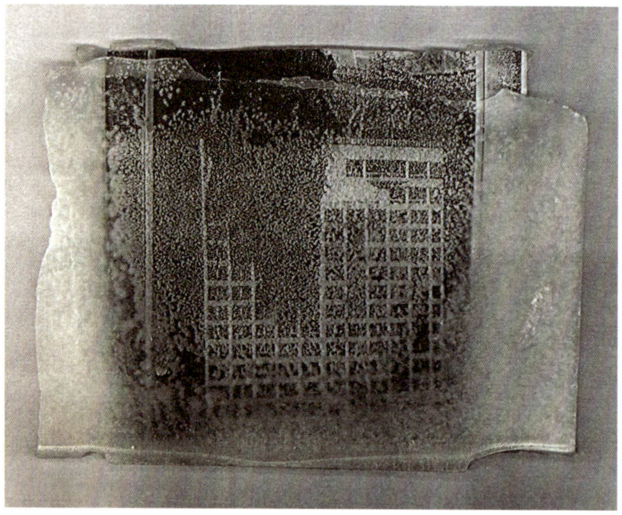

FIG.38 *Paola Yacoub, Mist (Holiday Inn), 1995. Wax, black & white photocopy, 12 × 15.7 × 1 cm.*

FIG.39 *Samir Khaddage, Untitled [Battle of the Hotels], c. 1975-1980. Graphite on paper, 2 × (100 × 70) cm.*

92 "Joint Forces back at the Murr Tower", *As-Safir*, 12 January 1976, p. 1.
93 FAYAD, interview of 24 July 2013.
94 The Phalangist military command had divided the city of Beirut into sectors. Sector 4 covered the hotel district and the Wadi Abu Jamil neighbourhood.
95 Former Phalangist party official, interview of 23 October 2013.
96 "La bataille du Holiday Inn rapportée par les agences internationales", op. cit.
97 *Ibid.*
98 Former Phalangist party official, interview of 23 October 2013.

SURVEILLANCE AND DEFENCE, FORTIFICATIONS AND FIRING POINTS

Fighters took advantage of the concrete construction, the depth of the buildings, the many windows and the views they commanded: "We could have held the Holiday Inn indefinitely, even with the Phoenicia and the Murr Tower on either side, with just thirty men. We had the very minimum in the way of fortification, no more than sandbags. All we'd have had to do was concrete off the ground and first floors."[99] However, there were not thirty but only six to eight men, with as many firearms, to defend the Holiday Inn during the final attack in March 1976:[100] "Two men on the second floor, two on the twenty-fourth, two at the entrance."[101] They used the intercom to communicate with one another, and when this was out of action a volunteer had to "go round the floors to check that everyone was still there."[102] The height of the building was an advantage for monitoring and controlling the surrounding terrain. From the very start of the battle, the two camps justifiably accused each other of using the towers as snipers' nests (FIG.42). One might wonder how the battle would have gone if these had been towers of glass.

FIG.40 *"Combatants hiding behind armchairs in the dining room at the 24th floor [of the Holiday Inn]", 1975. Photograph published in L'Orient-Le Jour, November 4, 1975.*

Inside, fighters moved about constantly to avoid being located. Positions would be improvised: "On a staircase landing, behind a broken window, swept by wind and rain. Behind this opening, they [women fighters] lay down on their bellies with their bipod machine guns."[103] The two sides played cat and mouse, as when bathrobes would be hung on a balcony, so as to encourage the enemy to fire and so find out their positions.[104] Positions were fortified with whatever was at hand – "beds, room-service trolleys, anything hard and non-flammable. The balconies were really useful. We'd put up a double barrier, the first on the balcony, the second in the room. The rockets they fired would hit the first barricade. The furniture we used for two things: rest and barricades."[105] Sandbags finished off the whole.[106] In a revolving restaurant on the twenty-fourth floor, the chairs and the tables draped in white linen allowed fighters to hide their presence from the marksmen in the Murr Tower (FIG.40).[107]

While the more elevated positions served for long-range fire, sniping and observation, those on lower floors controlled the approaches to the building and those on the ground floor defended the entrance. On this last, the most striking testimony is a photograph taken by Don McCullin in the lobby of the Holiday Inn in January 1976 (FIG.41). The bay windows around the entrance porch are divided by pillars behind which two fighters have stationed themselves. The window panes are broken, the curtains blowing in the wind, some rubble lies on the floor. On the right, the varnished wood "reception desk" is scratched all over, and behind it stands the cardboard cut-out figure of an Air France stewardess – because, in September 1975, the airline had thought it best to move its office from the Place Riad Solh, by then a battlefield, to the Holiday Inn, believed to be a safer location, only to have to leave the following month.[108] Three palms survive in their pots. On the left, a wooden panel in

99 FAYAD, interview of 24 July 2013.
100 FITCHETT, JOSEPH, "The Shootout at Beirut Holiday Inn", *Washington Post*, 23 March 1976, p. A13.
101 The commander of the Phalangist forces at the Holiday Inn, in "Who is in control of the Holiday Inn?", op. cit. A number of witnesses, testified that the meagreness of the force defending the Holiday Inn is explained by the fact that most of the fighters sent to the front had ended up looting city-centre shops and dockside warehouses rather than reporting to their positions. Looting of all kinds was endemic on both sides.
102 Former Phalangist party official, interview of 23 October 2013.
103 DUPLAN and RAULIN, *Le cèdre et la croix*, op. cit., p. 82.
104 Former Phalangist party official, interview of 23 October 2013.
105 *Ibid.*
106 UNITED PRESS INTERNATIONAL, "Conflicting Reports on Seizure of Strategic Holiday Inn in Beirut", *Times Union*, 22 March 1976, p. 3.
107 "Après (?) la guerre", *L'Orient-Le Jour*, 4 November 1975, p. 2.
108 DIAB, JEAN, "Air France a maintenu ses vols réguliers sur Beyrouth au cours des événements", *La Revue du Liban*, no. 881, 28 February 1976, pp. 36–8.

the foreground and a miscellaneous heap behind offer rare visual evidence of the defences constructed for the Battle of the Hotels. They are flimsy indeed compared to the fortifications on the Green Line.

FIG.41 *Don McCullin, Christian Phalange Gunmen in the Holiday Inn Hotel, Beirut, 1976. Photograph.*

VERTICAL COMBAT, FLOOR BY FLOOR

The final assault on the Holiday Inn took place on 21 March 1976, the theatre of hostilities first shifting inside the hotel and then moving upward, floor by floor. The operation began at night, at 2.45 a.m., with intense fire by 106mm artillery[109] which destroyed the defenders' only cannon and the breeze-block walls erected to replace the bay windows of the lobby.[110] One Christian fighter was mortally wounded on the twenty-fourth floor. "I carried him to the hotel entrance, on the ground floor,"[111] his commander recalled, without saying whether the lift was working or he had negotiated the twenty-four floors on foot. Arriving at the bottom, the commander was "surprised by a substantial enemy attack on the hotel entrance."[112] Armoured vehicles – five according to the Joint Forces,[113] twenty-five according to the Phalangists[114] – opened fire to cover the attackers' penetration into the interior. The commander goes on: "As we fought, we were cut off from the outside and unaware of what was going on elsewhere.

109 "Who is in control of the Holiday Inn?" op. cit.
110 Fitchett, "The Shootout at Beirut Holiday Inn", op. cit.
111 Commander of the Phalangist forces at the Holiday Inn, in "Who is in control of the Holiday Inn?" op. cit.
112 *Ibid.*
113 Spokesman for the Arab Socialist Union – Nasserist movement, *ibid.*
114 Commander of the Phalangist forces at the Holiday Inn, *ibid.*

Our ammunition ran out, but we succeeded in taking arms and ammunition from attackers who had fallen at the hotel entrance [the attack saw three killed and four wounded, according to the PLO[115]]. We carried on fighting until six o'clock in the morning."[116]

By then, one of the Phalangists had gone to join the two marksmen in the twenty-fifth-floor nightclub.[117] The five or six others went down to the cellars; there, they found themselves surrounded, though the attackers never managed to lay hands on them. Helped by a hotel employee who guided them through the dark and winding corridors, they managed to make their way to an exit. At 6 a.m., a motorised force arrived to "put a pincer on the neighbourhood" and evacuate the Phalangist escapees.[118] At that point, the fate of the three men on the twenty-fifth floor was unknown.[119] At 10.45 a.m., a Joint Forces detachment made its way in and at 1 p.m. the victors climbed to one of the upper floors and hung a Lebanese flag from a window.[120] After having combed the building without finding any sign of the men on the twenty-fifth floor, the *Murabitun* gave a press conference in the hotel lobby at 4.30 p.m.[121]

For all that, the battle for the Holiday Inn was not yet over. At dawn the next day, it was learned that an attack on it had been "launched from the Phoenicia, after an underground tunnel was dug between the two hotels. Militiamen are said to have used this to get to the Holiday Inn's car park."[122] A spokesman for the Phalange said that the Phoenicia had been recaptured after "the fiercest of battles", together with the Holiday Inn, from which a party flag now flew.[123] How had they managed to get into the Phoenicia, which they had lost four months earlier? How could they have dug a tunnel in such a short period of time, in enemy territory at that? One can only imagine that the Christian fighters had gained access to the basement of the Saint Charles Center from Fakhreddine Street, where the *Murabitun* had earlier tried to break in. A spokesman for the Left admitted the existence of "pockets" of invaders and fighting on the lower floors.[124] The Joint Forces had "set fire to the lower floors to eliminate any Phalangist pockets within."[125] The Phalangist attack had been facilitated by the three men left behind on the upper floors of the Holiday Inn.[126] Barricaded in the top-floor bar and prepared for combat on a vertical battlefield, they are said to have come up with "a device to make hand grenades survive intact the twenty-three-story descent (increasing air pressure made the grenades explode early) toward opposing combatants who were advancing upward from the ground floor. Using the objects available in the bar, they put grenades inside glasses, transforming them into cluster bombs once they reached the ground."[127] A PLO fighter tells how "a friend of ours, he wanted to go upstairs, they shot him from behind and he fell to the ground [on the stairs]."[128] These final efforts did not, however, prevent the failure of the counteroffensive. As *Time* put it: "The Christian Phalangists lost the hotel, won it back briefly, then lost it for good."[129]

---

115 Palestine Liberation Organisation (PLO), *Yawmiyat al harb al lubnaniyya*, Beirut, 1977, p. 144.
116 Commander of the Phalangist forces at the Holiday Inn, in "Who is in control of the Holiday Inn?" op. cit.
117 Fitchett, "The Shootout at Beirut Holiday Inn", op. cit.
118 Commander of the Phalangist forces at the Holiday Inn, in "Who is in control of the Holiday Inn?" op. cit.
119 *Ibid.*
120 Fitchett, "The Shootout at Beirut Holiday Inn", op. cit.
121 Spokesman for the Arab Socialist Union – Nasserist Movement, in "The Joint Forces occupied the Holiday Inn after clashes that began at dawn and lasted 10 hours", op. cit.
122 "Who is in control of the Holiday Inn ?", op.cit.
123 United Press International, "Conflicting Reports on Seizure of Strategic Holiday Inn in Beirut", *Times Union*, 22 March 1976, p. 3.
124 *Ibid.*
125 Yaghi, Zainab, "The Holiday Inn: a story interrupted by the war", *As-Safir*, 19 May 2014.
126 "Who is in control of the Holiday Inn?", op. cit.
127 Fregonese, Sara, "Between a Refuge and a Battleground: Beirut's Discrepant Cosmopolitanisms", *Geographical Review*, vol. 102, no. 3, 2012, pp. 316–36.
128 Forham, Alice, "Beirut's Holiday Inn: Once Chic, Then Battered, Still Contested", *Parallels*, NPR, 27 May 2014, radio report.
129 Prager, Karsten, "Beirut's Agony Under the Guns of March", *Time*, vol. 107, no. 14, April 1976, p. 31.

FALLING MEN

Time's report on the capture of the Holiday Inn goes on: "Moslem riflemen stormed into the shattered lobby, fought their way up from floor to floor and savagely tossed the body of a Phalangist sniper out a window as they climbed"[130] (FIG.43). The PLO member quoted earlier confirms: "When they got to the top, they saw the snipers. They picked up the snipers and they threw them from the top to the very bottom."[131] The story of one or more snipers thrown out of the window inflamed feelings among the Christians, as did that of the last defenders, whose "bodies, some of them decapitated, were brought down to the ground floor, tied by ropes to the backs of motor vehicles and dragged through the street."[132] This was a savage practice adopted by both camps. In *Bye Babylone*, the narrator learns that "a bruiser of a van-driver from Kattine[133] used to drag the bodies of Muslims behind his pick-up."[134] A year later, the photograph of a naked body was published with the caption: "The Holiday Inn sniper fell naked from the 22nd floor. Don't ask what happened to him, or what he did. . . Here he is!"[135] This body reappears in a collaborative painting by Seta Manoukian and Samir Khaddage (FIG.44). Other accounts claimed that at the Hilton "the Phalangist fighters were jumping out of the windows in a desperate attempt to escape. So they were jumping to their doom, but we should keep in mind that this occurred after the Black Saturday massacre."[136] Unlike the case of the occupants of the World Trade Center, who leaped into the void, rather than die in the fire on 11 September 2001, there is no picture of bodies in freefall from the Holiday Inn. The mismatch between the amplitude of the narrative and the number of lives lost – minimal compared to the massacres of the time – can be explained by the exceptional character of the event: defenestrations are a rare historical occurrence and remain taboo.[137]

FIG.42 *Ayman Baalbaki, The Sniper, 2009. Acrylic on fabric mounted on canvas, 210 × 125 cm.*

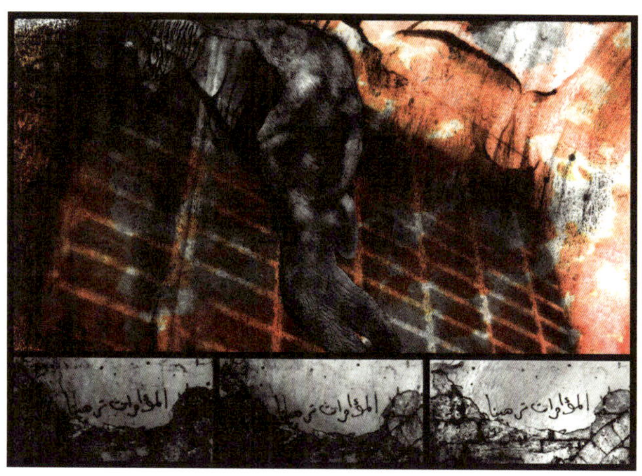

FIG.43 *Alfred Tarazi, Wishful Beginnings, 2013. Giclee Print.*

130 *Ibid.*
131 FORHAM, "Beirut's Holiday Inn: Once Chic, Then Battered, Still Contested" op. cit.
132 UNITED PRESS INTERNATIONAL, "Conflicting Reports on Seizure of Strategic Holiday Inn in Beirut", op. cit.
133 Kattine is the village in the Christian district of Kesrouan from which the author's family comes.
134 ZIADÉ, *Bye Bye Babylone*, op. cit.
135 ITANI, NAYLA, *Harb Lubnan*, Beirut, Dar al Massira, 1977, p. 112.
136 DAVID HEARST interviewed in ISSAOUI, OMAR, *Harb Lubnan (The War of Lebanon)*, episode 4, Al Jazeera, 2001. The Black Saturday massacre of 6 December 1975 involved the murder of possibly some 150–200 Muslim civilians in reprisal for the killing of four Phalangist militiamen outside Beirut.
137 THOMAS RICHARD, interview with the author, 19 May 2014.

FIG.44 *Seta Manoukian and Samir Khaddage, The City, 1979. Acrylic and airbrush on board, 220 × 121 cm.*

THE BONFIRE OF THE VANITIES

On 12 December 1975, the *New York Times* published a short backgrounder on "one of the most distinguished hotels. . . a haunt of prominent Middle East politicians and officials, of the international set, of visiting motion picture stars and literary figures."[138] A photograph of the blackened building completed what more resembled an obituary than a news article. The Saint-Georges had been heavily damaged by fire. Two months earlier, the politician Takieddin el-Solh had made efforts to prevent the fighting spreading to that district, because "the hotels symbolise what Beirut is all about."[139] His nephew Khaldun el-Solh had succeeded in arranging a meeting at the Holiday Inn between the warring factions, which resulted in a "gentleman's agreement" – a pact that came to nothing, as we have seen.

The destruction of the hotels followed that of the historic centre, begun in September 1975. During the early months of what were then called "the events", both the city centre and the hotel district were relatively distant from the fighting. One could long debate the reasons why the beligerents chose to shift the theatre of war, but there is agreement that the issues at stake were "more political than strategic."[140] While the city centre was a social space of encounter and intercommunal mixing, the hotels were emblematic of the cosmopolitanism and economic success of a Lebanon dominated by a financial oligarchy consisting of some thirty families, "the consortium" that had taken control of what was then known as the "Merchant Republic."[141] The bar of the Saint-Georges was the place where "the Gettys and Rockefellers went to meet everyone who mattered in the Middle East" in a city that in 1967 "had more commercial banks than New York."[142] The prosperity of this golden – or gilded – age was not without its dark underbelly.[143] At the heart of one of the world's most unstable and contested regions, it "became notorious for smuggling, arms-running, trading in drugs, black-marketing of contraband products, and other nefarious activities."[144] The cinema offers much evidence of this disreputable image: from the 1950s to the 70s, adventure films recounting the movements of smugglers and spies all took the same route: landing at the airport, then arrival at the Phoenicia, where the hero enjoys ogling the bathing beauties through the portholes of the Bar Sous la Mer, followed by a venture into the souks and an outing to an archaeological site. The reality was not so different. On 23 January 1963, Kim Philby settled down at his customary table at the bar of the Saint-Georges for his "five or six afternoon drinks."[145] It was the last public sighting of the most notorious Cold War spy before his escape to Moscow.

FIG.45 *Joana Hadjithomas and Khalil Joreige, Wonder Beirut, Part 1. The story of a pyromaniac photographer. Battle of the Hotels (Historical Process). Photographic print on aluminum, Diasec, 30 × 153 cm [9 versions of the postcard "Général view with mountains", "burnt from October 28 to December 16, 1975"].*

138 "Plush Beirut Hotel Is Victim of Strife", *New York Times*, 12 December 1975.
139 Aburish, *The St. George Hotel Bar*, op. cit., p. 203.
140 Saab, Edouard, "Tandis que l'État se désagrège : de violents combats se poursuivent dans plusieurs régions", op. cit.
141 Traboulsi, Fawwaz, *A History of Modern Lebanon*, London, Pluto Press, 2007, p. 115.
142 Aburish, *The St. George Hotel Bar*, op. cit., p. 110.
143 Samir Khalaf draws a distinction between "Golden" and "Gilded", titling his Chapter 6 "Lebanon's Golden/Gilded Age: 1943–1975" in *Civil and Uncivil Violence in Lebanon: A History of the Internationalization of Communal Conflict*, New York, 2002, pp. 151–203.
144 Khalaf, *Civil and Uncivil Violence in Lebanon*, op. cit., p. 198.
145 Aburish, *The St. George Hotel Bar*, op. cit., p. 3.

It has to be said that both sides involved in the conflict managed to find moralising justifications for the destruction. Amid the smoking ruins of Martyrs Square, a Phalangist official proudly declared: "We have succeeded in doing what the government has been incapable of doing over the years. In cleaning up these alleyways, this whole neighbourhood, a hotbed of vice, drugs and crime. A sanctuary for outlaws, for foreigners illegally in the country, for habitual criminals, for every kind of prostitution."[146] And it proved equally tempting, in a conflict said to be between the forces of Left and Right, to see some logic of social revolt at play: "I saw the destruction, the ruined hotels, but I asked myself who profited from them except for one or two per cent of the population. And what of the rest of the people?"[147] One witnessed the pleasure of those who "rose up as one and came together to sack the cities, the temples and the idols."[148] A *Murabitun* poster featured a colossal fighter striking the Holiday Inn with his rifle butt and the words: "On 21 March 1976, the *Murabitun* destroyed the symbol of fascist treason."[149] Beirut's grand hotels suffered the same fate as the Shepheard's Hotel in Cairo, which had "finally paid for its years of imperial glitter [when] angry Egyptian crowds burned it to the ground in 1952."[150]

Politics being the art of having it both ways, each side boasted of having cleansed the city – of vice, imperialism or whatever – while accusing the other of having reduced it to ashes. The *Revue du Liban*, aligned with the Christian camp, had no doubt about "the very clear criminal intent and the desire for destruction for destruction's sake. 'We have to destroy to rebuild a new Lebanon' is the arrogant claim of a Progressive leader who is clearly the enemy of progress."[151] It went on to argue – against the claim that "all who came from the poverty-stricken suburbs and countryside shared a hatred and a bitterness against the capital and wanted to destroy it"[152] – that this "indescribable frenzy is not a 'revolt of the disadvantaged' as some have sought to argue, but the criminal and utterly despicable doing of foreign elements and paid agents."[153] Quick to point out that the Christian forces were the first to enter the hotels, the *Murabitun* declared themselves astonished "to see the opposite camp occupy the Holiday Inn hotel and force the foreign tourists onto the roof, and attempt to occupy the Saint Georges, as if they wanted Lebanon to suffer what has happened to Cyprus. They oblige us to fire at these establishments and kill foreign tourists so as to tarnish our reputation."[154] Ten years later, an author hostile to the Christian Right lamented:

- *Your hotels, O Beirut, why have they destroyed you?*
- *They sought to occupy them, to violate them. They made their way in from the sea and they occupied them. My sons defended them against this attack. The sons of Metn, of Aley and of Shuf, the sons of the suburbs took part in the defence against the attacker and helped put him to flight. Their blood stands forever witness to their heroism. The enemy, before making away, demolished the hotels and set them on fire.*[155]

146 Helou, Nelly, "Au centre-ville de Beyrouth 48 heures avant l'arrivée des Syriens. Les batailles du Liban commencent et se terminent au centre-ville", *La Revue du Liban*, no. 896, 20 November 1976, pp. 44–5.
147 Nigolian, Sonia, "Quatre Miliciens libanais exposent les raisons de leur combat", *La Revue du Liban*, no. 879, 14 February 1976, pp. 58–9.
148 Benassar (Bechara Menassa), *Anatomie d'une guerre et d'une occupation : événements du Liban de 1975 à 1978*, Paris, Galilée, 1978, p. 66.
149 Maasri, Zeina, *Off the Wall: Political Posters of the Lebanese Civil War*, London and New York, I. B. Tauris, 2009, p. 105.
150 Fitchett, "From Khans To Khiltons", op. cit.
151 Diab, Jean, "The slow death", op. cit.
152 Rechmaoui, Marwan, paper given at *History of the Last Things Before the Last: Art as Writing History*, symposium organised by the Arab Image Foundation and the Centre Pompidou at Ashkal Alwan Home Workspace, Beirut, 30 November–1 December 2012.
153 Diab, "The slow death", op. cit.
154 "The 'Mourabitoun' and the Kataeb: Why are they fighting in the Kantari region?", *An-Nahar*, 28 October 1975, p. 6.
155 Al Zaib, Mohammad, *Lawhat al-ghadr, Lawhat al-tha'r*, Beirut, Dar al Farabi, 1986, p. 40.

It is hard to ignore the bad faith of those on one side who claimed to have sent their militia to occupy the hotels in order to protect them, and those on the other who said they besieged them to protect the lives of their occupants. The fate of the hotel district put an end to the utopian myth of a prosperous and cosmopolitan Lebanon, and this is perhaps one of the reasons why it has been taken up as a subject by so many artists of the so-called post-war generation. During the Mois de la Photo festival of photography in Lebanon in 1998, Joana Hadjithomas and Khalil Joreige showed *Beirut, Urban Fictions,*[156] later known as *Wonder Beirut: The Story of a Pyromaniac Photographer* (FIG.45). According to the accompanying text:

> *In a desperate attempt to reflect the Lebanese Civil Wars that began on 13 April 1975 and officially ended on 13 October 1990, the negatives of these post cards were burnt in places, over time, by Abdallah Farah himself [the photographer], to reflect the bombardments and the destruction caused by the armed conflict.*
>
> *[. . .]*
>
> *Published in 1969, the post card "General View with Mountains" was burned in parts between 28 October and 16 December 1975, during the first Battle of the Hotels. Abdallah photographed the image after each burn he inflicted, methodically tracking the day's events, producing a series of images that we call the "historic process."*

The nine versions of this image each bear on the back a date and a description of the events that took place on it. In the name of their fictional pyromaniac photographer, Hadjithomas and Joreige visited upon the images the destruction that befell the city.

Globally speaking, the Battle of the Hotels – whose character as an act of war was paradoxically denied by the New York court mentioned earlier, which ruled it to be a "series of 'civil commotions'"[157] – was one of the first terror acts to involve skyscrapers. It was the same year that J. G. Ballard published *High Rise*, a novel set in a residential tower whose residents split into hostile factions that carry out attacks on enemy floors. Unlike the Holiday Inn, Ballard's building is wrecked by its own inhabitants in an orgy of barbarism. The Battle of the Hotels also predates the 9/11 attacks by a quarter of a century. It has been said, rightly or wrongly, that the destruction of the World Trade Center was seen not just as an attack on a building, but as an attack on an ideological, political and economic system.[158] Yet neither the Battle of the Hotels nor the 9/11 attacks has put an end to extravagantly ambitious building projects. New York's World Trade Center has been rebuilt, and on the Beirut seafront the Phoenicia, the Holiday Inn and the Murr Tower are now dwarfed by the towers that have sprung up since. The race for the heights shows no sign of stopping.

156 *Juillet, Mois de la photographie au Liban*, Beirut, 1998, p. 168.
157 Lewin, "Beirut Insurance Ruling Favors Holiday Inn", op. cit.
158 Kocache, Moukhtar, "Up in the Air", in *Home Works II: A Forum of Cultural Practices*, Beirut, 2003, pp. 110–20.

CHAPTER 2

DEFENSIVE SPACE: THE GREEN LINE

FIG.46 *Steve McCurry, Beirut, 1982. Photograph.*

THE LINE AND ITS HISTORICAL ANTECEDENTS

FIG.47 *Rafic Charaf, Untitled, 1976. Ink on paper, 31 × 43 cm.*

Between 1975 and 1990, Beirut was cut in two by what was variously called the front line, the demarcation line, the line of confrontation or the Green Line. This divided West Beirut, dominated by the Left Forces and East Beirut, controlled by the Christian Right. The permanence of this line of division, in contrast to the mobility of the Battle of the Hotels, reflects a kinship with both the trenches of the Great War and the post-war condition, in which, Virilio tells us, "the dialectic of combat waged on the battlefield has. . . vanished, the instantaneity and ubiquity of the different means of action having completely distorted the geostrategic notions of *front* and *rear*, just as they have distorted the chronostrategic notions of *pre-* and *post-war*."[1]

In the 19th century, an earlier line separated the "rival communities [Druze and Christian] contending for control of rural space. Far from a solution that would bring an end to the fighting and the massacres, this division represented (. . .) an institutionalisation of the Civil War."[2] And in the 20th century, the construction of arterial roads linking central Beirut to the suburbs encouraged a process of fracture. Neighbourhoods such as Bashura and Zokak el-Blat found themselves cut off, isolated from their natural hinterlands. The troubles of 1958 thus saw the appearance of "a demarcation line between Muslim and Christian territories."[3] Yet, despite the force of these portents, "it was only with the war that these lines of separation became scored into the landscape. Communal separation did not arise of itself: while division existed, it was tempered by other factors; separation was imposed by force of arms."[4]

1 Virilio, Paul, "The Imbalance of Terror", in *A Landscape of Events*, translated by Julie Rose, Cambridge, MA, 2000, pp. 23–30.
2 Beyhum, Nabil, "Les Démarcations au Liban d'hier à aujourd'hui", in Kiwan, Fadia (ed.), *Le Liban aujourd'hui*, Paris and Beirut, 1994, pp. 276–7.
3 Brones, Sophie, "Al-Khandaq al-Ghamik ou la mémoire en ruine", in *Mémoires de guerres au Liban, 1975–1990*, Arles, 2010, pp. 447–8.
4 Beyhum, "Les Démarcations au Liban", op. cit., p. 285.

A BRIEF HISTORY OF THE GREEN LINE

On 13 April 1975, an armed attack on a busload of Palestinian militants led to fighting between the "Christian" neighbourhood of Ayn al-Rummana and the "Muslim" neighbourhood of Shiyah. In May, the area around Damascus Street saw "violent clashes."[5] While the Lebanese "preferred to speak only of 'events' (*hawadith* or *ahdath*)" and "it was only in the autumn that the word 'war' started to be used",[6] there was already talk of a "frontier zone" running through the heart of the city.[7]

After a summer lull, the city centre saw extensive fighting break out on 17 September 1975.[8] "In this labyrinth of streets and alleyways, combatants confronted each other almost eye to eye, fighting from shop to shop, from intersection to intersection, from window to window and from one hastily constructed sandbag barricade to the next."[9] A place where all communities met and mixed, the city centre witnessed its strength become its chief weakness, as "the militias began to see it as a 'legitimate' target of violence."[10]

The dismantling of the barricades in mid-October 1975[11] represented no more than a simulacrum of normalisation that was shattered by the Battle of the Hotels, whose end in April 1976 saw the stabilisation of the line of confrontation. In the years that followed, the two sides would engage in an ongoing violence, "never so great as to be militarily decisive, and never so attenuated as to allow Beirutis to forget the world they now lived in."[12]

Early 1977 saw the line vanish for a time, even as it remained "a psychological barrier for many Beirutis."[13]

In 1978, the Phalangists challenged the Syrians who had taken over the high-rises of Ashrafieh. The so-called Hundred Days' War in East Beirut brought a reorientation of the front as West Beirut came to serve as supply base for both camps.[14] The battle ended with the defeat of the Syrians and the re-establishment of the previous line of division.

In the summer of 1982, the Israelis imposed on West Beirut a "watertight blockade",[15] maintained until the deployment in late August of a multinational force to supervise the evacuation of the Palestinians and open the crossings.[16] Following the assassination of Bashir Gemayel and the massacres of Sabra and Shatila, the Israeli army then occupied the western part of the city. The way in which it was able to take "this whole urban territory from the rear brings to mind the radical difference of strategy, vision and practice that distinguishes the war of movement from trench warfare."[17] Be that as it may, they succeeded in this only after the withdrawal of the Palestinian resistance.[18] The Multinational Force returned and, on 1 October, the headline in *L'Orient-Le Jour* read, "The demarcation line no longer exists." President Amin Gemayel announced that "Beirut is again one single city" and his prime minister, Shafiq Wazzan declared "No longer any East or West."[19] A development plan was drawn up for "Greater Beirut"[20] and the demolition of the souks began. The decision taken then "gave material expression to the process of division. . . The 'neutral' territory of before the war was wiped off the map, as if to underline that the city was irremediably divided."[21]

---

5 "Violents affrontements dans tous les 'points chauds' entre 14 et 20 heures hier", *L'Orient-Le Jour*, 26 May 1975, p. 1.
6 Kassir, *Histoire de Beyrouth*, op. cit., p. 66.
7 "Halte à la démence : Enlèvements par dizaines et déchaînements sur tous les fronts", *L'Orient-Le Jour*, 31 May 1975, p. 1.
8 Oliver Saidi, Marie-Thérèse, "La ligne verte de Beyrouth 1975–1991", *Guerres mondiales et conflits contemporains*, no. 190, June 1998, p. 44.
9 Massabki, Jacqueline and Porel, François, *La mémoire des cèdres*, Paris, 1989, p. 447.
10 Beyhum, Nabil, "La place des Canons et la guerre", in *El Bourj. Place de la liberté et porte du Levant*, Beirut, 2000, p. 94.
11 Moukhaiber, Farid, "Tandis que l'on tente de démanteler les barricades, Yasser Arafat s'installe dans l'Olympe libanais", *La Revue du Liban*, 18 October 1975, pp. 7–9.
12 Beyhum, Nabil, "Beyrouth, histoire de deux villes où tuer est une pulsion qui se répète", in *Guerres civiles : Economie de la violence – Dimensions de la civilité*, Paris, 1999, pp. 132 and 136.
13 Prager, "Beirut: Better, But Not Yet Well", op. cit.
14 Fayad, interview of 4 February 2015.
15 "Les Israéliens soumettent Beyrouth-Ouest à un blocus hermétique", *L'Orient-Le Jour*, 4 July 1982, p. 1.
16 "Réouverture-test, à 8h30, du passage Sodeco", *L'Orient-Le Jour*, 2 September 1982, p. 1.
17 Jean-Yves Andrieux, email to the author, 11 August 2015.
18 "En 12 jours, 10 876 Fedaï et 2700 soldats syriens ont quitté Beyrouth", *L'Orient-Le Jour*, 2 September 1982, p. 1.
19 "Beyrouth : La ligne de démarcation n'existe plus", *L'Orient-Le Jour*, 1 October 1982, p. 1.
20 Arnaud, Jean-Luc, "Trop grand Beyrouth ?", in *Beyrouth, Grand Beyrouth*, Beirut, 1997, pp. 209–27.
21 Davie, Michael F., "'Beyrouth-Est' et 'Beyrouth-Ouest' : territoires confessionnels ou espaces de guerre? Essai d'interprétation", in *Beyrouth : regards croisés*, Tours, 1997, p. 40.

In the summer of 1983, the situation deteriorated and, on 6 February 1984, the Left militias pushed government forces out of West Beirut, re-establishing the demarcation line. On 27 September 1986, those same militias burst through the Sodeco crossing and entered Ashrafieh with the complicity of dissident elements of the Lebanese Forces, before the Lebanese Forces proper succeeded with the help of the army in regaining control.[22] The front then remained stable until 1990, when East Beirut found itself internally divided, with the northern districts, Ashrafieh among them, controlled by the Lebanese Forces and the southern part around the Museum in the hands of the army under General Michel Aoun. In the west, the forces of Amal, Hezbollah, the Progressive Socialist Party and the *Murabitun* attacked each other regularly, though there was there no such marked territorial division. Conflict between the army and the Lebanese Forces would continue until 13 October 1990, when the Syrian army attacked the presidential palace where General Aoun had taken up residence. This brought an end to the Civil War and, with that, to the Green Line.

Since then, the line has had no existence on the ground, but lives on in memory and imagination. One still frequently meets people "for whom to cross it was to enter an unknown world, one in which they had lost or never had their bearings."[23] In the 2000s and 2010s, there were clashes between Sunni and Shia factions within West Beirut itself. The Green Line of 1975–90 is no longer a boundary between hostile territories, but a frontier between zones, one safe, the other dangerous, with the production of geographies of danger informed by wars yet to come.[24]

LINES OF DIVISION

Ayman and Said Baalbaki like to recall that "the demarcation line ran between the statues of Riad Solh and Bechara el-Khoury, fathers of Lebanese independence, which form a triangle with the Martyr's Monument."[25] The line ran south from the port (FIG.49), through the vegetable market and across Weygand Street before dropping past the souks parallel to Martyrs Square, to then follow Damascus Street. At the level of the National Museum, it crossed the racecourse to pass through the southern suburbs before reaching the mountains.

The Arabic term *khutut al-tamas*, lines of confrontation in the plural,[26] reflects the fact that the line was, in reality, a ribbon whose width varied between the "real limits of no-man's land" on the one hand and the "psychological limits of no-man's land" on the other,[27] a zone where every metre could be vital: "fifty metres in an urban area is just one or two blocks that might be of strategic importance."[28] Becoming at night a band of darkness across the city, it also came to be known as the Green Line. In the first months of the war, the city centre had been dubbed the Green Zone; later, the destruction of the water mains would provoke "a cancer of bramble, sycamore and wild fig [where] the bulging ground is mossy. Trees raise their branches between the ruined walls. . . "[29] (FIG.46)

FIG.48 *Ginane Makki Bacho, Map of Beirut, 1985. Mixed media on paper, 28.5 × 38.5 cm.*

22 "Invasion of West Beirut to gain control of Achrafieh", *An-Nahar*, 28 September 1986, p. 1.
23 MERMIER, FRANCK, *Récits de villes : d'Aden à Beyrouth*, Arles, Actes Sud, 2015, p. 76.
24 BOU AKAR, HIBA, "Contesting Beirut's frontiers", *City & Society*, vol. 24, no. 2, 2012, p. 151.
25 AYMAN BAALBAKI and SAID BAALBAKI, interview with the author, 19 September 2014.
26 MØYSTAD, OLE, "Morphogenesis of the Beirut Green-Line", *Cahiers de Géographie du Québec*, vol. 42, no. 117, December 1998, pp 421–35.
27 ABIRACHED, ZEINA, *Je me souviens. Beyrouth*, Paris, Cambourakis, 2008, p. 11.
28 GEMAYEL, BASHIR, in ALAIN MÉNARGUES, *Les Secrets de la guerre du Liban : 1. Du coup d'état de Béchir Gémayel aux massacres des camps palestiniens*, Paris, 2004, pp. 201–2.
29 WALLET, BERNARD, *Paysage avec palmiers*, Paris, Gallimard, 1992, p. 67.

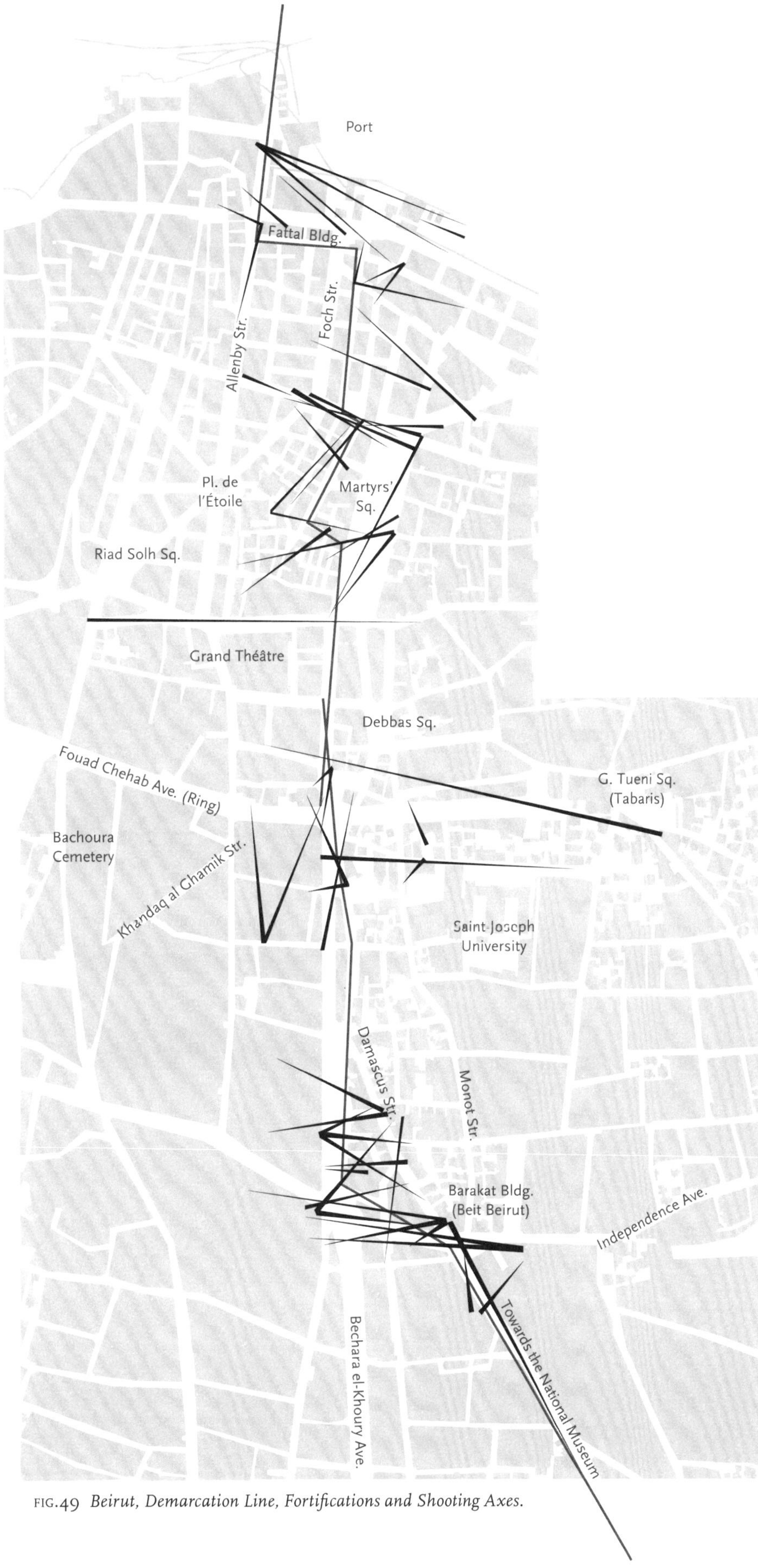

FIG.49 *Beirut, Demarcation Line, Fortifications and Shooting Axes.*

BARRICADES, EARTHEN BANKS, TUNNELS AND MINES

FIG.50 *Roger Moukarzel, Militiaman posing in a destroyed scene Beirut, 1984. Photograph.*

Between spring and autumn 1975, the urban space witnessed a balletic back and forth between partisans and the lawful authorities, as the militias imposed their rule by erecting barricades and the security forces deployed patrols and dismantled such obstructions. The latter sought to striate – control – or re-striate the space, this being "one of the fundamental tasks of the state" as it seeks "to establish a zone of rights."[30] At each "round", the balance went further against the state, which increasingly failed to impose its own control on movement. In May, there were roadblocks and barricades "by the hundreds" in "neighbourhoods transformed into fortresses."[31] In September, the militias again redrew the map, as when "all the streets linking Damascus Street and Monot Street were walled off by the NLP",[32] i.e. by the Tigers of the National Liberal Party.

The barricade is a constant in urban conflict. In the Middle Ages, "partisans attacked neighbouring positions, or defended them by raising barricades or stretching chains readied in advance."[33] An emblematic feature of 19th-century Paris, from Delacroix's *Liberty Leading the People* to Hugo's *Les Misérables* and from Meissonnier to Manet, it was resurrected by the Commune: "It extended across the great boulevards, often reached first-storey level, and sheltered the trenches situated behind it."[34] The barricades of the Lebanese Civil War were not raised by revolutionaries, but by factions who acted in accordance with "an unwritten consensus shared by the internal and external actors involved" to "rob the state of its sovereign functions without themselves becoming a state."[35]

"An accumulation of objects and materials serving to obstruct the passage of the enemy and to afford cover in street fighting" (FIG.50),[36] the barricade is to be distinguished from a fortification proper, which remained "by reason of both technology and cost the prerogative of the state."[37] A barricade might consist, among other things, of sandbags, barrels filled with concrete, blockhouses, banked earth[38] or transport containers filled with earth set across an alleyway.[39] It would form part of a larger system – no fewer than four thousand were raised in Paris in 1830[40] – and was deployed in depth at the front. One might then speak of defensive lines, completed by bunkers, trenches and tunnels.

FIG.51 *Varouj Malivian, "The Gate of Hell", 1975. Photograph published in An-Nahar, October 26, 1975. [Barakat building on the Sodeco front].*

30 DELEUZE, GILLES and GUATTARI, FELIX, *A Thousand Plateaus: Capitalism and Schizophrenia*, translated by Brian Massumi, Athlone Press, London, 1987, p. 479.
31 "En attendant que la situation se décante ; Les 'souks' paralysés et les quartiers transformés en forteresses", *L'Orient-Le Jour*, 25 May 1975, p. 1.
32 "On s'est battu sur tous les fronts, hier", *L'Orient-Le Jour*, 30 October 1975, pp. 1 and 4.
33 ROGUET, CHRISTOPHE-MICHEL, *Insurrections et guerre des barricades dans les grandes villes*, Paris, J. Dumaine, 1850, p. 5.
34 BENJAMIN, WALTER, "Paris – Capital of the Nineteenth Century", *New Left Review*, no. 48, 1968, p. 87.
35 BEYHUM, "Beyrouth, histoire de deux villes", op. cit., p. 133.
36 *Dictionnaire Larousse.*
37 PROST, PHILIPPE, "La ville et la guerre de Vauban à Napoléon Ier", in PICON, ANTOINE (ed.), *La ville et la guerre*, Besançon, Editions de l'Imprimeur, 1996, p. 89.
38 "Ils ont commencé à déminer les routes et les immeubles. Les Français progressent le long du no man's land entre l'Est et l'Ouest", *L'Orient-Le Jour*, 28 August 1982, p. 2.
39 ABIRACHED, ZEINA, *Mourir partir revenir. Le jeu des hirondelles*, Paris, Cambourakis, 2007, p. 12.
40 BEIK, WILLIAM, "*The Insurgent Barricade* by Mark Traugott", *American Journal of Sociology*, vol. 117, no. 2, September 2011, pp. 675–7.

At the Sodeco crossing, fighters left their vehicles in the car park and followed a protected route through buildings then took to tunnels, escaping observation or fire from enemy lines. The tunnels had been dug with pneumatic drills, and where it was impossible to dig, lines of barrels covered with sandbags served to secure safe passage.[41]

The warring parties also laid mines. During the dismantling of the front in 1982, the incautious were "killed or wounded by explosive booby traps."[42] Mine clearers were faced by systems that could be triggered by the opening or closing of a door, or lifting "the weight of an old jacket, a shoe or a hat."[43]

CROSSINGS

Punctuated by crossing points, this "site of fracture [was] also destined to unite."[44] From north to south, there were the Port crossing, located in downtown Beirut; the Fouad Shehab overpass, commonly called the Ring, where it was recommended to "hurl the car across at maximum speed. . . for the gunmen liked to do some target practice from time to time";[45] the Sodeco crossing[46] at the geographical centre of the city (FIGS.51, 54); the Museum crossing, "the most frequently used, and so the most dangerous",[47] which could be done by car or "on foot, taking different taxis on either side",[48] was also the site of demonstrations organised by civil society against the war and militia control;[49] the Franciscan crossing, via the racecourse; and the Galerie Semaan, south of the city.

FIG.52 *Samir Khaddage and Marc Mourani, The Bridge, 1983. Acrylic on paper laid on panel, 110 x 160 cm.*

In *Beyroutou el Lika* (*Beirut the Encounter*), Haidar, a young man from the south who has found refuge in West Beirut, has to "cross" to the east to meet with a woman friend. "Beirut does all it can to prevent encounters. . . so much does the city fail to get anything right, as on a morning after the night before."[50] Impossible in Borhane Alaouié's film, that meeting does take place for the couple of newlyweds captured by the cameras of Jay Ullal and George Semerdjian as they crossed the ruined and rubble-strewn Damascus Street. Faced by such obstruction and the ensuing division, Ginane Makki Bacho offers a double portrait of herself, the two images superimposed on a plan of the city and separated by the demarcation line, reflecting not only fracture, but the dichotomisation of a centre that no longer exists (FIG.48).

Vital for those who lived on one side and worked on the other, the crossings played an equally important role at times of mass exodus, as on the occasion of the Israeli invasion. The road bridge crowded with people in Khaddage's painting gives an idea of the density of such flows (FIG.52). In 1982, Fouad Elkoury took a poignant photograph at the Museum crossing, as figures carrying bundles fled West Beirut while another woman walked in the other direction, towards the camera, making for the besieged city (FIG.53). The black and white brings out the contrasts of texture, conferring an aura on the scene that recalls the Berlin of 1945.[51]

41 FAYAD, interview of 24 July 2013.
42 "Le monde démoniaque des engins piégés ", *L'Orient-Le Jour*, 12 October 1982.
43 *Ibid.*
44 OLIVER SAIDI, "La ligne verte de Beyrouth 1975–1991", op. cit., p. 51.
45 SEURAT, MARIE, *Un si proche Orient*, Paris, Grasset & Fasquelle, 1991, p. 205.
46 Sodeco is only one example of a toponym derived from a business location (the offices of building company Société de Construction et de Commerce). News bulletins would thus refer to exchanges of fire involving Gaumont Palace, Chevrolet , Galerie Semaan or Sodeco.
47 KANAFANI-ZAHAR, AIDA, "Le musée national de Beyrouth : Mémoire des contraires, frontière et passage, échafaud et liberté", in *Mémoires de guerres au Liban, 1975–1990*, Arles, 2010, p. 127.
48 OLIVER SAIDI, "La ligne verte de Beyrouth 1975–1991", op. cit., p. 51.
49 SLAIBY, GHASSAN, "Les actions collectives de résistance civile à la guerre", in *Le Liban aujourd'hui*, Paris, 1994, pp. 119–36.
50 "Les générations éclatées", *Le Monde diplomatique*, September 1982, p. 13.
51 BUCHAKJIAN, "Selecting, sorting, looking", op. cit., pp. 223–48.

FIG.53 *Fouad Elkoury, Museum Crossing, Civil War series, 1982. Photograph.*

CROSSCUTTING DIVISIONS

The demarcation line intersected others which also, each in its own way, represented scissions. The construction of the Ring Road in the early 1970s tended to cut the city centre off from its surroundings, while the Avenue Salim Salam, seen in the building in *Bayrout ya Bayrout* (FIG.6), sliced through existing neighbourhoods. In the master plan for the reconstruction of the city centre in the 90s, "Martyrs Square was conceived as part of a boulevard that carried off the condemned old city to the sea. . . The war continued after the war, but by other means, as Clausewitz might say."[52] Since then, the Ring has come to serve as the boundary between the secure and well-appointed Solidere zone and working-class districts such as Bashura. In the years 2000–10, and more especially after the outbreak of war in Syria, tensions mounted between Sunni and Shia and "the boulevard that separates this neighbourhood [Sunni Tariq Jadidah] from the mixed Sunni–Shia neighbourhoods of Mazraa [has become] a demarcation line as real and consequential as that which separated Ayn al-Rummana and Shiyah."[53]

In 1985, Alfred Kettaneh was seized on the Green Line while at the wheel of a Red Cross ambulance, never to be seen again. Decades later, his disappearance inspired his niece Lamia Joreige to make *Here and Perhaps Elsewhere*, a film in which she walks the old line, asking passers-by if anyone they knew was kidnapped during the war (FIG.54). The artist here draws up her own map of the city,[54] taking viewers on "a journey which does not end in either information or answers – a ghost hunt of sorts."[55] *Here and Perhaps Elsewhere* seems to mirror *Bayrout ya Bayrout*, the two films sometimes touring the same places as they contemplate the wounds of a city and a war still to come for one, already in the past for the other.

FIG.54 *Lamia Joreige, Here and Perhaps Elsewhere, 2003. Video.*

52 Beyhum, "La place des Canons et la guerre", op. cit., p. 95.
53 Mermier, *Récits de villes : d'Aden à Beyrouth*, op. cit., p. 72.
54 Joreige, Lamia, "Here and Perhaps Elsewhere", in *Out of Beirut*, catalogue of the exibition of the same title held at Modern Art Oxford, 13 May–16 July 2006, pp. 18–21.
55 Rogers, Sarah, "L'art de l'après-guerre à Beyrouth", *La Pensée de midi*, no. 20 – Beyrouth xxie siècle, March 2007, pp. 115–123.

STAYING, LEAVING, COMING BACK: LIVING ON THE GREEN LINE

Many of those who lived on what became the Green Line left. Some stayed, left, came back and left again. After the 1982 invasion, the Chemaitillys returned to find their Tayouneh apartment devastated and soiled with the excrement of Israeli soldiers. Hidden under a floor slab they found papers that had belonged to a Palestinian fighter: love letters to his girlfriend, a note on the use of weapons, personal reflections. In the grip of the prevailing mood of anxiety, they burned the documents for fear of their being found by the Israeli army and then left, never to return.[56] In *Je me souviens*, Zeina Abirached devotes two pages to her family's successive departures, between 1981 and 1990, from their home directly overlooking the barricades.[57] The last of these saw them leave for West Beirut on the occasion of the battle between the army and the Lebanese Forces. It was this same intra-faith conflict that destroyed the Boueiz building (bf2455, Mazraa), near the Museum, and with it the illusions of its residents. Having survived unscathed until then, it received a pounding in July 1990. The caretaker and an elderly lady (the tenant of a first-floor apartment) stayed on amid the ruins, having nowhere else to go. After the war, the owners ended up demolishing the whole building.[58] In *The Green Line*, made in 1988, the camera seeks out the residents who stayed on despite everything. The rector of St Joseph's University explains that "the demarcation line is a zone of relation as well as a zone of confrontation" and that "we cannot have a politics of the void. The unity of Lebanon will be forged in Beirut. We do not wish to leave the area that will be the zone of reunification."[59]

The Green Line also absorbed newcomers, refugees most of them; this suited the warring parties, who saw it, among other things, as a way of filling up a void in the face of the enemy.[60] In 1979, the diplomat and writer Tawfiq Yusuf 'Awwad moved into the Boueiz building mentioned earlier, his previous apartment having been devastated during the Battle of the Hotels. In 1976, the Lebanese parliament had moved not far from there, after abandoning its building in Place de l'Étoile on account of the fighting around it. A site accessible to deputies from both sides had to be found if it was to meet again, and the choice fell on the Villa Esseily-Mansour (bf630, Mazraa), a "vast, stately residence, architecturally vaguely reminiscent of Versailles."[61] Together with the Résidence des Pins next door, this became home to the only political institution on "neutral" territory. In 1990, the legislature returned to its building on Place de l'Étoile, leaving the Villa Mansour the only non-military site on the front line to be used in time of war and abandoned in time of peace (PL.37, 38).

War halted, residents who had left the Green Line began to return:

> *Then, one morning, the wall was no longer there.*
> *I discovered that my dead end was not one.*
> *And that it led to a network of other streets.*
> *Other stories, other lives.*
> *Since then, the city has entered into me.*[62]

NEIGHBOURHOOD LIFE: SOLIDARITIES, ENCOUNTERS, RELATIONSHIPS

In Ziad Doueiri's film *West Beirut*, there is a scene in a brothel in the neighbourhood of Zaytouneh, whose bars and nightclubs used once to be frequented by sailors seeking a tryst with the "artiste–hostesses": having made our way through the rubble, we enter a space where the madam welcomes clients from both sides of the line and weapons are banned. It serves as a metaphor for a certain tie that has always existed between the two sides. An episode no less outré occurred during the shooting of Jocelyne Saab's *A Suspended Life*, as war raged in Beirut,

56 Wassim Chemaitilly, interview with the author, 15 June 2015.
57 Abirached, *Je me souviens. Beyrouth*, op. cit., pp. 46–7.
58 Zeina Toutounji Gauvard, interview with the author, 6 November 2014.
59 Jean Ducruet in Hojeij, Bahij, *La Ligne Verte / The Green Line*, 1988.
60 Baalbaki and Baalbaki, interview of 19 September 2014.
61 "L'accès au nouveau parlement et le dispositif de sécurité : Les députés n'auront que quelques mètres à parcourir à découvert", *L'Orient-Le Jour*, 30 April 1976, p. 1.
62 Abirached, Zeina, *Beyrouth Catharsis*, Paris, Cambourakis, 2006.

when a group of young men burst into the Grand Théâtre brandishing guns and kidnapped the crew: "They locked us up in a café that functioned as a whorehouse and a gambling joint and sent my assistant to fetch a ransom, together with one of the kidnappers, while the others held us at gunpoint. She came back with a cheque for 3000 Lebanese pounds and they let us go."[63]

Beyond the comical aspect of these episodes where reality and fiction converged, life on the front line changed human relationships, generating solidarity between neighbours and blurring the distinction between public and private. Located 30 metres from the front, the Choueiris' apartment became both gaming club and military headquarters, officers arriving each evening to direct battle as they played cards.[64] The militias were variously a threat and a support. For the residents of the Museum sector, the Tyous or "Billy Goats" – a far-Right Christian militia that haunted the neighbourhood – were a presence "neither agreeable nor reassuring."[65] Elsewhere, having certain neighbours might be more fortunate, as witnessed by this letter to a woman who lived in the same building as Pierre Gemayel, founder of the Kataeb or the Phalange: "Because I knew who lived in your building, I was sure you had nothing to fear from rifles or artillery and that food and water would pose no problem."[66] In Maarad Street, right in the city centre, Madame Youssevitch and her daughters Wanda and Ida did not budge from the apartment that had been theirs since 1935. Their first instinct had been to destroy documents connected with their past, notably those relating to a circus the family had owned in Russia, for fear that the Left Forces should denounce them to the Soviet embassy.[67] Isolated and threatened by hunger and cold, they were assisted by the men in arms: "They gave us food. At first, we paid them the cost of the bread, the vegetables, the meat, the water. . . And even when we couldn't pay any longer, they still kept us in food."[68]

In neighbourhoods close by, the children "hung about with the fighters", who "one day, for a bit of fun, blew up the water main and bathed in swimsuits in their improvised pool."[69] The war seemed to have become a game, even a forbidden pleasure, as when in *High Rise* the apartment owners "enjoyed this breakdown of its services, and the growing confrontation between themselves."[70] One might ask how some hundreds of fighters held hostage a city of a million inhabitants for fifteen years. Nabil Beyhum reminds us that, "A militia doesn't exist without a surrounding society that supports it, even should it end up rejecting them."[71] Speaking of the French contribution to the construction of the Atlantic Wall, Paul Virilio emphasises that "strategic defense is only possible with the active and unconditional participation of the population, as the Chinese leader [Mao] once again put it", adding that mobilisation is tied to "psychological and political necessities, to the participation on the part of occupied populations in the defensive effort."[72] A documentary shot in 1989 has a sequence where women present the militiamen at a barricade with pastries:

> *"We live on the Green Line. We want to thank you because without your protection we wouldn't have been able to stay. We've made you these cakes. We used the baker's oven because we don't have gas any longer."*
> *"Thank you, that's kind of you, it's very touching. It reminds me of before, during the Two-Year War, when women would bring down coffee they made in their apartments."*[73]

There were women who made their homes available to fighters, even as they continued to live there. Madame Aida had an apartment overlooking the Ring: "Her home soon became a permanent observation post for around twenty young people, mostly men along with some young girls who were fighting in the Christian militias," and then a mini barracks. Nicknamed "Maman Aida", she prepared hot food to be eaten there or sent down to the barricades. Although she "lived and worked in the front for twelve years from 1975 to 1986, when her apartment was destroyed by shelling, "she never changed her lifestyle."[74] For Raed Charaf, the ruling-class women

63 Jocelyne Saab, interview with the author, 2 November 2015.
64 Choueiri, Michel, in "Mona's House" (SWR, n.d.).
65 Toutounji Gauvard, interview of 6 November 2014.
66 Marie O., letter to Victoria K., 15 June 1977.
67 Adolphe Youssevitch, interview with the author, 2 October 2014.
68 Khoury, Hala, "Les Youssevitch de la rue Maarad. Trois femmes qui n'ont pas quitté leur maison un seul jour", *L'Orient-Le Jour*, 11 October 1982.
69 Michel Raggi, interview with the author, 2 April 2015.
70 Ballard, J. G., *High Rise*, London, Jonathan Cape, 1975, p. 81.
71 Beyhum, "Beyrouth, histoire de deux villes", op. cit., p. 137.
72 Virilio, Paul, *Bunker Archaeology*, translated by George Collins, New York, Princeton Architectural Press 1994, p. 28.
73 De Maistre, Gilles, "24 Heures à Beyrouth-Est", *24 heures*, Canal Plus, 1989.
74 Karamé, Kari H., "Maman Aida, a Lebanese Godmother of the Combatants: fighting Without Arms", in Lamia Rustum Shehadeh (ed.), *Women and War in Lebanon*, Gainesville, FL, 1999, p. 203.

photographed decades later by Lamia Maria Abillama, wearing battledress in their opulent interiors, testify to the porosity between civil society, and the bourgeoisie in particular, and the world of combat and warfare.[75]

THE LAST OF THE LEOPARDS

FIG.55 *Fouad Elkoury, At Henri Pharaon's, Civil War series, 1984. Photograph.*

FIG.56 *Sophie Ristelhueber, Résidence des Pins, 1982. Photograph from Beyrouth, photographies (1984).*

Despite its location at the foot of the Murr Tower, Henri Pharaon's mansion, with its fine Damascus panelling and collection of antiquities, survived intact (FIG.55). That Lebanese elder statesman took no position on the conflict and paid vast amounts of money to different factions in order to save his house,[76] telling the *National Geographic*, "I tried to make my house what I wanted Lebanon to be."[77]

Pharaon was not the only "leopard" to remain on the Green Line. Tawfiq 'Awwad wrote his last books in a veritable museum of opalines, Japanese prints and modernist paintings.[78] His daughter and neighbour, the gallerist Samia Toutounji, organised exhibition openings that attracted "French ambassador Monsieur Hubert Argod, Chinese ambassador Monsieur Ming, Madame Assad Rizk, Madame Farid Raphael and an impressive number of painters and intellectuals."[79] On the other side of the barricades, the Schoucair family continued to reside in their villa until the Israelis besieged Beirut. In 1984, the house became a training centre for Amal,[80] and it was probably they who set fire to the room where the Schoucairs kept their archives, the remains of which still lie on the ground (PL.13).

Opposite the Villa Schoucair stands the Résidence des Pins. This historic building – where the state of Greater Lebanon was declared on 1 September 1920 – served as the residence of the French high commissioner and afterwards the French ambassador. From 1975, the diplomats struggled to maintain the property in the face of mortar and sniper fire and incursions into the gardens.[81] In 1981, Louis Delamare, who had revived the tradition of holding a big reception on 14 July, was assassinated just outside his residence. His successor Paul-Marc Henry did not give up the effort to "return the gardens to their former glory."[82] In May 1982, French prime minister Pierre Mauroy visited Lebanon, and an evening reception was held at the residence to which leading representatives of all the country's political tendencies were invited.

> *They all came, including Pierre Gemayel and his son Amine, who had no hesitation in making the dangerous*

75 Raed Charaf, interview with the author, 7 June 2015.
76 Farhat, May, "A Mediterraneanist's Collection: Henri Pharaon's 'Treasure House of Arab Art'", *Ars Orientalis*, vol. 42 (2012), pp. 103–13.
77 Ellis, William S., "Beirut – Up From the Rubble", *National Geographic*, vol. 163, no. 2, February 1983, p. 281.
78 Toutounji Gauvard, interview of 6 November 2014.
79 "Vernissage non-stop", *L'Orient-Le Jour*, 26 May 1977.
80 Georges Schoucair, interview with the author, 6 September 2011.
81 Fournié, Pierre and Ammoun, Denise, *La Résidence des Pins, Beyrouth*, Paris, ACR Édition, 1999, p. 89.
82 Henry, Paul-Marc, *Les jardiniers de l'enfer*, Paris, Olivier Orban, 1984, pp. 107–8.

traverse of the Green Line at the Museum crossing and entering the trap that the Résidence des Pins represented from a security point of view. That was probably the last big reception to be held there for a long time. . . It was possible to witness and to photograph the most improbable conversations, among them a discussion between Pierre Gemayel and Walid Jumblatt. . . An enormous and omnipresent security detail made up of several hundred Lebanese army paratroops and interior ministry special forces made this unlikely happening a truly special and unprecedented occasion, though one sadly never to be repeated. . . There was more than anything a sense of farewell to a past one would have preferred to be still alive, when the greatness of republican France was the one, true guarantor of Lebanese democracy. A few days later, the Israeli army crossed the border.[83]

The world of the Henrys, the Schoucairs, the 'Awwads and Pharaons was collapsing, and its swansong was in some ways not unlike the last moments of the Hôtel Saint Georges. The Résidence des Pins suffered its first injuries in late June. On 11 July, there followed "the complete destruction of the doors and of a significant part of the furniture and furnishings."[84] On 23 July, the ambassador entertained for lunch – for the last time – his "remaining colleagues in West Beirut, the ambassadors of Bulgaria, Canada and Morocco. There was heavy shelling. The poor building literally trembled on its foundations."[85] A ruin by late summer, the Résidence was one of the sites photographed by Sophie Ristelhueber (FIG.56). Ignoring the main building, her picture shows the empty swimming pool and "in the background, a multitude of skeletal pines", while "almost lost among the trees, the remains of a little temple of antiquarian appearance confer on the image a timelessness that prevents any precise interpretation."[86]

The Résidence des Pins would be restored in the 1990s. Some of the contents and décor had been salvaged, such as the monumental door removed by Émile Tarazi and transported to the chancellery in Clémenceau Street. Twenty years later, it was his son Michel who renovated and reinstalled it.[87]

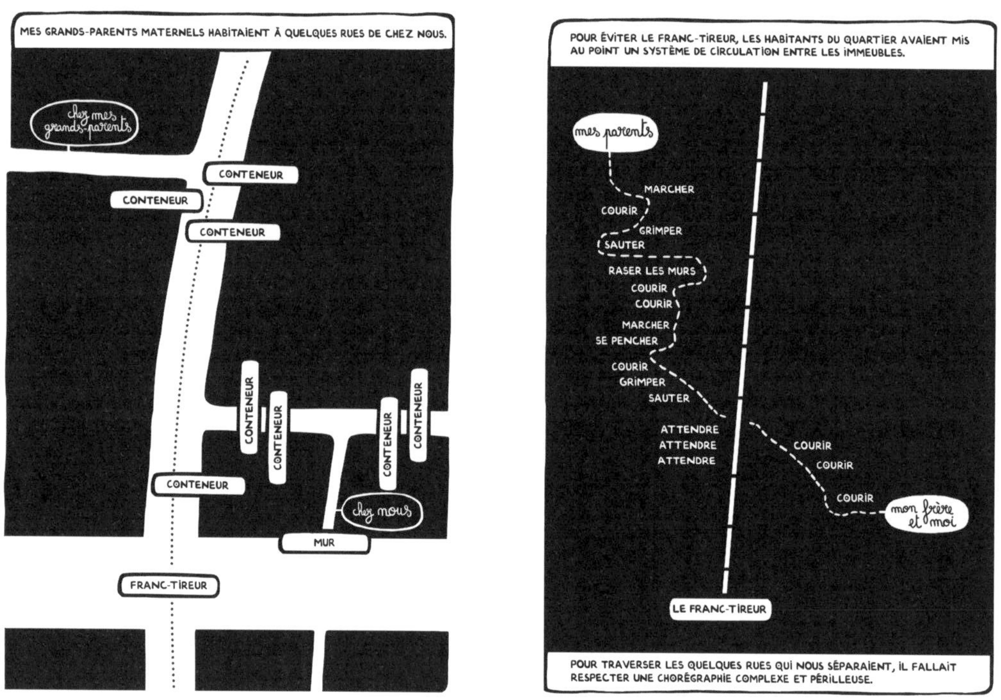

FIG.57 *Zeina Abirached, Mourir partir revenir. Le jeu des hirondelles, 2008. Graphic novel.*

83 *Ibid.*, pp. 122–3.
84 FOURNIÉ and AMMOUN, *La Résidence des Pins*, op. cit., p. 90.
85 HENRY, *Les jardiniers de l'enfer*, op. cit., p. 108.
86 POLLEDRI, "Photographier la ville, penser l'histoire", op. cit., p. 190.
87 TARAZI, CAMILLE, *Vitrine de l'Orient. Maison Tarazi, fondée à Beyrouth en 1862*, Beirut, Éditions de la Revue Phénicienne 2015, pp 246–7.

GETTING THROUGH ALIVE

Living in a war zone called for a rethinking of urban geography. The "streets were categorised by degree of danger and the mode of locomotion to be adopted."[88] Depending on the case, it might be better to pass on foot rather than in a car, or vice versa. Streets that were close to the front, but parallel to it were protected by the buildings between. Those perpendicular to it called for sail-like screens to be raised or containers upended and arranged to form a chicane if residents were not to be mown down by snipers. Passages were opened through buildings and gardens – not all of them abandoned – by knocking holes through walls. Zeina Abirached's albums describe, not without humour, these complex arrangements for getting about (FIG.57).[89] Snipers could also operate a regular timetable, one in the Museum sector starting work at midday. When Zeina Toutounji had to vacate her apartment, she arrived at six in the morning, did her packing and left before noon.[90]

A reorganisation of space was sometimes necessary at home as well. At the Abiracheds, "gradually, the bedrooms, the kitchen and dining room fell out of use. And the house started to shrink and shrink and shrink and shrink, until it was no more than the tiny square of the entrance hall." (FIG.58)[91] In 2008, on the 33rd anniversary of the outbreak of war, Nada Sehnaoui installed in the city centre her *Haven't 15 years of Hiding in the Toilets Been Enough?* An array of 600 lavatory pedestals with cisterns, this was a memento of the days when citizens would take refuge in the toilet.

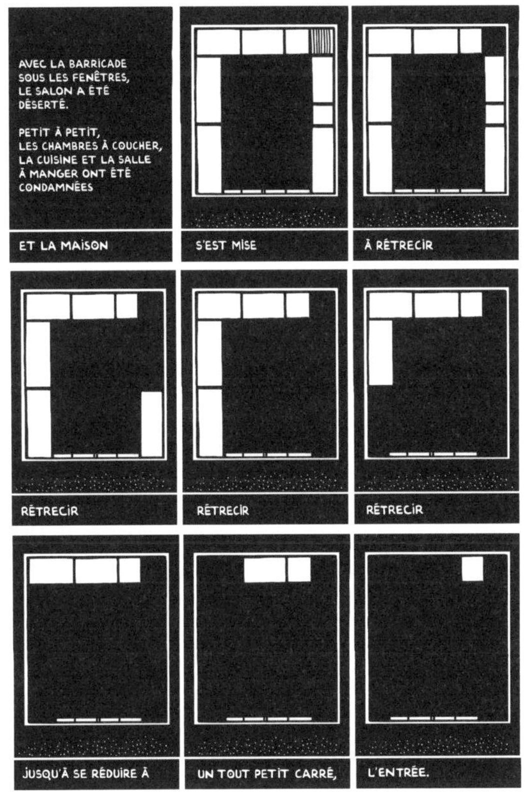

FIG.58 *Zeina Abirached, Mourir partir revenir. Le jeu des hirondelles, 2008. Graphic novel.*

HOUSES INTO FORTRESSES

In 1588, Paris saw "the windows of the houses filled with musketeers and arquebusiers."[92] And when the Green Line was established in Beirut, fighters took over the buildings. A more discreet presence than those who invaded the public realm, they had the function of what Virilio calls a "countermeasure": "Unlike defensive measures, unlike visible, ostentatious fortifications, countermeasures involve secrecy, the greatest possible dissimulation. The power of the countermeasure thereby resides in its apparent non-existence."[93]

88 Davie, Michael F., "Comment fait-on la guerre à Beyrouth ?", *Hérodote*, no. 29/30 (April 1983), p. 39.
89 Abirached, *Mourir partir revenir*, op. cit., pp. 13–14.
90 Toutounji Gauvard, interview of 6 November 2014.
91 Abirached, *Mourir partir revenir*, p. 34.
92 "Histoire très-véritable de ce qui est advenu en ceste ville de Paris", Paris, 1588, attributed to the Paris alderman Louis de Saint-Yon, a supporter of the Catholic Party of the Duc de Guise; cited in Richet, Denis, and Lapeyre, Marie-Claude, "Les Barricades à Paris, le 12 mai 1588," *Annales. Histoire, Sciences Sociales*, vol. 45, no. 2, April 1990, pp. 383–95.
93 Virilio, Paul, *The Vision Machine*, Bloomington and Indianapolis, Indiana University Press, 1994, p. 66.

DEFENDERS

Over a period of fifteen years, men and women camped out in abandoned premises. In a building on Martyrs Square, Jocelyne Khoueiry and her "girls" "did everything possible to make the place clean and almost comfortable. The tiles were white again."[94] The description of the state in which they found the building previously occupied by the opposing camp is unsparing: "Quite simply filthy. Their enemies had put a foam mattress on the ground. Not even an animal would have slept on it."[95] They made themselves at home with what they found to hand: "A two-metre-long table pushed against the wall served at the same time as a heavy shelf and as a kind of raised bed. They brought mattresses from the long-abandoned Hôtel Royal. They put out wooden and plastic boxes to sit on. There was running water and the toilets worked."[96] And as "an icon of the Virgin watched over them, a little candle always alight before it",[97] the war that had invaded the civil sphere brought its religious sanction with it.

The number of defenders fluctuated at around a thousand, taking both camps together. The estimate is based on a count in Sector 10, the section of the front most important to East Beirut, which identified some 160 men, suggesting between 400 and 500 for that side of the city as a whole. Of those 160, 40 were at the front, 12 on the barricades and the rest in reserve. The number rose at night and fell during the day.[98] Life at the front recalled the Phony War, as, for instance, when a direct telephone line ensured co-ordination between the Phalange and Amal.[99] Both sides screened "Super-8 films, blue movies often. Every barricade had its schedule."[100]

SNIPERS

In the popular imagination, there was some confusion between defenders and those who were called snipers, sometimes *francs-tireurs* or irregulars, who aimed to sow terror. The English word sniper, meaning "a person who shoots from a hiding place, especially accurately and at long range",[101] is not the same as *franc-tireur*, which signifies: "an irregular soldier; a guerrilla fighter."[102] The sniper helped bring the war to the city. This happened in Syria in 2011, and twenty years earlier with the slaughter conducted from the Sarajevo Holiday Inn – a horror portrayed by the final scene of *The Tornado*, in which men on top of a building fire down on a crowd assembled to commemorate the martyrs of the Lebanese Civil War. Like other film-makers, Samir Habchi chose to focus on death by sniper, "a death much more distant, which also has the effect of diminishing the potential for rekindling tensions among the viewers and diffuses guilt among an indeterminate 'they'."[103] Neither the government nor the warring parties put a stop to these indiscriminate killings – the former because it was impotent, the latter because it suited them not to. The destruction that could be wreaked by a single individual confirms Virilio's observation that "we have moved from *mass war* to *mass killers*, so much so that the miniaturisation of weaponry's destructive power has gradually made it possible for a single man or small commando to inflict damage comparable to that of the full-scale military operations of earlier centuries."[104]

"Begin", "Tarzan", "Gilbert" and "Catol" are among the nicknames whose traces can be found on the walls of the Barakat Building (bf1237, Achrafieh), also the haunt of a certain "Barakat-man." The legends surrounding him give the impression that he held the line all by himself. Builder and killer, he is said to have painted his own

94 Duplan and Raulin, *Le Cèdre et la Croix*, op. cit., pp. 85–7.
95 *Ibid.*
96 *Ibid.*
97 *Ibid.*
98 Fayad, interview of 22 May 2015.
99 *Ibid.*
100 *Ibid.*, 4 February 2015.
101 *Oxford English Dictionary.*
102 *Ibid.*
103 Richard, Thomas, "Mémoire de guerre et de résistance dans les films libanais", *Contemporary French and Francophone Studies*, vol. 18, no. 5, 20 October 2014, pp. 505–13.
104 Virilio, Paul, "De la géopolitique à la métropolitique", in Picon, Antoine, ed., *La ville et la guerre*, Besançon, Editions de l'Imprimeur, 1996, p. 226.

FIG.59 *Fouad Elkoury, The Sniper, Allenby street, Beirut City Centre series, 1991. Photograph.*

silhouette on the wall to create a decoy.[105] It is reported that "between 1979 and 1989 he never left the place, man and building becoming increasingly dependent on each other."[106] Barakat-man's inevitably tragic end comes in a number of different versions. When negotiations began, it is said, he was considered an obstacle to peace, and as none of his comrades could be persuaded to kill him, the task was assigned to a fighter from the west, who was sneaked in one night, knife in hand.[107] Another story has it that Barakat-man was loyal to the dissident Hobeika and allowed the forces of West Beirut to break through the front on 27 September 1986. After beating off the attack, the Lebanese Forces are said to have liquidated him.[108]

In a building overlooking the Ring (bf126, Saïfi), a sniper was tasked with shooting drivers when it was necessary to close the crossing. One day "a bullet. . . from the other side came through the hole he fired through and killed him."[109] Snipers, then, were not invincible. A resident of Ayn al-Rummana decided to avenge the deaths among his neighbours. He acquired a rifle more powerful than the weapon generally used by snipers – an SVD (*Snayperskaya Vintovka sistem'y Dragunova*) 7.62 mm, called the "Drago" – and installed a photographic detector system. That is to say, he mounted a camera on a tripod and, after nightfall, set it to B (for Bulb), which holds the shutter open as long as the shutter-release button is depressed, enabling him to capture on film the halo of light that accompanies a shot.[110] During the day, he shot exactly the same view, without moving the camera, and by repeating the process he obtained comprehensive coverage of the opposing line, with each pair of matching day-and-night photographs revealing, when superimposed, the origins of the rifle fire. Armed with this information, he picked off his targets.[111] Rifle and camera were united in being "point-and-shoot", and in his 1991 photo-exploration of Beirut city centre Fouad Elkoury forcefully evoked the analogy in a view of Allenby Street from above, entitled *The Sniper* (FIG.59).

THE INVISIBLE NETWORK OF FORTIFIED BUILDINGS

Four grids of fortified positions overlapped along the front: the first between different positions on the same floor, the second between different floors of the same building, the third between the different buildings along one section of the front and the fourth being represented by the front as a whole. The dominant rationale was not that of the megastructure, but rather that of the network, as in the case of the Atlantic Wall, distinguished form the Maginot Line by its "dispersion across the field."[112]

105 JAD GHOSTINE, interview with the author, 25 January 2013.
106 DIALA LTEIF, interview with the author, 10 January 2013.
107 LTEIF, DIALA, "Framing Barakat", *Transblog / Parsons*, 15 December 2011.
108 Fayad, interview of 24 July 2013.
109 ALAIN BRENAS, interview with the author, 9 March 2016.
110 SUESS, BERNHARD J., *Mastering Black and White Photography: From Camera to Darkroom*, New York, Allworth Press, 2003, p. 15.
111 ALEXANDRE MEDAWAR, interview with the author, 3 June 2015.
112 RICHARD, THIBAULT, "Les batteries fixes d'artillerie côtière allemande pendant la Seconde Guerre mondiale dans le Cotentin : principes de construction et choix des sites", *Guerres mondiales et conflits contemporains*, no. 165, January 1992, pp. 43–51.

It was on the eastern, northern and western sides of Martyrs Square that the most impressive system was to be found, contradicting the commonly accepted idea that the Green Line ran right down the middle (FIG.49). The no-man's land actually consisted of Souk al-Nouriyeh and Souk Sursock, between Martyrs Square and Place de l'Étoile. Four buildings on the west side of Martyrs Square represented the Phalangists' first line of defence: an unfinished modern building on the corner with Weygand Street (bf290, Marfa'), the Ezzedine Building (bf291), the Art Deco Opéra cinema by Bahjat Abdelnour (bf440) and the vast edifice of the Savoy Hotel (bf439). The Left Forces occupied this block for a time before abandoning it, leaving it to be taken over by a group of young women under Jocelyne Khoueiry. The "girls" took "the sandbags facing onto the square and put them on the other side", [113] reversing its orientation as a military position. The defence of these buildings underwent a radical change after 1982. In the days following the Israeli withdrawal, Rafic Hariri's Oger company demolished and cleared the maze of souks that made up the no-man's land,[114] creating an open space that scuppered any attempt at an incursion and eased the task of the defenders. On the eastern side of Martyrs Square stood the second defensive line, based on the police station and the brothel district of Mutanabbi Street. On the northern side of the square, the modern buildings encircling the Rivoli cinema completed the whole with an array of improvised blockhouses and afforded protected passage to the front line.

EAST AND WEST – A STRIKING ASYMMETRY

A quarter of a century after the end of hostilities, consultation of archive images from the war and the period immediately following and examination of the little that survives of the ground have led to the identification of more than thirty fortified buildings that stood on the front line. These are distributed as follows:

Zone	East	West
Port and city centre	17	6
Ring to Sodeco	8	3
Around the racecourse and the Museum	3	-

Is the disparity between the two camps attributable to chance variation in the availability of evidence, or does it reflect something in the balance of power? The Christians controlled a relatively unified but compact territory, often termed "the Christian redoubt." After 1976, no one could imagine them invading West Beirut, while the converse was a possibility realised one day in 1986 and then again on 13 October 1990. "We were more afraid than they were," confessed the Phalangist commanding the front,[115] relaying a sentiment already expressed by Pierre Gemayel in March 1976.[116]

As well as the fear, there was an ideological difference. The Christian parties were conservative and attached to ideas of land and such: Pierre Gemayel's *nom de guerre* was Al-Sakhra, the Rock, and they took the cedar of Lebanon as their emblem. Their opponents were Left-wing parties seeking to change the system, Palestinian organisations whose goals were in Palestine, the Syrian army – a foreign force – and, after 1980, the Shia militia whose ideology focused on the liberation of Israeli-occupied Southern Lebanon. No one but the Christian parties claimed to defend the Lebanese state, nor did anyone else do as much to take its place.[117] What was established on the Green Line was, to use the language of Deleuze and Guattari, an opposition between a "smooth" space in the west, where the militias existed in nomadic mode, and a once again "striated" space in the east, where the militias replaced the state. The Left parties were not concerned with building bunkers. They functioned as fugitive war machines, fighting as much against each other as against external enemies. In this reading, Beirut's Green Line was not heir to the symmetrical entrenchments of the Great War, but one of a series of fortifications unilaterally raised up against an elsewhere that was supposedly hostile and definite or indefinite to varying degrees: the Great Wall of China, the Atlantic Wall, the Berlin Wall or the Separation Wall built by the Israeli government.

113 Duplan and Raulin, *Le cèdre et la croix*, op. cit., pp. 85–7.
114 "Oger s'active", *L'Orient-Le Jour*, 2 October 1982.
115 Fayad, interview of 22 May 2015.
116 *Spéciale Liban*, INA Histoire, 15 March 1976.
117 Except perhaps for the Progressive Socialist Party in the Shouf district after the Mountain War of 1983–4.

MAKING USE OF THE ARCHITECTURE

The militarisation of the built environment offers a lesson in architecture in the form of a duel or involuntary collaboration between builders and the warriors who instrumentalise their works. Gunmen chose premises whose viewpoints commanded fields of fire covering a multiplicity of frontages, internal courtyards, entries, colonnades, etc. In the initial confrontations, the militias occupied all sorts of buildings. Together with her brothers, Jocelyne Khoueiry arranged the family home to provide "dormitories, canteen, food shop, armoury, infirmary, offices"; there, they would "stack sandbags, seal off windows, post sentries and stand duty in turn."[118] A documentary shot in 1994 showed what survived: a heap of rubble.[119] The lesson of the story was that if a building was to be fortified, it had to be sufficiently solid in the first place. Normally, "blockhouses were established in concrete-framed buildings. Experience showed that this type of construction stood up well to fire",[120] while older "sandstone buildings, constructed in the last [19th] century, stand on vaulted basements, and it doesn't take much for the whole structure to collapse."[121] The loss of the souks of the old town between 1976 and 1982 is explained in part by their construction, "the only buildings to have survived being cinemas, hotels and offices."[122] By introducing reinforced concrete into the structure of the Barakat Building, begun by Youssef Aftimus in Ramleh stone "from the quarries of Ramleh al-Bayda", which "arrived on camel-back",[123] Fouad Kozah was unknowingly preparing the ground for the fighters who would occupy the building four decades later.

MOVING UP AND DOWN

While men and much of their gear could go up by the stairs, getting an artillery piece to an upper floor posed more of a problem. To position a gun on the rooftop of a second-line building on the Sodeco front (bf788, Achrafieh), the Phalangists set up behind it a generator-powered electric hoist that raised a metal cage.[124]

What is more, the stairs might not even be there, as in the Barakat Building (FIG.60), where only the backstairs survived destruction. For this, some blamed the fighters, said to want to prevent the "well-heeled" occupants from coming back,[125] while others held responsible the crew that set about demolishing the building in the 1990s. A third theory has it that the fighters got rid of the stairs to secure the upper floors against attack, themselves using the service stairs further back from the entrance. But how then is the destruction of the stairs from the first to the second floor explained?

FIG.60 *Valérie Cachard, Barakat Building, Eastern staircase, 2012. Photograph.*

118 DUPLAN and RAULIN, *Le cèdre et la croix*, op. cit., p. 61.
119 ARACTINGI, PHILIPPE, *Chemins de Femmes*, 1994.
120 DAVIE, "Comment fait-on la guerre à Beyrouth ?", op. cit., pp. 36–7.
121 *Ibid.*
122 *Ibid.*
123 KOZAH, FOUAD KAMAL, *Chroniques du Levant : Mémoires d'un architecte libanais*, Paris, L'Harmattan, 2010, p. 115.
124 FAYAD, interview of 24 July 2013.
125 HALABI, AHMAD in RAKAN MAYASI, "Bineyet Barakat. Chahed Samet" [The Barakat Building: a silent witness], *Zakirat Makan*, Future News, 2007.

Part of the answer may be found in the bunker on the first floor, whose southern line of fire passed through the stairwell, which would have made aiming very difficult. Was the staircase destroyed to open up a line of fire, or was a loophole opened up on this line because the destruction of the stairs made it possible? The question remains open.

Fighters' accounts also mention that because the use of torches at night could attract enemy fire – men could be killed on account of the glow from their cigarettes – they would learn by heart the number of steps on "their" stairs.

MOVING HORIZONTALLY

An article written in May 2006 boasted of the Israeli army's use of an "inverse geometry" of the space of war inspired by the writings of Deleuze, Guattari and Debord. Faced with an enemy "who interprets space in a classical, traditional manner", a paratroop commander explained that, in order to avoid the danger of doors and windows, "we all walk through walls!"[126] Unless we are talking pure science-fiction here, this must mean knocking holes through with picks or explosives. Was it really necessary to read Deleuze to come up with that? Thirty years earlier, "to attack the enemy without breaking cover, the fighters smashed through the walls of buildings that were in addition emptied of their contents."[127]

During the Hundred Days' War of 1978, the Phalangists created paths through buildings by making holes in walls: "We'd smash the walls with a pick – in apartments full of furniture – and install signage and a battery-powered lighting system so that the men never went astray or fell into a hole."[128] The fighters "applied the history of the city to the building, creating a new system of connections. They passed through rooms by going through the walls."[129]

Shot after the war but before reconstruction, the film *Beirut of Stone and Memory* shows several routes of this type. Philippe Aractingi's camera advances through a succession of openings in the walls between the different commercial premises that occupied the ground floor of the buildings on the west side of Martyrs Square (bf290 et 291, Marfa'). These openings allowed fighters to make their way along their first line of defence in the city centre.

This passage through walls represents an appropriation of territory from within, in the manner of an infection spreading through the body. For forty years, Israel has confronted guerrilla movements whose patterns of organisation and movement stand opposed to those of the traditional regular army. The *Frieze* article cited above seeks to confer a conceptual aura on the practices of an army seeking to borrow the techniques of its enemy. Its publication preceded by two months the Lebanese War of July 2006, when that same army fought for thirty-three days, with notable lack of success, against an invisible enemy sheltered by a system of underground passages and natural vegetation.

MOVING AT HEIGHT

The front calls for submersion, hence the trenches, tunnels and holes in the walls. Aerial gangways, however, were needed when men had to move between buildings separated by a space between, or within buildings where floors had been destroyed. A news photograph published in August 1976 (FIG.61) shows a house whose roof and first floor have collapsed.

FIG.61 *Port area, fighter crawling on a wooden board placed on beams, 1976. Photograph published in La Revue du Liban, August 1976.*

126 WEIZMAN, EYAL, "The Art of War", *Frieze*, May 2006.
127 KHOURY, EDMOND, "Beyrouth Zone verte : un monceau de ruines", *La Revue du Liban*, 14 August 1976, pp. 44-45.
128 FAYAD, interview of 4 February 2015.
129 GHOSTINE, interview of 25 January 2013.

A collection of wooden planks of various sizes rest on an iron girder, and a fighter can be seen crawling along this improvised gangplank. He is making for the first floor of another house, where, tucked in against the base of an arch, a comrade has taken up a firing position.

CLASSES OF FORTIFICATION

A first fortification, with its walls, window frames, doorways, columns, balustrades, doors and shutters all offering potential shelter, the building itself had to be reinforced. Some walls were built only to protect both civilians and combatants. These are known as passive fortifications. Others, active fortifications, were provided with "loopholes making it possible to fire on the enemy without being spotted."[130] To afford maximum room for manoeuvring the weapon together with minimum exposure, these openings were splayed towards the inside, being lined with four trapezoidal pieces of wood. When time was short, cement pipe served.

A RANGE OF POSITIONS

FIG.62 *Fouad Elkoury, Port Street, Civil War series, 1982. Photograph. [Fortifications visible on floors 1 to 4 of Fattal Building].*

130 DAVIE, "Comment fait-on la guerre à Beyrouth ?", op. cit., p. 36.

Firing positions could be established "at street level, making use of shop premises, which would be entered through a hole in the back wall while the front would be replaced by sandbags or reinforced concrete some 75 to 100 cm thick."[131] There were, in addition, improvised blockhouses "installed on the upper floors of a building, even on the terrace."[132] Like a battleship, a substantial building might bristle with weaponry ready to fire in all directions. This was the case of the Fattal Building (bf105, Marfa'), which occupied an advanced position on the front, exposed on north, south and west (FIG.62). Firing positions within buildings varied in height and orientation and also in their distance from the outside. They could be located on a balcony, behind a window or a hole in the wall, even deep inside, depending on considerations of safety and efficacity.

On Martyrs Square, Phalangist fighters constructed "a very visible barricade"[133] as a decoy to draw enemy fire away from their blockhouse, itself "invisible from without."[134] This game, played by both sides, came to an end when each eventually came to see through the tricks and succeeded in identifying the enemy's true positions.

A feature in the *National Geographic* in 1983 opened with a photograph by Steve McCurry whose caption reads: "Sidewalk gossip returns to West Beirut after Israel's invasion last summer, as workers clear away older debris left from the height of Lebanon's Civil War – one of many scars on a city trying hard to heal its wounds."[135] Older men are seen smoking hookahs, presenting the clichéd image of the Middle East, while young boys sweep the street. In the background is a building (bf1018, Zokak el-Blatt) with three first-floor windows walled up. Flush with the outside wall and pierced by loopholes, their cast-concrete slabs do not reach full height and are topped by sandbags. Standing 700 metres from its target, Gemmayzeh, this is the only concrete fortification to the west of the line of which any trace survives.

It would have been impossible to identify, on the other hand, positions hidden deep inside, such as those in the Barakat Building (FIG.63). On the ground floor, the wall between an apartment and a shop space giving onto Damascus Street was fortified with cast concrete pierced with loopholes (FIG.63a). On the first floor, the hallway of the apartment saw a sandbag barricade erected between the living room and the dining room, some considerable distance from the exterior (FIG.63c). In the same apartment, another such barricade was installed in a toilet (FIG.63b), against a window opening onto a central void within the building. The line of fire passed through this air shaft, re-entered the same dwelling by another window, crossed a room and continued through another window giving onto Boulevard Bechara el-Khoury. The gunman would have been completely invisible. Finally, at one end of a corridor was a bunker with three loopholes: two facing west and one south (FIG.63d). The line of fire from this last crossed the central hall, passed through the door of the apartment, across the stairwell and out through a window to graze between two columns of the veranda opposite to reach Damascus Street. It served to deter any invasion from the direction of Ras el-Nabeh and to kill passers-by. The complexity of the lines of fire available from the Barakat Building makes it a "success" in terms of the integration of military with civilian architecture. The ground and first floors were constructed in 1924 to plans by architect Youssef Aftimus. In the early 1930s, on his recommendation, the Barakats entrusted the design for two further floors to Fouad Kozah. The combined efforts of Aftimus and Kozah offered very subtly worked perspectives onto the exterior from a building consisting of two masses set off at an angle from each other (PL.19). Yet Kozah thought of space not in terms of masses, but of voids and had the idea of uniting the two parts through conjoined and superimposed verandas.[136] These extended the available living space and reinforced its connection with the city outside (PL.15), while giving the impression of a peristyle. A masterpiece of dissimulation presenting an airy and delicate exterior, the building proved a solid and effective war machine.

There was one case where the opposite principle was applied, the building itself being surrounded by a continuous fortification (FIG.64). This was the headquarters of the Tyous militia (bf4150, Achrafieh). Four metres high and varying between 50 and 70 centimetres in thickness, the wall stood in places only a few centimetres from the building, at others 2 metres, depending on the façade.

131 *Ibid.*
132 *Ibid.*
133 Duplan and Raulin, *Le cèdre et la croix*, op. cit., pp. 89–90.
134 *Ibid.*
135 Ellis, "Beirut – Up From the Rubble", op. cit., pp. 262–3.
136 Kozah, *Chroniques du Levant*, op. cit., p. 116.

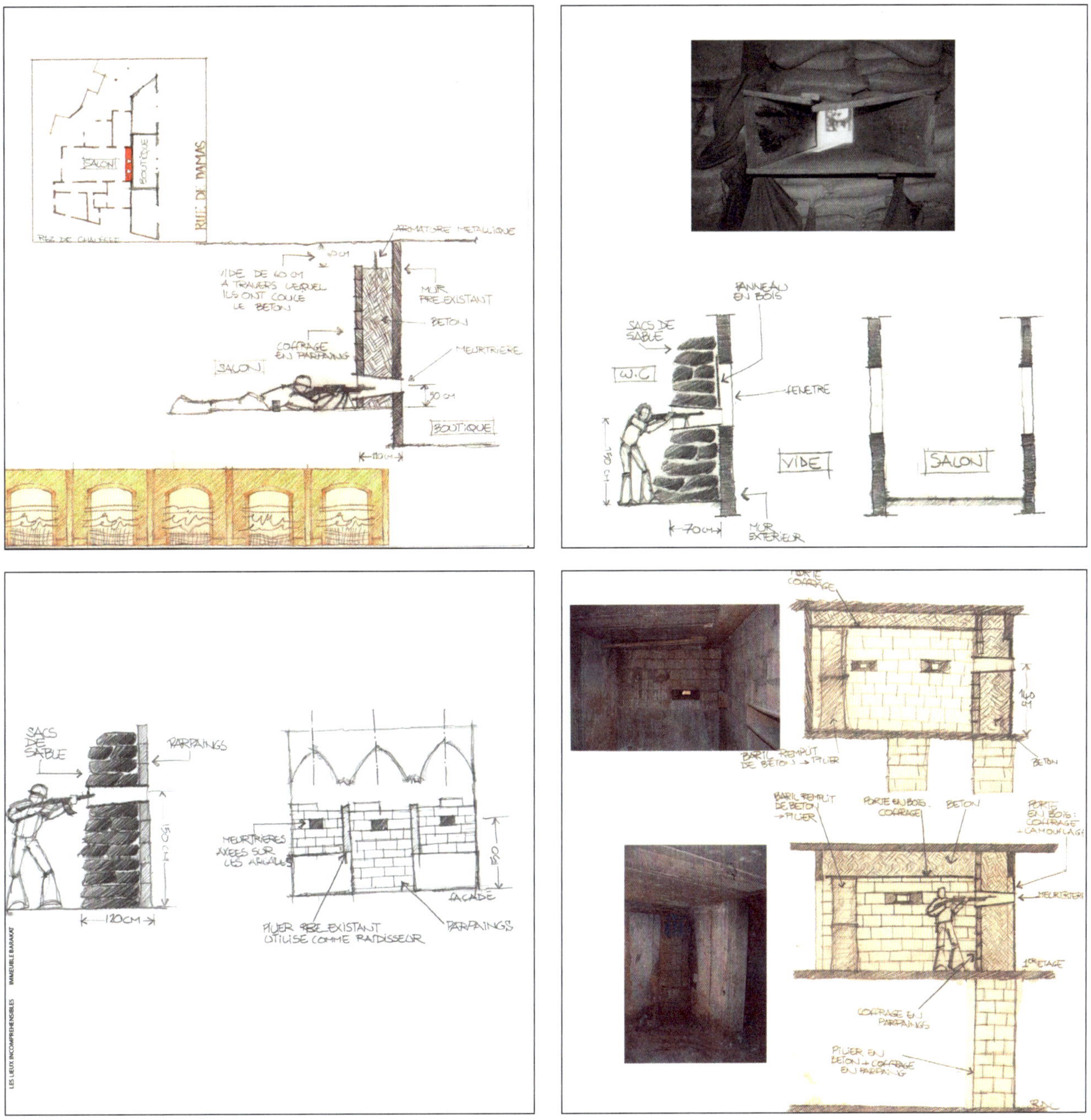

FIG.63 *Atelier de recherche ALBA/Yara Akl, Patricia Fakhry, Maher Fleyfel, Youssef Helou, Wissam Rachid. Machines Célibataires, Machine # 1, Incomprehensible places, 2000. Documentation of Barakat Building*

a. Blockhouse on Ground floor, plan and section;

b. Barricade in the bathroom;

c. Central hall Barricade;

d. Bunker on first floor.

FIG.64 *Yves Atalla, From the Car Series, 2008. Photograph.*

QUESTIONS OF MATERIAL, FORM AND STYLE

The fortifications may be divided into two classes – barricades and protective walls; the first being accumulations, the second constructions of cast concrete. The two types correspond to two different relationships to time, the first generally preceding the second. Fighters had first gradually assembled sandbag defences in the buildings they occupied. Then, in 1978, with the war seeming unlikely to end any time soon, they began to build bunkers. At advanced positions like the Fattal Building, it was impossible to bring in the required equipment and it was necessary to settle for sandbags.

The second line of defence for the Christian parties, the eastern side of Martyrs Square, was abundantly fortified. While a loophole in the neoclassical palazzo of the police station was surrounded by a motley assemblage of breeze blocks, sandbags and barrels, the *pièce de résistance* was to be found to the left. A frontal photograph by Gabriele Basilico has immortalised the Palace Hotel (bf827) and the Acra Building (bf831) with the fortifications installed in them: on the second floor of the Acra Building, breeze blocks flush with the façade alternate with sandbags stacked against the remains of the windows, while in the Palace Hotel next door a wall inside the first floor runs across its whole width. The gap of about a metre between the top and the ceiling was necessary for pouring the concrete for which the breeze blocks served as coffering. This was one of the largest blockhouses to have been constructed in Beirut (FIG.65).

On the Sodeco front, the western and southern sides of the bunker installed on the first floor of the Barakat Building were fortified by two conjoined structures raised right against the existing wall, the door in each of these remaining closed in place (PL.17). Concrete was poured between the apartment walls and a breeze-block coffering set a metre back. There was also a cast ceiling slab, coffered with doors, and a layer of concrete was laid on the floor.[137] This volume weighed between six and seven tonnes and, to avoid the risk of collapse, two pillars were inserted beneath on the ground floor, while a supporting column was created in a corner of the bunker using stacked barrels into which cement was poured (FIG.63d). This bunker could easily support the firing of medium-calibre weapons of up to 80 mm, or the B7 rockets very common at the time.[138] Given firing angles and the short distance from the enemy, the building was not exposed to heavy artillery. The bunker here is to be distinguished not only from the barricade but also from the simple protective wall, on account of its three-dimensional aspect: a box set into the larger box of the building. The two boxes were closely linked, but each retained a certain independence from the other. "While most buildings are embanked in the terrain by their foundations, the casemate is devoid of any, aside from its center of gravity," says Virilio, "which explains its possibility for limited movement when the surrounding ground undergoes the impact of projectiles."[139] At the Tyous headquarters, the defensive wall joined a balcony above, grafting itself onto the building like a second skin (FIG.64).

137 YOUSSEF HAÏDAR, email to the author, 10 February 2015.
138 *Ibid.*
139 VIRILIO, *Bunker Archaeology*, op. cit., p. 37.

The interior was lost within this sepulchral mass bristling with steel spikes, a defence that nonetheless proved insufficiently thick when it was holed by a shell.

There is a vast visual difference between the massive concrete of the Barakat Building or the Tyous HQ and the barricade set up about a hole knocked through the mosaic of the *Good Shepherd* in the National Museum (FIG.67). One shares in the brutalism of modern architecture, while the other recalls Arte Povera. What is more, the barricade is moveable, in both the legal and practical sense, while the wall is immovable – literally and metaphorically, an integral part of the building to which it belongs. It can only be removed along with the latter, but also it resists its demolition. Like the *anarchitecture* of Gordon Matta-Clark, the bunker precludes any return to the past. While Matta-Clark turned buildings into sculptures by reducing them to rectilinear, curved or conical forms, Beirut's fighters filled them in with breeze blocks and cement. In 1975, Matta-Clark took part in the Paris Biennale with *Conical Intersect*. Slicing into two 17th-century buildings on Beaubourg Street that were scheduled for demolition, he created an optical instrument that framed the urban space, somewhat in the manner of the colonnaded veranda of the Barakat Building. These lesions are symptomatic of a profound sickness affecting both the built environment and society. Highlighting the violent impositions of the ruling classes, Matta-Clark was "directing [his] attention... to the gap... between the self and the American Capitalist system."[140] The activities of the militias expressed the spilling over of this violence into the city and the collapse of social order.

FIG.65 *Gabriele Basilico, Beirut, 1991. Photograph. [Fortifications visible on floor 1 of Palace Hotel on left and floor 2 of Acra building on right]*

140 MOURE, GLORIA (ed.), *Gordon Matta-Clark: Works and Collected Writings*, Barcelona, Ediciones Polígrafa, 2006, pp. 57–8.

In October 1999, the Atelier de Recherche ALBA showed the first instalment of its study of the Barakat Building in the context of an exhibition on vernacular architectures. The vernacular here was in the interventions of the fighter–builders, located not in a style, but in their essentially functionalist logic. Yet it was precisely this logic of "form follows function" that inspired the emergence of the Modern Movement. The Atelier's approach was informed by two ideas. First, was the challenge to the thinking that associates the vernacular with the "good" and the "natural", as opposed to the evils of modernism. It took upon itself the role of the *franc-tireur*, in the literal sense, not without provocation, with a presentation entitled *Bien fonds 1237 : l'architecte, le vernaculaire et le franc-tireur*.[141] The second idea was to pose the question of style in relation to the architecture of war, as when in the central hall of the Barakat Building the firing positions were centred under three arches (FIG.63C). A few years later, J. G. Ballard would see in the relation between the "concrete tombs" of the Atlantic Wall and the Brutalist architecture of the 1950s the death of the modernist dream: "In its heyday between the wars, modernism was a vast utopian project, and perhaps the last utopian project we will ever see, now that we are well aware that all utopias have their dark side."[142]

FIG.66 *Atelier de recherche ALBA, Machines Célibataires, 2000. Installation.*

THE GREEN LINE AFTERWARDS: FROM WASTELANDS TO MUSEUMS

The reconstruction of the city in the 1990s saw the mechanical excavators swing into action and buildings fall one after another, their demolition sometimes revealing the concrete fortifications within. The rubble was dumped at the Normandy landfill. While much of the city centre has been rebuilt, Martyrs Square is still a wasteland a quarter of a century after the end of the war. One is reminded of Robert Smithson's thoughts faced with suburban Passaic in New Jersey, whose "center was no center – it was instead a typical abyss or an ordinary void", prompting him to wonder: "Has Passaic replaced Rome as The Eternal City?"[143]

141 Hage-Boutros, Pierre, Haddad, Rana and Buchakjian, Gregory, "Bien fonds 1237 : l'architecte, le vernaculaire et le franc-tireur", Atelier de Recherche ALBA website, 1999.

142 Ballard, J. G., "A Handful of Dust", *Guardian*, 20 March 2006.

143 Smithson, Robert, "A Tour of the Monuments of Passaic, New Jersey", *Artforum*, December 1967, reprinted in *Robert Smithson: The Collected Writings*, Berkeley, Los Angeles, University of California Press 1996, pp. 68–74.

FIG.67 *Good Shepherd Mosaic at the National Museum, 1990. Photograph.*

FIG.68 *Lamia Joreige, Good Shepherd Mosaic, detail, 2013. Photograph.*

With the loss of the Petit Sérail – built by Manouk Avedissian (commonly known as Bechara Effendi al-Muhandis[144]) in 1884 and demolished in 1950, an act that "forever deprived the city of a civic centre and symbolic emblem"[145] – and then of the Rivoli cinema that took its place, which Solidere had dynamited in 1994, the northerly view from Martyrs Square has been left desperately empty. The nascent city history museum, however, will provide it with a new focus. Commissioned by the Department of Antiquities in collaboration with Solidere, this building by Renzo Piano will incorporate the archaeological excavations on the site and offer an account of the city's natural and cultural history.[146] Ali Cherri – a "troubled" artist disquieted by the catastrophes of the past that he seeks to surmount and those of an expected future that he hopes to avert[147] – is equally concerned with loss and recovery, and has contemplated the future destruction of the museum before it has yet risen on its foundations.[148] Its creation is nonetheless among the ventures that may succeed in transforming what was a line of confrontation into a point of cultural contact.[149]

At the other end of the front line, the still ruined National Museum first reopened to the public in 1993, when visitors were able to view the priceless sarcophagi that Maurice Shehab, head of the Department of Antiquities, had had encased in concrete – bunkers in themselves, in a way – in order to protect them. They were also able to see the hole knocked through the *Good Shepherd* mosaic by a sniper (FIG.67), the inspiration for Lamia Joreige's installation *Under-Writing Beirut – Mathaf.* This includes a video that "puts us in the position to imagine what the sniper saw and whom he may have killed through the hole."[150] The artist also took pin-hole camera pictures of the same view – "ghostly, like faded echoes of another era, again toying with the notion of authentic representations of history and the present."[151] Part of the same installation, the sculpture *Object of War* represents a negative of the sniper's hole, cast in concrete from a digital model created from photographs and precise measurements on site, but envisaged as reformulation rather than replica[152] (FIG.69). Since 2013, it has been possible to see the *Good Shepherd* restored, but still bearing its stigmata, the missing part not having been replaced (FIG.68).

144 DAVIE, MAY, "Manouk Avédissian, alias Béchara Afandi al-Mouhandis. Itinéraire beyrouthin d'un ingénieur beyrouthin à la fin du XIXe siècle", in ANASTASSIADOU-DUMONT, MÉROPI (ed.) , *Médecins et ingénieurs ottomans à l'âge des nationalismes,* Istanbul and Paris, Institut français d'études anatoliennes and Maisonneuve et Larose 2003, pp. 219–329.

145 DAVIE, MAY, "La construction nationale et l'héritage ottoman au Liban", *Patrimoines culturels en Méditerranée orientale,* Maison de l'Orient et de la Méditerranée, Lyon, Université Lumière 2, Lyon and CNRS, 2009, p. 5.

146 ANNE-MARIE AFEICHE, interview with the author, 9 January 2016.

147 PICARD, ANDRÉA, "Ali Cherri: Gazing at the catastrophe", *Cinema Scope,* January 2016, p. 68.

148 ALI CHERRI, public interview with the author, Sursock Museum, Beirut, 19 May 2016.

149 WRIGHT, ROBIN, "Beirut's Museums of War and Memories", *New Yorker,* 12 October 2016.

150 JOREIGE, LAMIA, "Under-Writing Beirut – Mathaf", Lamia Joreige website.

151 WHITING, REBECCA, "Records for Beirut's Uncertain Times", *Al-Akhbar,* 26 April 2013.

152 JOREIGE, "Under-Writing Beirut – Mathaf", op. cit.

Opposite the National Museum, on land belonging to St Joseph's University, APEAL – the Association for the Promotion and Exhibition of the Arts in Lebanon – is spearheading the creation of BeMA, the Beirut Museum of Art, due to open in the 2020s. Designed by Hala Wardé, the building will be set into the earth, its presence signalled by a 120-metre-high campanile. Not very far away, the MIM Museum opened in 2014, housing founder Sélim Éddé's renowned collection of minerals. Designed by Fadlallah Dagher and located on the University's Innovation and Sport Campus – the work of architect Youssef Tohme – this too is an underground museum. Finally, at the intersection of Damascus Street and the Avenue de l'Indépendance, the Barakat Building has been restored to become Beit Beirut.

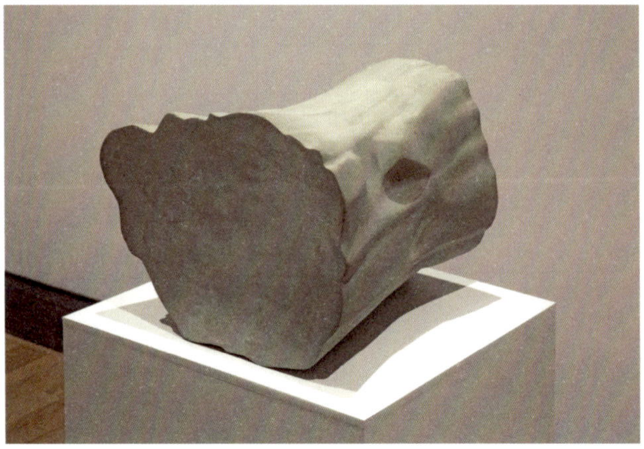

FIG.69 *Lamia Joreige, Object of War, 2013. Concrete, 40 × 45 × 40 cm.*

A BUNKER TURNED INTO A MUSEUM: FROM THE BARAKAT BUILDING TO BEIT BEIRUT

In the 1990s, architect Mona Hallak, photographer Sophie Haluk and artist Greta Naufal set about documenting the Barakat Building. Naufal herself was injured by sniper fire from this precise location in 1975.[153] In 1997, Hallak noticed that "someone had started removing all the iron and art-deco tiles. I was told that the building was being gutted and there was only two weeks left before it would be completely demolished."[154] She launched a campaign to save it, and persuaded Pierre Hage-Boutros, Rana Haddad and myself to visit the site. This was the beginning of the Atelier de Recherche ALBA project *Bien-fonds 1237: l'architecte, le vernaculaire et le franc-tireur*, the building helping "reveal the 'shared singularity' that makes new relationships to the city possible."[155] In 2000, the Atelier de Recherche showed *Machines Célibataires*, a grid of 300 visuals exploring the building's neighbourhood, its architect, Youssef Aftimus and its successive transformations (FIG.66). The installation reawakened ghosts that many would have preferred to banish. Danielle Arbid observed at the time that "officially, in Beirut, the war did not take place. Or almost. It is fantasized, invented, bought and sold."[156] Philosopher Christian Delacampagne saw in *Machines Célibataires* "a work in many voices that draws on the shared imaginary of a whole generation that grew up during the war, but is capable of touching people anywhere in the world."[157] In this early 21st century, Oliver Rohe began a novel "amid the cracked yellow walls" of a building that – even though it was not identified, any more than was the city – could not be more recognisable. A fixed point, "all the great avenues, all roads lead there, whatever the route taken. . . it is impossible to pass it by."[158] Yet the wound seemed invisible: "In everyone's mind, it was as if this building – what it might represent – did not exist . . . No doubt they had got so used to it as to forget it. Even before it vanished."[159]

153 Greta Naufal, interview with the author, 25 May 2015.
154 Mona Hallak, cited in Zada, John, "Hallak on 'Beit Beirut'" *The Planisphere*, 12 August 2012.
155 Hage-Boutros, Haddad, and Buchakjian, "Bien fonds 1237 : l'architecte, le vernaculaire et le franc-tireur", op. cit.
156 Danielle Arbid (director), *Seule Avec La Guerre*, 2000.
157 Delacampagne, Christian, "À propos de Machines Célibataires", Atelier de Recherche ALBA website, 22 September 2004.
158 Rohe, Oliver, *Terrain vague*, Paris, Allia, 2005, pp. 8–11.
159 *Ibid.*

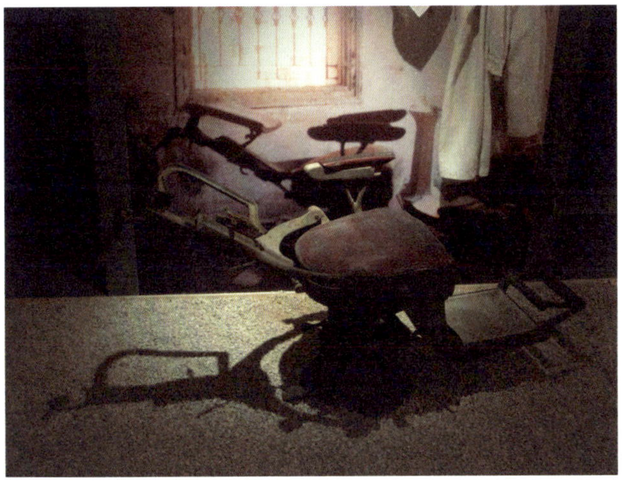

FIG.71 *Mona El Hallak, Dr. Nejib Schemali's dentist chair, 2001. Installation.*

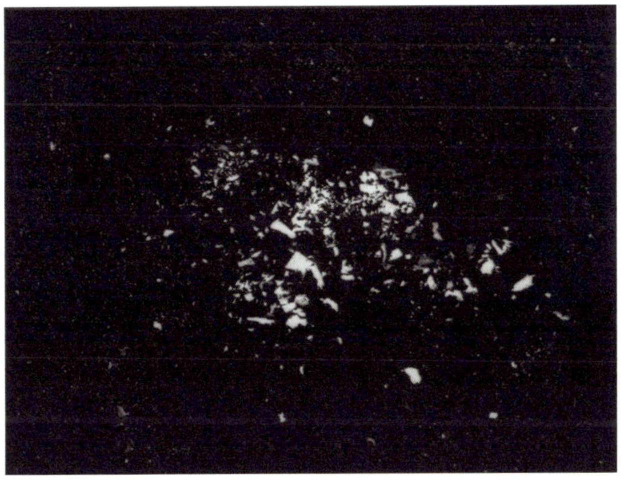

FIG.72 *Vartan Avakian, Suspended Silver, 2015. Photograph.*

In 2001, Mona Hallak drew together the results of her explorations in *Visages Perdus*[160] (FIG.71). Relics of the past from the apartment of Dr Nagib Schemali, a first-floor tenant, were exhibited like artefacts in an archaeological museum. *Visages Perdus* was staged at the Grenier des Artistes, a restaurant, bar and gallery in Phoenicia Street. On leaving, visitors found themselves confronted by a photograph of the façade of the Barakat Building, pasted onto a walled-up window of the Excelsior, formerly one of the jewels of the hotel district. A triple *mise en abyme*: the picture of an abandoned building mounted on the façade of an abandoned hotel to be seen on leaving an abandoned restaurant. A few years later, the Grenier was demolished. The Excelsior, the Barakat Building and the photograph survive.

Since then, the Barakat Building has continued to inspire art-making. Following the investigation of the premises of the "Photo Mario" studio on the ground floor, Vartan Avakian was inspired by the materiality of the silver particles he found among the film debris to scan them and enlarge and print the images to make *Suspended Silver*[161] (FIG.72). The stock of negatives and prints Hallak discovered there went on to form the basis of the *Photo Mario Archive Project*, intended to recapture the memory of the studio's clients, the people of the neighbourhood. This was presented at an exhibition marking the tenth anniversary of the Arab Fund for Arts and Culture (AFAC), held in the building itself in 2017.[162] In the meantime, a visit to the premises and the memory of the *sunduq al-ajaib* – the "box of wonders" that was a primitive form of animated image device – inspired in François Sargologo the slow but inexorable production of a series of tondos whose proliferating bruises suggest a process of constant decomposition[163] (FIG.73).

In 2003, Hallak persuaded the Beirut city authorities to purchase the building with a view to turning it into a museum and cultural centre to be known as Beit Beirut, the "House of Beirut." The commission was given to Youssef Haidar, who decided to treat the structure as "a living being with lacerated face and missing limbs, left with no more than stumps, whose disabilities we sought to help overcome."[164] Work began in 2012, and was completed four years later. At the time of writing, the associated cultural project has not yet got off the ground, the events that have been put on there not forming part of any ongoing programme. The very idea of Beit Beirut deserves closer examination, however. In its unrestored condition the Barakat Building resembled the Genbaku Dome, the ruin that is now the Hiroshima Peace Memorial.[165] Testimony to traumatic pasts, such places – the Nazi extermination camps and the Tuol Sleng prison in Phnom Penh among them – have been opened to the public without significant architectural transformation, and a visit is gripping and troubling in itself. "Fundamentally vestiges", they are a necessity in the face of what Pierre Nora calls the "acceleration of history." "*Lieux de mémoire*", he says, "arise out of a

160 SINGH-BARTLETT, WARREN, "Ayloul Festival breaks from the past and presents many Faces of Truth", *Daily Star*, culture section, 31 August 2001.
161 CORNET, LAURENCE, "Collapsing Clouds of Gas and Dust: Vartan Avakian at Marfa'", *Ibraaz*, 25 November 2015.
162 "Ten Years Later: AFAC Celebrates Its 10th Anniversary with More than 40 Artists from 15 Arab Countries", Arab Culture Fund Bulletin, 26 October 2017.
163 BUCHAKJIAN, GREGORY, "Introduction", in *Beyrouth Empire. Sunduq Al-Aja'ib*, catalogue of the exhibition of the same title at Galerie Janine Rubeiz, Beirut, 2018, pp. 7–11.
164 MAKAREM, MAY, "Rempart contre l'amnésie, Beit Beirut figé comme Pompéi", *L'Orient-Le Jour*, 5 March 2014.
165 SAITO, HIRO, "Reiterated Commemoration: Hiroshima as National Trauma", *Sociological Theory*, vol. 24, no. 4, December 2006, pp. 353–76.

sense that there is no such thing as spontaneous memory, hence that we must create archives, mark anniversaries, organise celebrations, pronounce eulogies and authenticate documents, because such things no longer happen as a matter of course."[166]

Monuments already in existence are to be distinguished both from those raised after the event, such as Peter Eisenman's Holocaust Memorial, and from museums, sites of history rather than of memory. Beit Beirut, however, seems intended as both museum and relic to be preserved with its stigmata. How does one introduce the new into the old, without impairing the latter? In Cologne, on the site of two churches destroyed by bombing, stands the Kolumba Museum designed by Peter Zumthor. Both auratic and functional, the Kolumba is an autonomous construction that envelops the ruins within its perforated brick façade, while Beit Beirut is itself a relic. Nuremberg has seen a Documentation Centre by Günther Domenig grafted onto Albert Speer's Reichsparteitagsgelände: "a light, airy wedge driven through the thin granite skin into the heavy brickwork arches of the Nazi Party congress building."[167] But Nuremberg is not Beirut. While both cities have a painful past, the two buildings do not deliver the same experience or the same message. Unlike Speer's folly, the Barakat Building has no intrinsic link to violence. It is, more than anything, a survivor in a city that is continually reinventing itself. Maurice Halbwachs insisted that "were the relationship between streets, homes, and groups inhabiting them wholly accidental and of short duration, then men might tear down their homes, district, and city, only to rebuild another on the same site according to a different set of plans. But even if stones are movable, relationships established between stones and men are not so easily altered."[168]

On 15 January 2015, French ambassador Patrice Paoli invested Mona Hallak with the insignia of a Chevalier de l'Ordre National du Mérite. The ceremony took place in the great drawing room of the Résidence des Pins, a building whose eventful history has been alluded to above. In her acceptance speech, Mona Hallak declared:

> *Finally, I still dream, as I always have, of Beit Beirut – the "Yellow House" so named for its blond stone – as a place of unity in the historic centre, a place of peace and hope, an urban cultural centre dedicated to the memory and history of the city; a place where each can listen to the story of the other, and to the story that is shared; a place that might inspire civic engagement and a sense of shared belonging.*[169]

166 Nora, Pierre, "General Introduction: Between Memory and History", in Nora (ed.), *Realms of Memory*, translated by Arthur Goldhammer, New York, 1996, vol. 1, pp. 1–20.
167 Erlanger, Steven, "Nuremberg Journal: The Architect Who Speared His Own Nazi Demon", *New York Times*, 8 November 2001.
168 Halbwachs, Maurice, *The Collective Memory*, translated by F. J. Ditter and V. Y. Ditter, New York, 1980, [1950], p. 133.
169 Mona Hallak, speech on the occasion of being made Chevalier de l'Ordre National du Mérite, 15 January 2015.

FIG.73 *François Sargologo, Beyrouth Empire, Scène IX, 80e jour de printemps. Analogue assemblage from personal and archival works on paper, 50 × 50 cm.*

CHAPTER 3
AUXILIARY SPACE: BARRACKS AND PLACES OF DETENTION

FIG.74 *Samar Mogharbel, Hamra, 2014. Ceramic, 34 × 33 × 30 cm.*

CONTROLLING TERRITORY

On the Green Line, as earlier in the hotels, living space was militarised, becoming part of the field of battle. However, even in the rear, "everyday city life was transformed by the war", as Jean-Louis Cohen observes of World War II, adding that "a new geography emerged, its centres the places directly administered by the military."[1] It is furthermore illuminating to note the role played by the military in the shaping of the city even when it was not at war. The 20th century saw an expanding Beirut endowed with "highways leading in and out that France, the former mandatory power, saw fit to control by the implantation of barracks in a semi-circle around the city."[2] A radial organisation that answers to the endeavour "to striate space" – "the response of the State to all that threatens to move beyond it";[3] a vain attempt, as we saw in the previous chapter, as ineffective in 1958 as in 1975. From 1975 onwards, the breakdown of government saw the development of a militia society in which each organisation sought to rule a fragment of territory. The cosmopolitan modern city slid into "a close linkage of space and ethnos, a tight intertwining of civil and military, a psychological state and a menacing contiguity that produced in the besieged a psychological reflex of resistance."[4]

From 1991 on, the monopoly of arms was held, in principle, by the Syrian army (until 2005), the Lebanese army and the various government security services: "Beirut has been crisscrossed with a variety of security mechanisms. . . deployed for surveillance, constraining and limiting activities, at times blocking activities altogether."[5] In the 2010s, painter Omar Fakhoury combed the city looking for concrete blocks, barrel barriers, camouflage material, sandbags, sentry boxes and watchtowers – "temporary, yet solid and omnipresent."[6] It was at this time, too, that Tagreed Darghouth produced *Vision Machines, Shall You See Me Better Now?* – paintings looking at cameras, drones and other such instruments of surveillance. Both series followed a decade after *I Only Wish That I Could Weep*, a video from Walid Raad's Atlas Group, "attributed to Operator #17, a Lebanese Army intelligence officer who was assigned to monitor the Corniche, a seaside boardwalk in Beirut. From 1997 on, the officer decided to videotape the sunset instead of his assigned target."[7] Coming after the Civil War and reflecting on both local situation and global trends, the work of Raad, Fakhoury and Darghouth is symptomatic of the way in which 21st-century urban societies have been subjected to an intensified system surveillance by authorities that see them as potential battlefields.[8]

MILITARISING BUILDINGS

What makes a site attractive, from the military point of view? In the 19th century, it was held that "the defensive military quarters selected should as much as possible dominate the rest of the city and its exterior and communicate easily with them without intervening defiles."[9] As on the front line, vision and communication are a necessity. Once the highest point in Ashrafieh, the thirty-storey Rizk Tower (bf808) represented a strategic position for the Syrians in the Hundred Days' War of 1978. It later passed into the hands of the Christian forces, for which it became the eastern equivalent of the Murr Tower, a surveillance tower and potential snipers' eyrie.

Buildings of lesser height might also command panoramic views, thanks to their elevated location relative to the surrounding landscape. This was the case of the Kuwaiti Embassy in the southern fringes of Beirut, which looked down on Sabra and Shatila. When massacres were carried out in these two Palestinian refugee camps on 16–18 September 1982, Israel laid the entire blame on the

1 Cohen, Jean-Louis, *Architecture in Uniform: Designing and Building for the Second World War*, New Haven, Yale University Press 2011, p. 43.
2 Davie, "Comment fait-on la guerre à Beyrouth ?", op. cit., p. 34.
3 Deleuze and Guattari, *A Thousand Plateaus*, op. cit., p. 426.
4 Kemp, Percy, "La cité-État. Beyrouth entre deux formes de résistance", *Esprit*, vol. 50, no. 5–6, May 1983, pp. 53–67.
5 Fawaz, Mona, Harb Mona and Gharbieh, Ahmad, "Living Beirut's Security Zones: An Investigation of the Modalities and Practice of Urban Security", *City & Society*, vol. 24, no. 2, 2012, pp. 173–95.
6 Amaya-Akkermans, Arie, "The Here of the Elsewhere", *The Mantle*, 2 September 2014.
7 Raad, Walid, "Operator #17" under "Files Type FD", at The Atlas Group Archive website.
8 Graham, Stephen, *Cities Under Siege: The New Military Urbanism*, London and New York, Verso, 2011, p. 63.
9 Roguet, *Insurrections et guerre des barricades*, op. cit., p. 96.

Christian militias. Yet the Israeli army had taken over the embassy and it was difficult to believe them when they claimed that "they did not know what was happening in the camps. . . They did not see the wanton murder of innocents through their telescopic binoculars."[10]

Another situation was presented by the coastline. Relatively unscathed until then, in 1982 the Beirut waterfront was targeted by the Israeli navy. In riposte, "tense but determined, defenders armed with anti-tank rockets, AA guns, artillery pieces and automatic weapons ruled the coast from Ain el Mreisseh to Khalde, where no one any longer dared or was able to venture."[11] In the Ain el Tineh sector, a self-propelled anti-aircraft gun was sited outside the Salha Building (bf1203, Ras Beyrouth) where my own family lived. Tenants and fighters shared the basement stairwell, gathering there for protection during the ensuing shelling. A few days later, on a vacant lot opposite, a bulldozer created an earth bank behind which would be positioned a 120 mm gun.[12] This scaling-up of the military presence was a signal to the residents that it was time to leave.

COMING HOME TO A BARRACKS

During the 1980s, both sectors of Beirut saw internal struggles that varied in intensity from fisticuffs to wide-ranging military conflict. An example is the so-called "Battle of the Flag" that broke out between Amal and the Progressive Socialist Party in November 1985.[13] Following that confrontation, the two parties formed a Joint Strike Force – *Al qouwa al-dariba* – whose task was to restore order and to enforce "withdrawal of the militias",[14] a paradoxical project given that the joint force itself was made up of party militias. For some reason, it decided on the Salha Building for its quarters, having been preceded there in 1982 by the Palestinian–Progressive forces and then the Israeli army, who had positioned a Merkava tank on the entrance ramp. The Joint Strike Force with its weapons and vehicles moved into the ground-floor car park and the main entrance lobby, both blocked off from the rest of the building. A metal grille installed between the lobby and the stairwell following the outbreak of war was now locked permanently in place, establishing a demarcation line between civilian and military space. Residents and visitors had to use the basement car park to come and go. They would take the stairs – the lifts being out of service – meeting the gaze of the militiamen as they passed, or observing them at rest, lying on the floor, cleaning their weapons or at their own ablutions.

To this cohabitation common to all the building's residents must be added another particular to my own family. On 19 May 1986, my father, Sarkis Buchakjian, was kidnapped and held for a month. During his captivity, our apartment found itself unexpectedly transformed into a semi-public space. Throughout the day, an unbroken stream of visitors dropped by, in a ritual very reminiscent of the visits of condolence that are a well-established custom in Lebanon. The visitors were friends, relatives, neighbours and acquaintances come to comfort the family and to take comfort themselves from not being in my father's place. There were also police officers and representatives of the political parties who came to offer their "good offices." Sitting on the drawing-room sofas, society figures, the heads of militias that had been killing each other the night before and police officers would face each other tight-lipped. It wasn't at all rare for the detective superintendent to discreetly mention to my mother that a guest seated opposite was one of the kidnappers. Such visits also allowed the armed elements another incursion into private space, crossing the line that still separated it from the realm they had already made their own.

10 Friedman, Thomas L., *From Beirut to Jerusalem*, New York, Anchor, 1990, p. 163.
11 "Les défenseurs de la capitale attendent de pied ferme. . . ", *L'Orient-Le Jour*, 11 June 1982.
12 Kheireddine el-Ahdab, email to the author, 29 July 2014.
13 "Beirut Battles Mark Independence Day", *New York Times*, 23 November 1985.
14 "The 'strike force' has withdrawn the militiamen and arrested the offenders", *An-Nahar*, 21 November 1985.

VULNERABLE TARGETS

To be in the vicinity of fighters could be dangerous. One example among many is that of the building in which they "climbed the stairs to the roof, installed a rocket launcher and fired before hurtling back down the stairs, only to go up and fire again a few minutes later, in complete disregard of the residents who might have had to suffer the enemy's response."[15] During the 1982 invasion, which saw a quarter of West Beirut's buildings seriously damaged or destroyed,[16] some were specifically targeted and reduced to rubble. A year before, the Israeli air force bombed the Rahmeh building, where Fatah, the Democratic Front for the Liberation of Palestine (DFLP) and the pro-Iraqi Arab Liberation Front had offices.[17] The seven-storey building collapsed with its residents inside. The Israeli prime minster declared that "any civilians who get in the way of attacks on Palestinian guerrillas will have to bear the consequences."[18]

Military buildings were also at risk of suicide bombers, who claimed victims among all the parties involved, notably the Multinational Force in Lebanon when, on 23 October 1983, truck bombs destroyed both the Drakkar Building occupied by the French contingent and the barracks of the American marines, who suffered their greatest losses "since the Battle of Iwo Jima."[19]

URBAN CITADELS

In the face of these dangers, militias and security services sought to establish "safe" zones around barracks and the homes of their respective leaderships. Their headquarters "were surrounded by walls of sandbags, metre-high concrete cubes and containers bolstered by sandbags; the entrances were guarded by barriers reinforced by small-arms posts."[20] Since then, technological progress has brought about a proliferation of surveillance devices: cameras, monitors, detectors and electronic gates. The most typical fortification of the post-war period, or of this time of latent war – or however the present may be described – is the concrete wall to be found surrounding public buildings and embassies, sometimes entire blocks. These walls are rows of tall concrete blocks in the form of inverted Ts, pre-cast, delivered and craned into place in front of the premises to be protected. There is no cementing or assembly and the blocks can be removed and taken elsewhere: they are moveable and nomadic. Often, they obtrude upon the public realm, obstructing the passage of pedestrians. Here, on a reduced scale, is the principle of the fortified city that the Americans tried to apply (with a well-known lack of success) in the ultra-protected Green Zone of Baghdad.

These concrete-block fortifications are a contemporary version of the walls of sandbags, which have not disappeared. During the years of war, they acted as a politico-military barometer, rising in times of tension and falling again in periods of calm. A surprising discovery was made in a villa once occupied by the Guardians of the Cedar militia (bf4229, Achrafieh). The garage, closed off from the street by breeze blocks, was full of sand (PL.2). Unlike Robert Smithson's *Partially Buried Woodshed,* its outside heaped with earth, here, it was the interior space itself that had been filled with sand – a little like Kolmanskop in Namibia, where the dunes have invaded the houses. Here, the floor, raised by around 80 cm, dips suddenly facing the breeze blocks. Several hypotheses have presented themselves as explanations for this mysterious phenomenon: an unloading platform for building materials? An arms cache? A mass grave? No, this was a sandbag factory.

15 "Assez de combats", *L'Orient-Le Jour,* 8 January 1982, p. 1.
16 "En trois mois, des destructions pour 10 milliards de LL", *L'Orient-Le Jour,* 31 August 1982.
17 "The Bombing of Beirut", *Journal of Palestine Studies,* vol. 11, no. 1, autumn 1981, pp. 218–25.
18 Cobban, Helena, "The Rahmeh Building", *New Statesman,* 14 July 1981.
19 "Beirut Marine Barracks Bombing Fast Facts", CNN website.
20 Davie, Michael F., "Les marqueurs de territoires idéologiques", L'Affiche Urbaine, Ndeg. 2, 1992, Groupe EIDOS et Maison des Sciences de la Ville, Tours, 1992.

This sand store shared its invisibility with many other installations, of which few ever suspected their existence, even among the neighbours. In the huge storerooms in the basement of the "Sector 10" building (bf1118, Achrafieh), the Phalangists organised a training centre and firing range, soundproof and secret. Some 150 members attended from July 1978 to 1992, two years after the war's end.[21] In more recent times, in an apartment in a partially abandoned building in Koraytem (PL.25), an equally invisible mini barracks was installed for the men tasked with the protection of a minister living close by.

INTERIOR AND EXTERIOR DÉCOR: FROM IDEOLOGY TO PERSONAL EXPRESSION

FIG.75 *Gregory Buchakjian, Hajj Zuheir Schehadeh Mural House, 2013. Photograph.*

FIG.76 *Gregory Buchakjian, Mustapha Massoud Schoucair Cenotaph-house, 2013. Photograph.*

The various parties to the conflict made use of the architectural and graphic elements available to them to proclaim their hegemony: signs, emblems, banners, portraits, flags, graffiti, posters.[22] So, "far from being innocent vehicles of political activism or simple, coercive tools of propaganda, posters were a constitutive element of the hegemonic articulation of political communities during the Lebanese Civil War."[23] In militarised buildings, they progressively invaded the immediate surroundings, the façade, the entrance, the stairs and the interiors. In 2013, a building in Bashura (bf325) was more or less covered by a portrait of Sayyed Hassan Nasrallah, the head of Hezbollah, with the slogan *Al-Muqawama* (the Resistance). "Presented by the young people of the region", this banner coexisted with another, smaller, that was as an advert for "DVD Store Asmer" and its "Movie – Ps2 – PC – DVD – Xbox – Wii – Ps3." The juxtaposition of the two messages testifies to a certain proximity between the world of political partisanship and social life more generally. On another façade of the same building was the inscription *Qaat el-Sayyida Tawaa* – Hall of the Lady Tawaa. She was the woman of the city of Kufa who took in an emissary of Imam Hussein's who was pursued by the Umayyads.[24] It is from this interpenetration of the martial, the political, the civil and the religious that a cult of the martyr has emerged to which no party is immune – for "[his death] is a testament to the justice of the cause."[25] This cult is so essential to partisan mobilisation that abandoned buildings have been transformed into commemorative monuments. At Basta, the home of Mustapha Massoud Schoucair (bf325, Bachoura) is a cenotaph, the interior empty, the exterior draped in black cloth and bearing a commemorative plaque (FIG.76). In a once luxurious

21 FAYAD, interview of 4 February 2015.
22 DAVIE, "Les marqueurs de territoires idéologiques" op. cit.
23 MAASRI, *Off the Wall*, op. cit., p. 17.
24 "Al Sayyida Taw'a", *Haya'*, 2 November 2008, p. 39.
25 CHAIB, KINDA, "Une figure de martyr au Sud-Liban", in MERMIER, FRANCK, and VARIN, CHRISTOPHE (eds), *Mémoires de guerres au Liban, 1975–1990*, Arles, Actes Sud / Sindbad, 2010, p. 260.

late-19th-century dwelling (bf471, Zokak el-Blatt), a wall formerly covered with painted decoration in imitation of a stucco relief now has a fresco portraying "the martyr commandant Hajj Zuheir Shehadeh", on his right a landscape with a red sun over a tented camp, an aircraft in the foreground, and atop a crest a blazing watchtower whose flames compose the words *Al Muqawama al-Islamiyya* – Islamic Resistance. These two funerary monuments differ in that the first is located in the public realm, the second in an interior (FIG.75).

Reserved for partisans, the interior is decorated with a variety of political images and personal testimonies expressing, as Tanya Traboulsi puts it, "the hopes and dreams" of these men.[26] Messages left on the walls of the Barakat Building (bf1237, Achrafieh) have the air of confessions, as, for example, one fighter's declaration that "If love of Gilbert is a crime, let history show that I am a dangerous criminal." In 2011, one bedroom inside an abandoned building (bf1281, Bachoura) disclosed images related to martyrs, empty beer cans, swimming trunks and women's underwear (PL.9). It is but a step from ideology to leisure and fantasy. At the various sites occupied by armies and militias, the walls present a patchwork of blessed virgins, cars, motorbikes, sportsmen and women in varying states of undress (FIG.77).

FIG.77 *Tanya Traboulsi, Collection 1983, #3, 2010. Photograph.*

LOOTINGS AND RESTORATIONS

The different forces did not hesitate to cannibalise the buildings in which they made themselves at home, removing furniture, tiles, doors, windows, electrical installations, taps and pipes. In 1976, Raymond Eddé, head of the Lebanese National Bloc, wrote to the Syrian prime minister to complain of looting at Sawfar – that of his own home in particular. He deplored "the theft of an old brass bed I am attached to, for it belonged to my father M. Émile Eddé, who was president of the Lebanese Republic and who was born at Bab Tuma in Damascus in 1884", asking the prime minister to "be so kind as either to return it to me, or to present it in my name to President Hafiz Assad, or to have it sent to Mazzeh prison so as to provide for all eventualities."[27] No less outlandish was the theft of a Cessna from the Beirut flying club, by two Israeli soldiers.[28]

In general, setting up home in an abandoned building involved the same sort of work whether a person was a fighter or a squatter, such as partitioning the internal space and isolating it from the exterior for warmth and protection from the elements (FIG.78). Certain militarised buildings were as picturesquely sordid as any occupied by poverty-stricken refugees, while others were repaired and refurbished. In the late summer of 1982, the US Marines brought with them "prefabricated showers with running hot water" while their French counterparts had to be content with "showers improvised from mineral water bottles."[29] In the Drakkar, the French took possession of a "no doubt once luxurious building in a very bad state. There was no water or electricity, and no windows" and so they embarked on a programme of "refurbishment and weather-proofing."[30] When they took over a villa as their HQ (bf4229, Achrafieh), the Guardians of the Cedar did not stint, installing ultra-modern offices with broadcast equipment and covering the walls of the drawing room with a fresco depicting a world map.

26 TRABOULSI, TANYA, "Collection 1983", Tanya Traboulsi website.
27 "Au lieu de maintenir l'ordre, les Syriens détruisent et pillent Sofar", *L'Orient-Le Jour*, 29 June 1976, p. 4.
28 MÉNARGUES, *Les Secrets de la guerre du Liban : 1*, op. cit., p. 351.
29 "Forces multinationales (II) La vie quotidienne en photos", *L'Orient-Le Jour*, 5 September 1982, p. 4.
30 HEMAR, JEAN-LUC, "Attentat Drakkar à Beyrouth, Liban, le 23 Octobre 1983", Camp Militaire d'Idron.

CACHES OF ARMS AND AMMUNITION – HOLES AND WALLS

FIG.78 *Guy Le Querrec, Shatila. 6th Regiment of parachutist fighters, Section Ghesquière, 1982. Photograph.*

For decades, arms caches had been the subject of wild rumour. In an apartment fire in 1972, firefighters came upon an arsenal of "Kalachinkoff [*sic*] machine guns in jute bags; 1 Herstal light machine gun; 40 cartridge cases; 400 'Kalachinkoff' bullets; 940 assault-rifle bullets; 40 machine-gun magazines; 20 assault-rifle magazines; 17 revolver loaders; 9 bayonets, not to mention the belts, cartridge holders, binoculars and holsters."[31] In 1982, we learned that "Beirut stood on a volcano of munitions",[32] and that "HQs and arms depots were linked by a fairly dense network of concrete tunnels."[33] However, as a general rule, stores of arms and ammunition remained hidden. As Gaston Bachelard says, "He who buries a treasure buries himself with it. A secret is a grave and it is not for nothing that a man who can be trusted with a secret boasts that he is 'like the grave'."[34]

The cleanly dug holes seen in many abandoned buildings raise all kinds of questions. Two houses (bf479 and 610, Saifi) with holes of this kind were part of a network providing additional logistics behind the early front lines. The two holes are so similar that their photographs look like inverted versions of the same image (FIG.80-81). During ceasefires and tactical retreats, combatants had taken to digging holes in which to deposit – bury – arms, ammunition and equipment for use at a later time. Once again, these arms caches reflect the entanglement of military and civilian activity. After the Israeli retreat in 1985, Ain el-Mir in South Lebanon became a front line and Ali Hachicho was part of a group of fighters who took over a house newly abandoned by its residents. In 1991, when the war was over, he wrote them a letter and put it in a mortar case, which he buried in the garden. In 2002, Akram Zaatari made the video *In This House*, in which the letter is dug up (FIG.79). In this film, "the story told to the film-maker by the fighter invests an object in absentia with a functional strangeness. When activated, the recovered note is already uncanny and has no need of a tangible surface to state, redundantly, that this is a land suspended."[35]

Just as enigmatic as the excavated houses are those that are walled up. The most fascinating example is a luxury

FIG.79 *Akram Zaatari, In this House, 2005. Vidéo.*

31 "Découverte d'un véritable arsenal grâce à. . . un incendie", *Le Soir*, undated (probably July 1972), p. 2.
32 Helou, Nelly, "Beyrouth reposait sur un volcan de munitions", *La Revue du Liban*, no. 1192, 25 September 1982, pp. 72–4.
33 Davie, "Comment fait-on la guerre à Beyrouth ?" op. cit. , p. 25.
34 Bachelard, Gaston, *The Poetics of Space*, translated by Maria Jolas, 4th edition, Boston, Beacon, 1994, p. 88.
35 Sadek, Walid, "Collecting the Uncanny and the Labor of Missing", in *Archives, Museums and Collecting Practices in the Modern Arab World*, Farnham, Ashgate, 2012, pp. 211–24.

FIGS.80-81 *Gregory Buchakjian, Excavations inside houses in Saifi, 2012. Photograph.*

apartment block built during the French Mandate in Pasteur Street (bf 11, Medawar) and known for having housed on its ground floor the headquarters of *Ketleh Wataniyeh* (the National Bloc Party), founded by Émile Eddé. On the first floor, in the devastated central foyer with its blackened walls, a sofa and seven armchairs upholstered in khaki were set out on the rubble, the doors were walled up and a statue of the Virgin Mary stood on a small table. All entrances to the eastern side of the house were filled in with breeze block reinforced with cement (PL.11,33). The uncanny impression created was compounded by regular crashing sounds like doors banging. These were made by pigeons that lived on the third floor and frequently flew into the walls. A single hole in one of the blocked openings led into the "hidden" part of the house, which looked like a perfectly ordinary office from the 1970s. The separation of this part of the building from the rest had not, in fact, been done to create a hiding place for some treasure, but in an effort to preserve the rooms that remained undamaged when the lounge went up in flames by separating them from the rest. An external staircase linked these rooms to a garden, so they continued to function independently before being abandoned in their turn. Despite this disappointing conclusion, the walled-up doors, the statue of the Virgin Mary, the vestiges of former splendours and the blackened ceiling radiated an aura that we also found in Peter Zumthor's description of a work by Per Kierkeby:

> *The house had no entrance. Its interior was inaccessible and hidden. This mystery, in combination with other characteristics of the work, gave it a profoundly mystical aura. I think the elements supporting the frame of a house should be arranged in such a way as to maintain the finished object in a state of internal tension and vibration. This is how violins are made – they remind us of living bodies in nature.*[36]

PLACES OF INCARCERATION AND TORTURE

> *But the body is also directly involved in a political field; power relations have an immediate hold upon it; they invest it, mark it, train it, torture it, force it to carry out tasks, to perform ceremonies, to emit signs.*[37]

The Lebanese security forces recorded four thousand kidnappings for the period 1975–90, but estimates put the total number of missing people at between 20,000 and 34,000,[38] in addition to those who were released from a detention that lasted anywhere between a few minutes and several years. Imprisonment, that "other form of

36 Zumthor, Peter, *Penser l'architecture*, expanded 2nd edition, Basel, Birkhaüser, 2010, pp. 18–19.
37 Foucault, Michel, *Discipline and Punish. The Birth of the Prison*, translated by Alan Sheridan, New York, Vintage, 1977, p. 25.
38 Courbage, Youssef, "Labaki (Boutros), Abou Rjeily (Khalil) — Bilan des guerres du Liban. 1975-1990", *Population*, 50, no. 1, 1995, pp. 217–21.

exclusion of the other",[39] was not covered by any legal framework, although some armies and militias acted as states within a state, complete with accompanying bureaucracy and paperwork. The floor of a cell run by the Guardians of the Cedars is still covered in the remains of documentation in which each "arrest" is recorded, with spaces for many categories of information, but leaving out the sufferings inflicted. Here, as elsewhere, in "this absurd situation that makes murder coincide with sacrifice",[40] the Geneva conventions that are supposed to govern the treatment of prisoners of war were readily flouted.[41]

Those abducted were most frequently taken in the street, notably at roadblocks. At the start of the conflict, "flying checkpoints" – so called because they were temporary and therefore unexpected – seized their victims on the basis of their adherence to a particular religious faith. Alongside these abductions "by identity card" there were targeted kidnappings, where the victim was specifically sought out. Wadad Halwani describes how her doorbell rang one day and, when the door was opened, she saw two pistols pointing at her husband's head. "They said, 'Don't be frightened, we're going to question him for five minutes'." Mr Halwani never returned.[42]

FIG.82 *Dalia Khamissy, Driving license belonging to Aziz Dirawi who was taken away by force in 1982, 2010. Photograph.*

UNIDENTIFIABLE PRISONS

Since the places of incarceration scattered across Lebanon had no legal existence, they are impossible to identify or quantify. Two films by Maroun Bagdadi present improvised prisons of different kinds. In *Land of Honey and Incense*, a doctor is held in a pigeon loft on the terrace of an apartment building, while in *Outside Life*, a photographer is successively imprisoned in the classroom of an abandoned school, the stables at a racecourse, a child's bedroom in an deserted apartment and the home that his kidnappers' leader shares with his wife and son. The hostage is held in a tiny storage room that serves as a larder. As it has no window, it is the most secure room in the house, where the child also goes to shelter from the bombing. The wife finds the situation unbearable, saying, "We are just as much hostages as that poor wretch!"

FIG.83 *Gregory Buchakjian, Khiam Detention Center, 2011. Photograph.*

39 TRABOULSI, FAWWAZ, "Société violente ou système de guerre ?" in *Guerres civiles : Économie de la violence – Dimensions de la civilité*, Paris, Karthala, 1999, p. 143.
40 RICŒUR, PAUL, *History and Truth*, translated by *Charles A. Kelbley, Evanston, Northwestern University Press, 1965*, p. 244.
41 The Geneva Convention (III) relative to the treatment of prisoners of war, 12 August 1949, replaced the 1929 Convention relative to the treatment of prisoners of war.
42 *House of Memory*, OR TV, 26 February 2001.

Sarkis Buchakjian was held captive for a month, in the bedroom of an inhabited flat: "I heard women's voices and children reciting their lessons for homework." The places where others were held included their own homes, abandoned buildings and a space already given over to military use. A sniper surveyed the neighbourhood of Saint Joseph University from an apartment block (bf1079, Bashura) that also contained a "chamber of answers." Stories tell of abuses perpetrated in the meandering underground spaces of the Holiday Inn, the perfect setting for a horror film, while another account explains that in the Murr Tower:

> *The torture chamber is in a dark antechamber. An iron triangle comes down from the ceiling and is hooked up to an electric battery. The "guilty person" is put in there and gradually electrified. A kind of metal spoon is used to brand him and burn his body. A long metal rod probably fulfils a similar function.*[43]

After the Battle of the Hotels, these two buildings became *Markaz* (centres), used at once as political headquarters, barracks and, when the need arose, prisons. So there were potentially as many prisons as there were *Markaz*.

A SEASON IN THE UNDERWORLD

FIG.84 *Fouad Elkoury, A Makeshift Prison, Civil War series, 1983. Photograph.*

In 1983, Fouad Elkoury managed to photograph Israeli prisoners held by Palestinians (FIG.84). It is hard to know what to make of this image of a man in a keffiyeh cheerily serving tea to smiling young people. Most prisoners would not have been treated with such consideration. They could be held in "damp and mouldy"[44] cells that measured between 0.5 × 1.5 m and 2 × 2 m.[45] The furniture included a small bowl which, in the absence of water "served as decoration" and a "heap of woollen blankets giving off a nauseating smell."[46] Food was minimal – usually one meal a day. It was also disgusting, and recalcitrant eaters were beaten. Toilet visits were similarly confined to one per day. Alone in their cells, sometimes with their hands bound, prisoners would hear the voices of others being beaten.

The beatings were conducted in the cells, or in the offices where prisoners were interrogated, or else in specially equipped rooms, such as the one in the Murr Tower described earlier. The job of moving prisoners could also become a form of torture, such as when the captors told them to "run" up and downstairs with their faces covered.[47] "Muscular" interrogations involved blows, threats, insults and humiliation. These would be followed by torture of a more explicit kind. The countless methods used are the stuff of nightmares, including jets of icy or boiling water and the *douleb* or tyre that would be placed over the victim, who was then rolled around and beaten.[48] Electric shocks were widely used,[49] notably in association with the Balango method, where the captive was bound and suspended above the floor to be beaten by the torturers, who were sometimes armed with iron bars (PL.7).

43 HADDAD, SCARLETT, "La tour Murr a cessé de tuer", *Nouveau Magazine*, no. 1313, 2 October 1982, pp. 20–31.
44 AL-KOURANI, WALID, "What the Syrian Reatreat has left behind in Lebanon", *An-Nahar*, 26 April 2006, p. 15.
45 CHAYA, MANAL, "Four detainees in Syrian intelligence centre tell of their ordeal", *An-Nahar*, 28 April 2005, p. 13.
46 *Ibid.*
47 AL-KOURANI, "What the Syrian Reatreat has left behind in Lebanon", op. cit.
48 AL-AMIN, RAMI, "Beau Rivage, Hotel of Tortures", *Al-Jadeed*, 2010.
49 SHERRY, VIRGINIA N., "Syria/Lebanon: An Alliance Beyond the Law. Enforced Disappearances in Lebanon", Human Rights Watch, 11 May 1997, p. 4.

VISIBLE AND INVISIBLE

Physical violence relates to an archaic state, where the body is "tortured, dismembered, amputated. . . symbolically branded on the face or shoulder, exposed alive or dead to public view."[50] In 1975–6, the corpses of enemies dragged along behind cars served as eloquent examples. Where kidnappings were carried out to obtain a prisoner exchange or a ransom, another form of display developed, involving sound and sometimes also vision. The kidnappers would communicate with the family or authorities by phone or would send them audio cassettes or videotapes in which the hostage would read out their demands. These provided confirmation that the hostage was alive and in the hands of a particular group. *The Bachar Tapes* by the Atlas Group record the personal story of Souheil Bachar, "the only Arab held with Western hostages."[51] This "experimental" video attributed to Bachar and dated 2001[52] is part of the work undertaken by Walid Raad to fictionalise the archive and its narratives. In their negotiation process, the kidnappers also sometimes sent audio recordings of the prisoner being tortured. Between the sounds of blows and cries of pain, the hostage would call for his torturers' conditions to be met as quickly as possible.

Imprisonment remained a secretive, invisible practice. Prisoners were held in concealed places, hence the creation of underground cells. However, secrecy was never absolute. Locked away in the dark, detainees developed a heightened sensitivity to sound. Based on accounts from survivors, Lawrence Abu Hamdan used the sounds heard in a space as a means to reconstruct the architecture of the prison and what happened there.[53] In a city like Beirut, neighbours and passers-by could not fail to notice when a person was unloaded from the boot of a car, such as the woman who was thrown from a vehicle and had to stand up with her head inside a bag.[54] Nor could they fail to hear the cries of pain. In Charif Majdalani's novel *Villa des femmes*, one night "insane howls came from the factory. . . It seemed obvious to us that someone was being tortured in the buildings."[55] As a teenager, Francis Najjar would often visit a friend. At first sight, "nothing about the building was any different from any other. There were guards at the door. I thought it was for the protection of a minister who lived nearby."[56] There was a sense that something was not quite right, but the residents carried on as if all was well. In 2005, Najjar learned that the building next door to her friend's was the headquarters of Syrian intelligence. In 2007, she made a short film called *Le Beau Rivage*.[57] Inspired by David Lynch's *Eraserhead*, the film shows the life of a family who hear sinister sounds in their apartment and question whether they should live in such a building.[58]

WHAT FUTURE FOR HOMES WITH SUCH POWERFUL MEMORIES?

Alongside the people who disappeared, there are places that now exist in name only, such as Beau Rivage, Anjar and Khiam. The sites of imprisonment are absent, even when they still physically exist. Their place in the collective imagination is at once vague and traumatic. Their history has not been written; they are gone, but not buried.

Many homeowners reclaimed buildings that were empty but bore traces of their terrible past. How can such a legacy be managed in a country where the political class, the elites and much of the population have turned collective amnesia into a necessity? This policy of forgetting is underpinned by an amnesty law passed in parliament on 26 August 1991, which pardons all war crimes committed before

50 Foucault, *Discipline and Punish*, op. cit., p 8.
51 Respini, Eva, *Walid Raad*, New York, The Museum of Modern Art, 2015, p. 90.
52 Raad, Walid, "Files Type A", The Atlas Group Archive website, 2002.
53 Abu Hamdan, Lawrence, "Saydnaya (the Missing 19db)", Lawrence Abu Hamdan website, 2017.
54 Al-Kourani, "What the Syrian Reatreat has left behind in Lebanon", op. cit.
55 Majdalani, Charif, *Villa des femmes*, Paris, Seuil, 2015, p. 266.
56 Nina Frances Najjar, interview with the author, 10 September 2014.
57 Najjar, Nina Frances, *Le Beau Rivage*, 2007.
58 *Ibid.*

28 March 1991.[59] Noting that the "boundary between forgetting and forgiving is crossed surreptitiously to the extent that these two dispositions have to do with judicial proceedings and with handing down a sentence", Paul Ricœur observes that:

> *Amnesty, as institutional forgetting, touches the very roots of the political and, through it, the most profound and most deeply concealed relation to a past that is placed under an interdict. The proximity, which is more than phonetic, or even semantic, between amnesty and amnesia signals the existence of a secret pact with the denial of memory which. . . distances it from forgiving after first suggesting a close simulation.*[60]

Many of the people questioned by Danielle Arbid in *Alone with War* seem content with a denial that must necessarily be forced, since it is hard to be without a parent, friend or neighbour who was killed, injured or kidnapped, or a house that was destroyed or occupied. Many owners did nothing to reclaim their homes; others were more determined. In 2005, the Jabre family retrieved their villa, in the Bois de Boulogne locality, after thirty years during which the place served as a centre for command and detention. In September of that same year, they organised a bucolic lunch in the garden of their villa, which became an act of catharsis.[61] The house became a place of pilgrimage: "People came there to show their families the places where they had been imprisoned."[62] Later, the architect Nabil Gholam suggested razing the house to the ground, but Philippe Jabre wanted to preserve it. In addition to wanting to hold on to family memories, Jabre had a particularly strong connection to the memory of the war, which led him to acquire photographs by Don McCullin relating to three of its episodes: the Battle of the Hotels (FIG.41), the Karantina massacre and the massacres of Sabra and Shatila.[63] Architect and client came to a compromise: the building's external envelope was preserved.[64] The walls and floors were completely demolished to "cleanse" the house of its tragic history.[65] When the works were completed their symbolism became apparent. As Zaza and Philippe Jabre explain, "When people see this house – which was in ruins ten years ago – they see a message."[66]

In Beirut, the Beau Rivage hotel survives in a state of lethargy; the neighbouring concrete structure whose basement had served as a prison was partially demolished and the apartment block that had served as a headquarters strove to return to anonymity.

Khiam in South Lebanon is the only detention centre that has become a museum. Opened to the public after the Israeli withdrawal in 2000, bombed in 2006 and reopened in its ruined state, it presents the narrative and rhetoric of one party only: Hezbollah. The Lebanese government is not part of it, and other organisations involved in the resistance are excluded. The absence of other input is compensated by writings and images based on personal accounts, notably those of Souha Bechara, a communist militant who was imprisoned here, and preserved in films such as *Souha, survivre à l'enfer* (*Souha, surviving hell*) by Randa Chahal-Sabbagh and *Khiam* (2000) and *Khiam 2000–2007* (2008) by Joana Hadjithomas and Khalil Joreige.[67]

---

59 Smaira, Dima and Cassehgari, Roxane, "Failing to Deal with the Past. What cost to Lebanon?" New York, Beirut, International Center for Transitional Justice, January 2014, pp. 9–10.

60 Ricœur, Paul, *Memory, History, Forgetting*, translated by Kathleen Blamey and David Pellauer, Chicago, University of Chicago Press, 2004, p. 453.

61 Khoder, Patricia, "Quand l'esprit de résistance est plus fort que les horreurs de l'occupation. La villa Philippe Raymond Jabre, ancien siège des SR syriens au Metn, se remet à vivre", *L'Orient-Le Jour*, 27 September 2005.

62 Jabre, Philippe, in Brooke Anderson, "Damaged by War, a Villa in Lebanon Gets a Transformation", *Wall Street Journal*, 22 January 2015.

63 Philippe Jabre, interview with the author, July 2013.

64 Nabil Gholam, interview with the author, 12 October 2013.

65 "work . private residence . j house", Nabil Gholam Architects website.

66 Anderson, "Damaged by War, a Villa in Lebanon Gets a Transformation", op. cit.

67 Launchbury, Claire, "Staging Khiam: documentary, theater, and archive in postwar Lebanon", *Contemporary French and Francophone Studies*, 18, no. 5, 20 October 2014, pp. 514–22.

FIG.85 *Gregory Buchakjian, Hôtel Beau Rivage, 2014. Photograph.*

CHAPTER 4

SPACES REGAINED: UNSTABLE HOMES AND MULTIPLE USES

FIG.86 *Ayman Baalbaki, Ciel chargé de fleurs, 2004. Acrylic on fabric mounted on board, 180 × 180 cm.*

A BRIEF HISTORY: TWO CENTURIES OF MIGRATORY FLOWS

"Our age – with its modern warfare, imperialism, and the quasi-theological ambitions of totalitarian rulers – is indeed the age of the refugee, the displaced person, mass immigration", wrote Edward Said.[1] Alongside wars these movements reflect a search for economic opportunities: the abandonment of the countryside for "social and political reasons", notably "family and cultural constraints… restricted land access or a low level of female independence" and the myth of the good life are also factors that drove human beings en masse to the cities.[2]

Marwan Rechmaoui's *Beyrouth Caoutchouc* (2004), a gigantic floor-based rubber map in relief, reveals the strange shapes of the city and its development – how Armenian, Palestinian and Iraqi refugees have moved in, how a giant refuse dump became reclaimed land.[3] Since the mid-19th century Beirut has constantly absorbed new arrivals. The troubles of 1860, first in the mountains and then in Damascus, drove a frightened population to the city. During this time, Beirut overflowed its mediaeval walls, its area massively expanded, and it promoted itself to capital of the Ottoman *vilayet* or province.[4] As a population of newcomers moved into the historic centre, the old families moved further out into new residences built around a central hall, with red roof tiles and three arched windows.[5]

During the Great War, the population of Mount Lebanon was decimated by famine.[6] In Beirut, the authorities of the French mandate counted "more than ten thousand women and children wandering the streets. They are given shelter in convents and empty buildings."[7] During this time, survivors of the Armenian genocide were placed in Mar Mikhael and Burj Hammud. These camps of tents, subsequently replaced by shacks made of wood and corrugated iron and military huts,[8] formed the basis of the shanty towns that later surrounded the capital.[9] In 1926, the authorities released money for the construction of Armenian neighbourhoods,[10] initiating the only process to turn "refugees" into "citizens" in the history of modern Lebanon.

In the 20th century, as Maronite farmers left the countryside in their droves, the Shia in the south formed a new poverty belt.[11] Lebanon played its role as a land of asylum for persecuted minorities, political militants, intellectuals and rich families,[12] and similarly absorbed some of the workless Palestinians cast into exile by the *Nakba* (catastrophe) of 1948 and the *Naksa* (reversal) of 1967. Beirut was surrounded by six refugee camps: "Their great sprawling camps are an eyesore which no visitor can bypass… In Beirut, refugee encampments are clustered only a ten-minute drive from the hotels and night clubs of the city's 'Riviera' area."[13]

In 1976, a year after the start of the conflagration, "half the million inhabitants of Beirut had sought refuge in the interior of the country or abroad."[14] In the end, more than half a million people were entering or leaving Beirut or moving from one sector to another in "highly elastic" movements: "Every time there's an Israeli attack, the south climbs towards the north. Then, every time war starts again in Beirut, Beirut emigrates southwards, to Beqaa or the mountains."[15] The net inward migration to the capital can be explained by the fact that battles left greater scars

1 Said, Edward, "Reflections on Exile", *Granta*, no. 13: After the Revolution. Essays and Memoir (1 September 1984), p. 159.
2 Soliman, Ahmed M., "Diversity of Ethnicity and State Involvement on Urban Informality in Beirut", *Theoretical and Empirical Researches in Urban Management* 3, no. 9 (November 2008), p. 19.
3 Wilson-Goldie, Kaelen, "City Limits", *The Review*, 23 April 2009.
4 Davie, May, "La millat grecque-orthodoxe de Beyrouth 1800-1940", doctoral thesis, Paris IV Sorbonne, 1993, p. 51.
5 *Ibid.*, p. 48.
6 Eddé, Carla, "La Première Guerre mondiale : une catastrophe sans précédent au 'Liban'", in *Les "petites écoles" du Mont-Liban. Joseph Delore, s.j. (1873-1944)*, Beirut, Presses de l'Université Saint-Joseph, 2003, p. 97.
7 *Lisan el-Hal*, 30 October and 26 December 1918, in Eddé, Carla, *Beyrouth, naissance d'une capitale : 1918-1924*, La bibliothèque arabe. Hommes et sociétés, Arles, Actes sud / Sindbad, 2009, p. 64.
8 Tachjian, Vahé, "Des camps de réfugiés aux quartiers urbains. Processus et enjeux", in Kevorkian, Raymond, Nordiguian, Lévon and Tachjian, Vahé, *Les Arméniens 1917–1939 : La quête d'un refuge*, Beirut, Presses de l'Université Saint-Joseph, 2006, p. 120.
9 Pharès, Joseph and Bourgey, André, "Les bidonvilles de l'agglomération de Beyrouth", *Revue de géographie de Lyon* 48, no. 2, 1973, pp. 118.
10 Tachjian, op. cit., p. 130.
11 Beyhum, "Les Démarcations au Liban d'hier à aujourd'hui", op. cit. p. 280.
12 Beyhum, Nabil, "Population Displacement in the Metropolitan District of Beirut: Are the Displacements Over?" *Center for Migration Studies Special Issues* 11, no. 4, 1994, p. 14.
13 Peretz, Don, "The Arab Refugee Dilemma", *Foreign Affairs;* an American Quarterly Review, 33:1/4, 1954/1955, p. 134.
14 "Beyrouth abandonné par la moitié de ses habitants", *L'Orient-Le Jour*, 19 May 1976.
15 Hamadé, Marwan, in "Beyrouth… La Vie Quand Même", *Grands Reportages*, TF1, 1990.

in rural areas;[16] where the departure of "the other" was regarded as a "purification", a "miracle" even.[17]

When hostilities ended, the government set up a ministry with the laborious task of repatriating displaced persons.[18] The 1990s were also a period of return, which Ghassan Kotait identifies as a dominant theme in the cinema of the time, with films such as *Around the Pink House* and *Histoire d'un retour (Story of a Return)*, a nightmarish return in *The Tornado* and a revisiting of personal traumas in *Phantom Beirut*.[19] In a short film by Kotait, a mother and daughter meet up in their house, which has been ruined in the bombing:

> *"They're going to start the demolition tomorrow. Doesn't that hurt you? It was kind of a last chance, the only place where I could re-establish contact. Tomorrow they're going to start destroying it all."*
> *"Yes, who knows where they'll start. In two days it'll all go up in smoke."*[20]

In the 1990s, Lebanon absorbed a mass of foreign workers in an "ambiance verging on that of the African slave trade."[21] Many illegal residents lived in pockets of temporary housing.[22]

On 12 July 2006, Israel began a war that emptied the south of the country and the southern suburbs of Beirut. The cessation of hostilities on 14 August 2006 was followed by the immediate return of the displaced.[23] At the start of the conflict, many chose to express feelings such as anger, fear and resilience through writings, drawings and films uploaded to the internet. These were followed by a great many art projects. Hadjithomas and Joreige took Catherine Deneuve and Rabih Mroué on a road trip to South Lebanon. At Bint Jbeil, "Rabih recognises nothing, he can't find his grandmother's house. They feel blinded by the scale of the destruction, the human and physical loss."[24]

In Beirut's southern suburbs, Gilbert Hage photographed the damaged remains of buildings (FIG.87) and published *Toufican Ruins?* with Jalal Toufic.[25] In Ayman Baalbaki's work, the same dismembered apparitions serve as headstones in an architectural graveyard, following his previous paintings of squatted buildings. Meanwhile, Rechmaoui made *Spectre (The Yacoubian Building, Beirut)*, a sculpture reproducing a modernist apartment building (bf670, Ras Beyrouth) of the 1950s. Rechmaoui created this duplication in order to recognise the transformations

FIG.87 *Gilbert Hage, Toufican Ruins #5, 2006. Photograph.*

FIG.88 *Marwan Rechmaoui, Spectre (The Yacoubian Building), 2006-2008. Non-shrinking grout, aluminum, glass, fabric, 225 × 420 × 80 cm.*

16 Toubi, Jamal, "Social Dynamics in War Torn Lebanon", *Jerusalem Quarterly*, no. 17, autumn 1980, pp. 83–109.
17 Traboulsi, "Société violente ou système de guerre ?" op. cit., pp. 144–5.
18 On this subject see Kanafani-Zahar, Aïda, "La réconciliation du Mont-Liban : La raison d'État et la légalisation communautaire au détriment de la mémoire", in *Mémoires de guerres au Liban, 1975–1990*, Hommes et sociétés 128, Arles, Actes Sud / Sindbad, 2010, pp. 285–312.
19 Ghassan Kotait, interview with the author, 17 September 2015.
20 Kotait, Ghassan, *Après le silence*, Académie Libanaise des Beaux-Arts – ALBA, 1995.
21 Medawar, Alexandre, "Domesticité et sous-traitance", *La Furie des Glandeurs*, 24 July 2012.
22 Deboulet, Agnès and Hily, Marie-Antoinette, "Les migrants de Beyrouth. Emplois à bon marché et zones refuges", *EchoGéo*, no. 8 (March 2009).
23 UNHCR's 2006 Global Report – the situation in Lebanon. Report of the United Nations High Commissioner for Refugees, 1 June 2007.
24 Hadjithomas, Joana and Joreige, Khalil in Max Silverman, "Entretien avec Joana Hadjithomas et Khalil Joreige : je veux voir", *Contemporary French and Francophone Studies* 18, no. 5 (20 October 2014), p. 533.
25 Hage, Gilbert and Toufic, Jalal, *Toufican Ruins?* Beirut, Underexposed, 2010.

and unformalised uses of the building apparent since 1975. While the piece was supposed to be shown at the São Paulo Biennale, Lebanon again found itself under fire from the Israeli army. Rechmaoui decided to make in Brazil a "replica of the replica."[26] On his return, he completed the original version. Virtually identical cells, differing only in the details of the inscriptions and signs they show, are delicately balanced to form a structure that manages to remain standing (FIG.88).

In 2011, Syria tipped over into chaos. In Lebanon, refugees were spread across the entire country. A comparative graphic of their presence over three years was used by Tiffany Chung in a drawing that is part of a series of pieces based on the cartography of the Syrian crisis.[27] In 2015, Lebanon was top of the list for the ratio of refugees to population: 232 per 1000 inhabitants.[28]

BUILDINGS OCCUPIED BY LAW OR BY FORCE

Housing described as temporary or informal ranged from land or dwellings rented from the owner by migrants to squats or buildings occupied by force and the refugee camps, representing a temporary solution for a massive influx of people, who were housed with the help of NGOs and the government.[29] The informal use of buildings in central Beirut began in the late 19th century, when "the old low houses with a central courtyard gradually changed use and thus usually their appearance. They were used for business or rented to individuals."[30] Jewish families left Wadi Abu Jamil in 1967. Their vacant homes were taken over at low cost by Kurds, who rented apartments that then turned into "internal shanty towns" housing "four to six families in the same apartment."[31] This was the start of the "pauperisation and, indeed, ruralisation of the urban landscape"[32] which was rampant in the 1980s:

> *For me the most poignant thing was not the destruction so much as the abandonment. I see it on walls that have been restored many times in the last decade, but never repainted, in the little mounds of rubbish that the road-sweepers don't fully remove, the resigned responses to pavements occupied by cars, the terrible aging of abandoned construction sites, the dilapidated state of luxury buildings with bare entrances that were once brightly lit and filled with flowers, and many things like that.*[33]

Throughout the various conflicts, refugees were taken in by residents. What has happened with the Syrians since 2011 is reminiscent of 1860, when families from Damascus "were kidnapped [*sic*] by Beirutis to offer them hospitality."[34] In the 1970s, displaced people fleeing violence who had nowhere to go would rent apartments and hotel rooms. As their exile continued, they stopped paying, remaining in occupation without the owners' consent.[35] This situation of unauthorised occupation led the owners to call them *muhtallin* – occupiers – rather than *muhajjarin*, which comes from *hajara*, meaning "has migrated", often under duress. This shift redefined the displaced as usurpers rather than passive victims, and even as the cause of the problem.[36] To ward off such difficulties, some property owners housed their acquaintances in the home they had been obliged to leave, others hired the services of a "gunman [who] will guard an apartment against other gunmen."[37] In June 1982, in West Beirut, there were "many families with bundles over their shoulders, arms full of packages and anxious faces, wandering the streets in search of empty apartments."[38] They were "often preceded by militiamen in battledress who, if necessary, would force

26 *Spectre by Marwan Rechmaoui*, Words on Works, Saradar Collection website, 2017.
27 ENWEZOR, OKWUI (ed.), *All the World's Futures: 56 International Art Exhibition. La Biennale di Venezia*, Venice, Marislio Editori, 2015, pp. 260–1.
28 MCCARTHY, NIALL, "The Countries With The Most Refugees Per 1,000 Inhabitants [Infographic]", *Forbes*, 18 June 2015.
29 SOLIMAN, op. cit., p. 22.
30 DAVIE, "La millat grecque-orthodoxe de Beyrouth 1800–1940", op. cit., p. 48.
31 PHARÈS and BOURGEY, "Les bidonvilles de l'agglomération de Beyrouth", op. cit., p. 109.
32 KASSIR, SAMIR, *La guerre du Liban : de la dissension nationale au conflit régional, 1975–1982*, Hommes et sociétés, Paris/Beirut, Karthala, CERMOC, 1994, p. 46.
33 BEYDOUN, AHMAD, *Le Liban : itinéraires dans une guerre incivile*, "Hommes et sociétés" series, Paris/Amman, Karthala, CERMOC, 1993, p. 160.
34 MADAME DE PERTHUIS, *Voyages en Orient. 1853–1855, 1860–1862. Journal de la Comtesse de Perthuis. Manuscrit inédit découvert par Fouad Debbas*, Beirut, Dar An-Nahar, 2007, p. 13.
35 "Hotels protest against proposal to consider displaced persons as refugees", *An-Nahar*, 24 February 1984, p. 6.
36 SAWALHA, ASEEL, *Reconstructing Beirut: Memory and Space in a Postwar Arab City*, Austin, University of Texas Press, 2010, p. 112–13.
37 RANDAL, JONATHAN C., "Illegal Building Booms Despite Lebanon War. Army Buffer Serves Fragile Beirut Truce", *Washington Post*, 17 December 1975.
38 "Dans Beyrouth-Ouest, où l'espace habitable s'est réduit de moitié, la chasse aux logements vides a commencé", *L'Orient-Le Jour*, 10 May 1982, p. 2.

the owner of a building to accept refugees."[39] The plot of Charif Majdalani's novel *Le Dernier seigneur de Marsad* centres on the home of a Greek-Orthodox merchant. The militias pressure Chakib Khattar to leave. But, in fact, the house (bf1184, Mazraa) on which the novel is based was never abandoned. Myrna Majdalani still lives there, surrounded by precious objects and though her "paintings of nudes were found shocking",[40] she never felt under attack. Even so, throughout the war years the arrival of refugees was synonymous with terror, particularly as when people fled a zone where they were part of a minority group, their homes were taken over by groups from the opposing community. Criticisms were also levelled at the lucrative business pursued by a new kind of "estate agent", who "impose their law, ensuring that refugee families are housed but also protecting certain special buildings whose owners have the means to pay generously for their services."[41] In addition to the "protection" of the manager, "any person seeking shelter or a place to occupy could in a sense buy the 'right' to occupy an apartment from the person who was already occupying it."[42]

The reconstruction and the return of refugees form the backdrop to the film *Around the Pink House*. It was shot in Wadi Abu Jamil, a neighbourhood that saw different waves of incomers after the Kurds and which the Lebanese development company Solidere began to evacuate in 1994.[43] The evacuation was an absurdly complicated process, involving a great many stakeholders – including the refugees and property owners, Solidere, the central refugee council, the forces of order and Shia parties. The refugees did all they could to inflate compensation payments to a level that earned the neighbourhood the name "*Wadi al-Dahab*" (Valley of Gold).[44] Meanwhile Solidere made life there impossible, destroying pipes, lifts and generators.[45] In February 1996, the company demolished a building (bf999, Minet Hosn) on top of its inhabitants as they were waiting to cash in their compensation and leave.[46] In April of the same year, it took advantage of an Israeli attack on the south to demolish ten houses that were still standing.[47] At the end of this saga, Wadi Abu Jamil was empty.

The owners of squatted buildings could either rebuild them, sell them or leave them to "sleep." Many buildings were "padlocked, the doors and windows walled up and the ceilings and parts of some walls destroyed."[48] This was deliberate damage intended to prevent further occupation. Others were left habitable and rented out. Former refugees could come to an agreement that would legitimise their presence. Since 2011, abandoned houses have taken on a new life as temporary housing for Syrians.

FIGS.89-90 *A Suspended Life, film by Jocelyne Saab, 1985.*

39 *Ibid.*
40 MYRNA MAJDALANI, interview with the author, 16 March 2014.
41 HERBOUZE, GEORGES, in MENASSA (Benassar), *Anatomie d'une guerre et d'une occupation*, op. cit., pp. 12–13.
42 CHARARA, WADDAH, "Journal de G.S., déplacée de guerre", in MERMIER, FRANCK, and VARIN, CHRISTOPHE (eds), *Mémoires de guerres au Liban, 1975–1990*, La bibliothèque arabe, Arles: Actes Sud, Sindbad, 2010, p. 414.
43 "The refugee compensation fund has begun the evacuation of Wadi Abu Jamil", *An-Nahar*, 28 September 1994, p. 4.
44 ABOU AL-AYNAYN, SAHER, "Wadi Abu Jamil or the Valley of Gold", *An-Nahar*, 2 September 1995, p. 11.
45 KOBEISSI, FATEN, "The Wadi Abu Jamil refugee movement grows", *As-Safir*, 19 October 1995.
46 "Political opprobrium and calls for those responsible to be prosecuted", *An-Nahar*, 16 February 1996, p. 6.
47 GEBRANE-BADLISSI, ELIANE, "Patrimoine urbain à Beyrouth après la guerre. Entre modernité et tradition", *Confluences Méditerranée*, no. 24, winter 1997–8, p. 147.
48 BRONES, SOPHIE, "Beyrouth et ses ruines (1990-2010). Une approche anthropologique", doctoral thesis, University of Paris X, 2010, p. 240.

HOME

FIG.91 *Aline Manoukian, Refugee woman in a building in Hamra, Beirut, 1983. Photograph.*

Temporary housing might last for a few hours, months or decades. Squatting means living in the unknown with, as this refugee put it:

> *Boundless confidence in the future that has enabled us to make a derisory kingdom out of these doorless apartments which are impossible to keep clean or tidy. . . Anyone who has shared our situation would be unable to find a place to go, having been ejected from what they thought would be their home forever.* [49]

Jalal Toufic and his family left their home during the Israeli invasion. "Did this turn the apartment into a ruin?" he asks, and answers in the affirmative, explaining that "it was because these houses became ruins when they were abandoned that ruin spread until they were explicitly turned into ruins, manifesting their existence as ruins." He goes on, "Will we ever learn to live in a place without inhabiting it, so that the act of abandoning it doesn't turn it into a ruin?"[50] The refugees organised themselves in these ruins where, because they were poor, "the least expenditure on a repair, however crucial, became a pointless waste in their eyes."[51] They used their wits to acquire water and electricity, creating "spider webs" of illegally connected cables.[52] Winter was not a comfortable time in these buildings where, as their occupiers describe, "nothing is done to block up the openings through which the wind whistles and which keep all of us in a state of flu and colds for the four months of winter."[53]

49 CHARARA, "Journal de G.S., déplacée de guerre", op. cit., p. 412.
50 TOUFIC, JALAL, "Ruins", in *Tamáss. Contemporary Arab Representations*, 1. Beirut/Lebanon, Barcelona, Fundació Antoni Tàpies, 2002, p. 19.
51 CHARARA, "Journal de G.S., déplacée de guerre", op. cit., pp. 415–16.
52 BAALBAKI and BAALBAKI, interview of 19 September 2014.
53 CHARARA, "Journal de G.S., déplacée de guerre", op. cit., pp. 415–16.

SHARED SPACE

In any society "neighbourhood behaviour is a shared convention that is tacit, unwritten," in which "any submission to the codes, or any infringement, is immediately a matter for comment."[54] In unofficially occupied buildings, overcrowding, trauma, ethnic tensions, reciprocal animosity, economic difficulties, the importance of religion and the omnipresent militias were all potential sources of tension. Members of the community were obliged to follow a certain number of rules to "enable partners to coexist in the same area."[55] In the unwritten contract that was a feature of this society, "No intimacy between us is permitted. Nothing can hide you from the countless eyes of the neighbours, nor their ever-listening ears."[56] Individuality was erased by the "triumph of the social power of the group."[57] In *Beirut the Encounter*, Haïdar's brother is preparing to distribute propaganda materials for a particular party. When Haïdar tries to stop him he is told:

> *"These people hold the whole neighbourhood. We can't live here and be against them, [. . .] after all, they helped us. If they ask a little service of us, we can't refuse. Besides, they're going to install a water pump in the building. Isn't that better for my wife who is wearing herself out bringing up the water on foot?"*[58]

Those who did not play the game ran the risk of exclusion. The group was held together by *asabiya* – esprit de corps – the rise of which conflicted with modern, individualised urban life and played into the hands of the political parties. In *Around the Pink House*, Maher announces, "We're going to ask the party for help." Souheil replies, "What party? That clique of fascists you hang around with?"[59] Here, the tension is ideological, but it could also be caused by a failure to respect the rules, as when Um Hussayn "put her rubbish against the stairs of the building instead of taking it to the dump. . . And as the building is a playground for the local cats, they opened the bag, scrabbled around inside it, ate what they could and scattered the rest in the stairwell."[60] At the Heneiné Mansion, the Qarut criticised the Majid for living in their own refuse, while the Majid observed that the Qarut repainted their rooms every six months, which must have cost a lot of money. "It's obvious that each side was exaggerating."[61]

No less apparent were the tensions between the refugees and "original" residents of the buildings or neighbourhood. The latter saw the refugees as invaders, blamed them for the deterioration of property and, if "they don't know how to use the lift, we make them take the stairs."[62] Here, we find a conflict between the *factors for maintenance* (the residents) and *factors of transformation* (the refugees) characteristic of this social change.[63]

54 Mayol, Pierre, "Habiter", in de Certeau, Michel, Giard, Luce and Mayol, Pierre, *L'Invention du quotidien. Vol. 2 : Habiter cuisiner*, Paris, Folio, 1994, p. 26.
55 *Ibid.*
56 Charara, "Journal de G.S., déplacée de guerre", op. cit., pp. 434–5.
57 Gebrane-Badlissi, Eliane, "Réfugiés et résidents anciens dans deux quartiers de Beyrouth : Ramlet el- Baïda et Raouché" in *Beyrouth : regards croisés*, Tours, Centre de Recherches et d'Etudes sur l'Urbanisation du Monde Arabe (URBAMA), 1997, p. 145.
58 Alaouié, *Beirut the Encounter*, op. cit.
59 Hadjithomas and Joreige, *Around the Pink House*, op. cit.
60 Charara, "Journal de G.S., déplacée de guerre", op. cit., p. 433.
61 Bodenstein, Ralph, "Qasr Heneiné. Memories and History of a Late Ottoman Mansion in Beirut", Master's dissertation, Rheinischen Friedrich Wilhelms-Universität, 1999. p. 147.
62 Resident in Gebrane-Badlissi, "Réfugiés et résidents", op. cit., p. 147.
63 *Ibid.*, p. 142.

RITUALS AND LEISURE

Once the men had gone out to work, the women set about doing "tasks seemingly devoid of any visible completion, never likely to be properly finished – maintaining the family's things, maintaining their bodies."[64] Cooking was a means of generating solidarity between women. In the Saab palace, they made freekeh – grilled green wheat – and invited the owners to share the meal.[65] At the Heneiné Mansion, the magnificent drawing room was used for the shared preparation of leaves for *mulukhiyah* – a dish based on the plant *corchorus olitorius* – orchestrated by the women and children of the Majid family, and also to smoke the hookah[66] and drink coffee. Life was given shape by everyday rituals, such as the *sobhiyyeh*, or morning meeting, and other less regular events, such as births, deaths and celebrations.

> *At Eid al-Adha, they would slaughter a sheep outside the entrance to the building. After the festivities, there would be a celebration for the return of pilgrims to Mecca. They would dip their hands in the sheep's blood and put their prints on the wall to the entrance, which was decorated with palms, lights, garlands and flags. Those leaving on pilgrimage would hang up two date palm branches. If, when they returned, the branches had fallen down, it was sacrilege. This belief is reminiscent of Jewish practices.*[67] (FIG.92).

FIG.92 *Abdel-Hamid Baalbaki, Pilgrims returning from Mecca, c. 1974. Oil on canvas, 133 × 99 cm.*

In addition to these "manipulations and gesticulations, a whole gymnastics"[68] that ensured the perpetuation of the community's way of doing things, there were also more down-to-earth events, such as meetings – frequent in the mid-90s – to enable the "co-owners" to agree on what to do next and ideas for the future. Their children, meanwhile, would seize every chance to escape and play on the stairs, in the courtyard or elsewhere in the neighbourhood.

> *We built a stone house out of rubble resulting from an Israeli rocket attack and dug ditches. We played King Kong and bombarded our little stone house from the top of the apartment building. In 1984, the French contingent left vestiges of fortifications and barricades. We took them over for our games. Another game involved finding orange plastic pipes and softening them using the heat from the sun caught with a bottle top. Then we'd bend them into hearts and other shapes.*[69]

Television brought everyone together, during or after the evening meal. Noting that the poorest inhabitants would watch American programmes showing the total opposite of their own living conditions and lifestyles,[70] Mona Hatoum made *Hidden From Prying Eyes* in 1987, an installation made from corrugated iron and a television screen, showing an excerpt from the TV series *Dallas*.

64 GIARD, LUCE, "Cuisiner", in DE CERTEAU, MICHEL, GIARD, LUCE and MAYOL, PIERRE, *L'Invention du quotidien. Vol. 2*, op. cit., p. 220.
65 JOCELYNE SAAB, interview of 2 November 2015.
66 BODENSTEIN, "Qasr Heneiné", op. cit., p. 151.
67 BAALBAKI and BAALBAKI, interview of 19 September 2014.
68 BOURDIEU, PIERRE, *Sociology in Question*, translated by Richard Nice, London, Sage, 1993, p. 143.
69 BAALBAKI and BAALBAKI, interview of 19 September 2014.
70 HATOUM, MONA, in *Audio Arts: Volume 8 Nos 2 & 3*, vol. Side D, London, Tate website, 1987.

MAKESHIFT HOUSING

The refugees' building is a "blot" on the city. It is named and shamed as a stigma – that "decaying property with its empty windows, its breeze-block add-ons, its ragged plastic sheeting flapping in the wind, in among normal buildings and normal people."[71] These jerry-built additions serve to repair damaged walls or sections, to create extra rooms on balconies – possibly toilets or showers – and to compartmentalise spaces. They are built either using "hard", "permanent" construction materials (breeze block, cement, concrete, stone) or "lightweight", "temporary" materials (wood, plywood, sheet metal), the choices varying in accordance with the financial resources available, the envisaged duration of occupancy and popular practice at the time.

In the summer of 1999, students of Atelier de Recherche ALBA (Lebanese Academy of fine Arts – research workshop) studied a 1950s' building (bf676, Bachoura) which was then being squatted, and witnessed its evacuation and subsequent demolition – after which it was referred to as the "ghost" building. Its cracked façades – across which a tree had grown – had been repaired with breeze blocks, wood and plywood (FIG.93). Sand-filled barrels, left over from its former military occupancy, were used to shore up a plywood wall. Windows had been set into these flimsy walls. The same materials were used to create additional rooms on the balconies. "Every floor is a street",[72] noted the students, observing the partitions constructed by the families sharing the apartments. Poverty's three layers

FIG.93 *Atelier de recherche ALBA/Yara Akl, Patricia Fakhry, Maher Fleyfel, Youssef Helou, Wissam Rachid. Machines Célibataires, Machine # 1, Incomprehensible Places, 2000. "Phantom" building.*

71 CHARARA, "Journal de G.S., déplacée de guerre", op. cit., p. 412.
72 AKL, YARA, et AL., "Machines Célibataires. Machine # 1 [the incomprehensible places]", Atelier de Recherche ALBA website, 2000.

were superimposed on the façade: the ruined building, the patchwork repairs, the washing hung out to dry. To complete the picture, we might add to this the portraits of political leaders and party emblems stuck to the walls, and the mountain of refuse on the north side of the building.[73]

In 2010, Marwa Arsanios created *All About Acapulco*, an installation encompassing the various stages in the life of Acapulco, a beach resort in Ouzai, in Beirut's southern suburbs.[74] The installation focused on Chalet Raja Saab, designed by Ferdinand Dagher and nicknamed the "spaceship" or the "doughnut" as it was built around a central open space. The chalet was occupied by Palestinians in 1976, and then by refugees from South Lebanon. The squatters "extended" it, filling the ground-floor space with rooms partitioned by breeze-block walls.

VEILED BUILDINGS

FIG.94 *Emily Jacir, Memorial to 418 Palestinian Villages which were Destroyed, Depopulated and Occupied by Israel in 1948, 2001. Refugee tent and embroidery thread, 243 × 305 × 366 cm.*

As a signal, washing hanging out to dry is to informal settlements what sandbags are to militarised buildings. We could track a dialectic relationship between the "neatness", associated with the dominant "urbanised" and "civilised" classes and the "chaotic", associated with poor people who "hang out any old how" this washing "which never dries."[75]

73 *Ibid.*
74 Wilson-Goldie, Kaelen, "In Focus: Marwa Arsanios", *Frieze*, March 2013.
75 Resident, in Gebrane-Badlissi, "Réfugiés et résidents", op. cit., pp. 146–7.

FIG.95 *Mari Meen Halsøy inside Barakat building, 2012.*

FIG.96 *Mari Meen Halsøy, Wounds: Beit Beirut / Sniper´s Room, 2012. Installation.*

The fact of the matter is that several families are living in one apartment; an entire family is living in one room: with this many people there is a lot of washing relative to a small amount of space. The iconography of hanging washing has its counterpart in the piles of clothes that evoke exodus, departure, escape and destitution, lending their resonance to Michelangelo Pistoletto's *Venus of the Rags* and Christian Boltanski's installations.[76] Having grown up as a refugee, Said Baalbaki painted "heaps, piles, mountains of suitcases, bags, bundles, scattered clothes, a lovely, simple jacket on a headless mannequin, a wardrobe."[77]

If, in the Arab imagination, displacement and textiles converge in the tent – the nomad home – then with washing this textile architecture is replaced by an architecture enveloped in textiles. Even though the displaced people initially inhabited permanent structures, the conflation is straightforward. Emily Jacir picked up on this connection, in reverse, in her 2001 work in New York: *Memorial to 418 Palestinian Villages which were Destroyed, Depopulated and Occupied by Israel in 1948*. On 29 November 1947, in the same building where Jacir's installation was displayed, the United Nations General Assembly met to vote on Resolution 181 (II) on the partition of Palestine.[78] *Memorial to 418 Palestinian Villages. . .* consists of a tent on which the names of 418 villages depopulated and destroyed in 1948 have been embroidered (FIG.94). With not enough time to complete this project on her own, Jacir opened her studio to anyone who wanted to sew with her. More than 140 people showed up:[79] the project became a collective work, acquiring a social dimension.[80] In Beirut, in 2012, Mari Meen Halsøy set up her loom in the Barakat Building (FIG.95). Having taken casts of the impact holes on the walls, she wove pieces of fabric to fill in the missing areas.[81] Her project, combining this act and the presentation of these "wounds" on an immaculate wall, explores themes of caring and reparation (FIG.96). Mira Chelala, meanwhile, draws on the traces of war to inform her experimental textiles practice; by means of various techniques, textile becomes a communications tool in its own right, materialising the chaotic aesthetics of war[82] (FIG.97).

FIG.97 *Mira Chelala, Haillons, 2013. Ripped clothes and textile threads, 25 × 30 cm.*

76 BUCHAKJIAN, GREGORY, "Une Venus et un tas de chiffons" in *Michelangelo Pistoletto in Beirut*, Beirut, Beirut Exhibition Center, Galerie Tanit, Galleria Continua and Citadellarte-Fondazione Pistoletto, 2014, p. 17.
77 CACHARD, VALÉRIE, *Nos* âmes *en chantier*, Berlin, 2015, artist's book (lithographs by Said Baalbaki).
78 BUCHAKJIAN, GREGORY, *War and Other (Impossible) Possibilities. Thoughts on Arab History and Contemporary Art*, Beirut, Alarm, 2012, pp. 80–82.
79 JACIR, EMILY, in "Emily Jacir", Station Museum website.
80 MENICK, JOHN, "Undiminished Returns: The Work of Emily Jacir, 1998-2002" in *Belongings*, O.K Centrum für Gegenwartskunst, Linz, 2003.
81 "Wounds", Mari Meen Halsøy website.
82 MIRA CHELALA, interview with the author, 26 December 2014.

In informal settlements, hanging washing becomes a second skin, challenging modernity's sleek transparency. It clothes the building, functioning, effectively, as a *mashrabiya* (balcony enclosed with a carved wood lattice), and is used in a similar way: "Looking across the washing, the refugee women can also watch the comings and goings of the neighbourhood or answer the calls of street vendors."[83] The 1990s saw squatters' washing supplanted by construction tarpaulins, generally green, which shrouded buildings destined for renovation – or, more often, for demolition. Said Baalbaki features several of these ghostly façades in artists' books and sets of lithographs (FIG.98).

Every building is emptied of its inhabitants.
Then, every façade is veiled – hidden.
Each building is emptied of its entrails. It is a patient in an operating room or the dead body in Rembrandt's anatomy lecture.
All the components are expelled through barrels, as though from stomachs. Next, the veiled façade disappears for good.[84]

In today's informal settlements, this veiling has become systematic, incorporating not just permanently closed curtains and hangings, but tarpaulins salvaged from building sites, advertising panels and UNHCR survival kits. Fabrics, netting and tarpaulins are overlayered: the epitome of the veiled building.

FIG.98 *Said Baalbaki, Wadi Abou Jmil, 2015. Lithograph, 66 × 50 cm.*

83 GEBRANE-BADLISSI, "Réfugiés et résidents", op. cit., pp. 146–7.
84 BUCHAKJIAN, GREGORY, *Wadi Abou Jmil*, Berlin, 2015, artist's book (lithographs by Said Baalbaki).

INTERIOR SPACE RECLAIMED

Set within an immaculate space, the indoor scenes of *Beirut the Encounter*, convey a sensation of emptiness far removed from the usual overpopulation of squatted buildings. The story takes place after 1975–6, when "there was still plenty of space and people could move in wherever they wanted."[85] Subsequently, "people started to co-habit, with several families to an apartment."[86] In hotels and apartment hotels, it was one household per room, as in 1860, when refugees in the city were accommodated in *khans* – inns – in individual units which had the name of the resident family displayed on the door.[87] Alongside the increase in the number of users, each unit now served multiple functions, too. Two rooms – or even a single room – served as living room, dining room and bedroom(s).

As a result, the building is reconfigured into semi-public spaces people pass through (entrance hall, staircase, landing, corridor, gallery, even the central hall in Ottoman-style residences), semi-private spaces where women talk and children play[88] – as well as in the central hall or the living room – and private spaces, where people sleep. Sometimes translucent membranes of voile or nylon netting are put up to create a psychological boundary – yet it is common to see walls of wood, plasterboard or even concrete installed, too. In buildings made of friable materials, and buildings that have already incurred damage, such structural additions inevitably constitute a stability risk. For residents below, like the Baalbakis, "because of – or thanks to – the water damage we could see the outline of the partitions on the floor above marked out on the ceiling of our apartment."[89]

These reconfigurations give the squatted building the character of a village, reinforcing the idea of a ruralisation of urban space. Within each unit, spaces are redesigned according to three needs: segregating one household from another, marking off a private space and creating areas for functions – washing, cooking – which might not have dedicated fittings provided. A living room might become the "village square" – but could also be divided into units for sleeping or cooking. A bedroom might retain this function or become a living room or a kitchen. A kitchen might be decommissioned and converted into a bedroom. And a balcony can be closed off to fulfil all kinds of functions, as on the first floor of El Khoury palace (bf501, Zokak el-Blatt), where the galleried façade has been partly walled in with the construction of two breeze-block kiosks, one for toilets and one for showers. In some instances, residents – not necessarily squatters – have blocked openings to give their house a more private character. One owner, for example, blocked the door connecting the living room to the corridor and created another, smaller door so that people seated in the living room would not be able to see his wife at work in the adjacent kitchen.[90] Walls are the unifying theme here: the residents of a building "entrench themselves in their domestic dwelling space – since that is what it is called – and they would prefer nothing to emerge from it."[91]

A VILLAGE IN A PALACE

Built for Count Todorsky in the 19th century, behind its discreet façade, the Heneiné Mansion (bf622, Zokak el Blatt) conceals a décor worthy of the *Thousand and One Nights*. From the entrance door, visitors find themselves in an atrium, facing two flights of stairs leading to the first floor – a scene of splendour reminiscent of Versailles (PL.42). The first staircase leads to a vestibule, a transition space opening onto the dining room, a corridor accessing the bedrooms and the main living room, the central hall. This main room is structured on a T-shaped floor plan, connected with its adjacent areas or *liwans* by triple arcades (PL.41). "This atypical spatial organisation [of the first floor]

85 Baalbaki and Baalbaki, interview of 19 September 2014.
86 *Ibid.*
87 Perthuis, *Voyages en Orient*, op. cit., p. 156.
88 Bodenstein, "Qasr Heneiné", op. cit., p. 150.
89 Baalbaki and Baalbaki, interview of 19 September 2014.
90 Chakar, Tony, "The Suburbs and the Vocabulary of Urbanisation: Violence as an Architectural Language", in *Tamáss. Contemporary Arab Representations*, Barcelona, Fundació Antoni Tàpies, 2002, p. 53.
91 Perec, Georges, *Life: A User's Manual*, translated by David Bellos, Boston, David R. Godine, 2009.

FIG.99 *Gregory Buchakjian, Heneiné Mansion, 2011. Photograph.*

is striking evidence of the bourgeois European lifestyle of the original builder of the house, a Russian nobleman living in Beirut."[92] The count was also "responsible for the exceptional interior decoration, most particularly the Alhambra-inspired *grand salon* with its marble fountain, multifoil arches, *muqarnas*, friezes and lavish stucco ceilings inlaid with mirrors. It is an 'imagined Orient' turned into stone and plaster, and one of the earliest examples of such a Mauresque interior in Beirut."[93]

After Todorsky, this residence was occupied successively by a French doctor (Dr Justin Calmette), the consulates of the United States and the Netherlands, Marie Mezher "Barbar" and her husband, Dr Joseph Heneiné, and the restaurant Le Petit Palais, managed by Mme Heneiné, until her death in 1970. During this time, the second floor was rented to Georges Haddad and his wife, Marie *née* Chiha, one of the first women painters in Lebanon. In 1942, the couple became followers of Salim Moussa Achi, more widely known by the name Dahesh, the founder of a new religion. The Haddads were his most fervent disciples and through to the 21st century their home became a temple to the glory of this self-proclaimed prophet, a controversial and mythologised figure.

In 1976, the first floor, which was already empty, was occupied by six refugee families, totalling more than forty people in all and distributed as follows:

- The Majid family: occupying the northern half of the building (i.e. the most attractive rooms, but also those most exposed to bombardments), the Majids created walls to separate the central hall from its two *liwans*; subdivided the western *liwan* into two and constructed a wooden room in the middle of the central hall, gaining four habitable rooms while retaining the rest of the hall as a collective living space. They created a kitchen in the west gallery.
- The Qarut family: the Qaruts took possession of the bathroom and three bedrooms. The bedroom at the end of the corridor became their living room. They also controlled part of the kitchen, which became an additional bedroom, and converted a small bedroom into a kitchen – cooking fried foods on the wooden walkway over the entrance door.[94] Later, when the family became larger, they constructed a wooden compartment in a corner of the vestibule.
- The Al-Zayn family: the Al-Zayns lived in the dining room, which was divided into two, and also had the southern half of the east gallery, separated by a wall from the Majids' northern half, as well as a wooden room in the north-eastern corner of the vestibule. These were the darkest rooms, but also the safest in the event of bombardment.
- The Fatunis family had a wooden room in the north-western corner of the vestibule.
- The Sha'ban family lived in a bedroom bordering the corridor.
- The Ibrahim family lived in a vaulted room on the ground floor.

92 Bodenstein, Ralph, "The Heneiné Mansion", in Gebhardt, Hans et al., *History, Space and Social Conflict in Beirut: The Quarter of Zokak El-Blat*, pp. 193–4.
93 *Ibid.*
94 Bodenstein, "Qasr Heneiné", op. cit., p. 150.

The Majids, who arrived first, occupied the central hall and its adjacent rooms, which they designated as *juwwa* (inside), as opposed to the rooms on the south side, which they referred to as *barra* (outside). [95] A subdivision between the Majids and the other families was established both on the ground and in the collective memory. In his monograph on the building, Ralph Bodenstein writes: "It is important to note that the distinction between *juwwa* and *barra* is used by all inhabitants of the first floor, and in this way reflects the social segregation in a spatial concept or a mental map."[96] As well as disputes and resentment, this reorganisation generated new pathways through the building. As the main door was blocked, access was via a secondary door opening onto the corridor – the main circulation route for *barra*, the southern part of the building. This led to the vestibule, which became both a demarcated space shared by three families, who each had a wooden room, and the entrance to *juwwa*, the northern part occupied by the Majids. Facilitated by an unconventional floorplan, this subdivision of the building into a village inevitably calls to mind the cliché of Abdallah, son of the Emir Mohammed Ben Kalish Ezab, setting up camp with his followers in the principal state room of Marlinspike Hall, much to the chagrin of Tintin, Haddock and Nestor.[97]

A Suspended Life (1985) by Jocelyne Saab tells of a love story between fifteen-year-old Samar and Karim (Jacques Weber), a painter from a bourgeois background. Samar's family, originally from South Lebanon, have taken refuge in the Heneiné Mansion. The father collects bricks, harbouring a hopeless dream of rebuilding the disintegrating city, the mother cooks and cleans and the younger brother keeps watch on his sister, suspecting her of improper behaviour. The idea of making a film about refugees came to Saab after housing refugees in her own family home, where the shooting was intended to take place. Then the Saabs' home was bombed and burned down during the 1982 Israeli siege of Beirut.[98] Following this tragedy, the production was divided between several locations: the Heneiné Mansion for Samar's family, Ziadeh Palace for the interior of Karim's studio and Maison Rose (Pink House) in Manara for the exterior. Jocelyne Saab secured the collaboration of the Majid family, who played themselves. The images of women working, talking, drinking coffee, and those of the family gathered around the television set, are very close to reality. More striking still are the images of Samar producing candyfloss and the surgical operation in the kitchen when the girl has her virginity restored "and will be more beautiful than a gold sovereign." "A space of safety, of trust", in contrast to the street, which is associated with all kinds of dangers,[99] the building is perceived as a vibrant, living space, as if to conjure up the lost buildings cherished by the director – both buildings in the city centre and her own family home (FIGS.89-90).

After the last refugees left in the 2000s, the construction company building a tower block on the adjacent plot occupied the building, setting up an office in one bedroom, which was repainted and furnished with computer workstations. On its white walls, the developer's son drew an image of the future skyscraper. In the central hall, workers slept on mattresses placed on carpets; their belongings were piled up on the floor and in the niches of the Moorish décor, hung on nails banged into the wall, and stowed away on shelf units (FIG.99). Alongside their washing, hung to dry on lines stretched between the columns, were a television set, a cooling fan and a basketball hoop. The mansion has since been cleared and in 2016 was listed on World Monuments Watch, the World Monuments Fund[100] programme that aims to identify endangered cultural sites and secure technical and financial support for their preservation. The project, involving rights holders, the local community and the state authorities, has the goal of saving the building from irreversible decline.[101]

95 *Ibid.*, p. 145.
96 *Ibid.*, p. 147.
97 Hergé, *The Red Sea Sharks*, translated by Leslie Lonsdale-Cooper and Michael Turner, London, Methuen, 1960, p. 6.
98 Jocelyne Saab, interview of 2 November 2015.
99 Rouxel, Mathilde, *Jocelyne Saab. La mémoire indomptée*, Beirut, Dar An-Nahar, 2015, pp. 212–14.
100 "Heneine Palace / World Monuments Fund", World Monuments Fund website, 16 October 2015.
101 "Endangered Heneine Palace in Zukak el-Blat Placed on 2016 World Monuments Watch", *Naharnet*, 23 October 2015.

IN AND AROUND THE PINK HOUSE

FIG.100 *Around the Pink House, film by Joana Hadjithomas and Khalil Joreige, 1999. [Souheil's Historical Wall].*

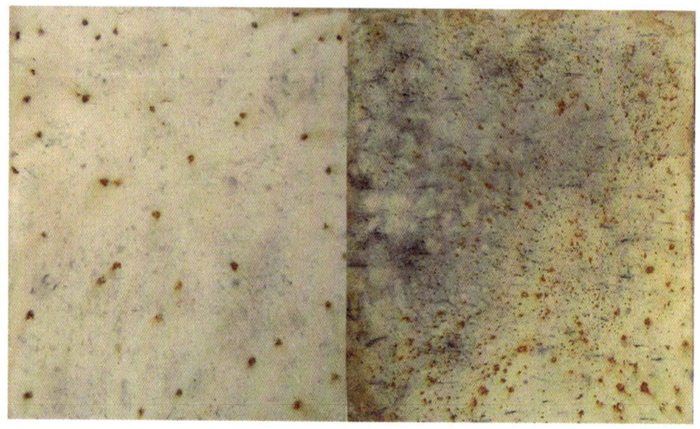

FIG.101 *Hanibal Srouji, Rust Rush, 1995. Iron particles and acrylic on canvas, 2 × (122 × 105 cm).*

Around the Pink House by Joana Hadjithomas and Khalil Joreige centres on a building inhabited by refugees at a time when the city is in the throes of reconstruction – one vast building site, revealed as the camera pans out in the final shot. The building in question is a montage combining a pink decorative façade, featuring a central *iwan*, specially designed by Fadlallah Dagher and Sophie Khayat, with interior scenes filmed "in abandoned buildings, left in their original condition."[102] It is accessed via three steps on the pavement – an encroachment on the public thoroughfare that underscores the film's central theme – and all the action takes place either on the street or in the building. At the end, when the building is demolished, it is on this pavement that the characters sell off its furniture and fittings. It is here, too, that the final banquet takes place. The Pink House interior is accessed with the absolute minimum of ceremony: a vestibule adorned with statues in niches opens directly – miraculously – onto the central hall, a space shared by two refugee families. The former owners' furniture, bronzes and paintings seem to have survived all the upheavals. When Matar, the developer, makes his entrance, each family is arranged around a sofa occupying one of the corners of the main room – the Adaimis to the right, the Nawfals to the left. The angled arrangement of the furniture is designed solely for the shot where Matar faces his audience. The other place where people gather is the kitchen – a dark space, its contours difficult to discern. The sequence showing an architect's visit plays a key role in delineating the boundary between semi-public and private: the man tries to enter a bedroom, but is stopped in his tracks by Madame Adaimi. This sequence also reveals the mansion's secret treasure: dimly, by moonlight, we see an immaculate marble neoclassical sculpture surrounded by fluted columns. This sanctuary-like, contemplative space is pure caprice. Contrasting with the film's Felliniesque overall mood, and without the slightest architectural justification, the scene was shot in the palace built by Alfred Sursock (bf358, Remeil).

The building and the film contain two further curiosities. Every day, the character of Mounir (Rabih Mroué) photographs a photograph of his lost sweetheart and sticks the print to the wall. He moved here in pursuit of this woman, while she vanished into thin air to escape him. Souheil (Issam Bou Khaled), another character, regularly updates a "history wall" riddled with cracks and bullet holes, each marked with a label indicating the date and nature of the event that caused the damage (FIG.100). This wall seems to link up with *Let's Be Honest, the Weather Helped* (1998). In this series of photographs by Walid Raad, dilapidated façades are covered with coloured marks (FIG.102). The artist explains that he collected used shells embedded in buildings in Beirut in the 1980s, cataloguing their locations. Years later, he says, he discovered that arms manufacturers use colour codes that leave marks – and realised that he had amassed an inventory of seventeen munitions-producing countries that had, indirectly, devastated Lebanon.[103]

102 Hadjithomas, Joana, in Mével, Quentin, *Le cinéma de Joana Hadjithomas & Khalil Joreige*, "Les Petits Entretiens", Paris, Indépendencia, 2013, p. 21.
103 "Walid Raad/The Atlas Group. *Let's Be Honest, the Weather Helped* (Finland, Germany, Greece, Egypt, Belgium)", Guggenheim Museum website.

Symptomatic of Beirut's "interminable destruction, or of its unfinished reconstruction",[104] these various fictitious walls are echoed in the project undertaken by Paola Yacoub in the same period. Having previously taken part in archaeological excavations in the city centre, Yacoub used the same technique to produce imprints and casts of projectile impacts collected along the Green Line (FIG.103). These archaeologies were created shortly before the *Machines Célibataires* installation by Atelier de Recherche ALBA. One of the *Machines, #7, imaginary stories and tales*, uses the eponymous work by Théophile Gauthier as a tool for reading and rewriting the Barakat Building (FIG.104). In a series of images, the installation sets up encounters between details of damaged edifice and sections from a copy of the book on which Riad Damien has inflicted similar mutilations.[105]

Souheil's project also seems to anticipate some works by Lamia Joreige, such as *Under-Writing Beirut – Mathaf* (FIG.69) and *Beirut, Autopsy of a City* – as well as offering a reflection on the artworks produced by Joana Hadjithomas and Khalil Joreige themselves. It has a negative counterpart, meanwhile, in the work of Hanibal Srouji. Haunted by cracked and shattered buildings, by walls riddled with bullet holes from automatic weapons, Srouji produced a series of paintings entitled *Particles*, in which he burned the canvas with a blowtorch – using the act of burning to sublimate the violence[106] (FIG.101).

These artists reconstitute the traces of war in order to erase them more effectively. When Khalil Joreige asserts that "Beirut does not exist" this is really a stratagem for evading its definition. In reality "its existence is endless."[107] In the film, the squatters in the Pink House decide to outmanoeuvre the developer who plans to demolish the building, while preserving its façade "for the honour of Lebanon." They borrow a digger and, taking turns, destroy it. This gratuitous act, with its echoes of *auto-da-fé* and sacrifice, bears witness to the attachment these people have developed to the physical structure they have occupied for more than ten years. Whether you are an owner, a tenant or a refugee is irrelevant: to live in a place is to appropriate it.

FIG.102 *Walid Raad / The Atlas Group, Let's be honest, the weather helped. Belgium, 1998. Archival color inkjet print, one of a series of 17 prints, 46,4 × 71,8 cm.*

FIG.103 *Paola Yacoub, Casts of bullets holes, 1995. 35 elements, wood paste, variable dimensions.*

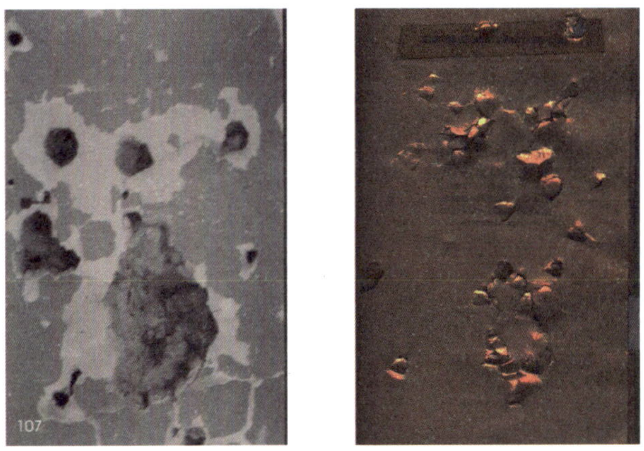

FIG.104 *Atelier de recherche ALBA/Riad Damien. Machines Célibataires, Machine # 7 Imaginary Stories and Tales, (2) face to face : bf 1237 / The Book, 2000.*

104 MONGIN, OLIVIER and PAQUOT, THIERRY, "Beyrouth", in JOUSSE, THIERRY and PAQUOT, THIERRY, *La ville au cinéma*, Encyclopédie, Paris, Les Cahiers du Cinéma, 2005, p. 335.
105 DAMIEN, RIAD, "Machines Célibataires : Machine # 7 imaginary stories and tales", Atelier de Recherche ALBA.
106 BUCHAKJIAN, GREGORY, *Hanibal Srouji. Peindre le feu, l'eau, la terre, la mer*, Beirut, Galerie Janine Rubeiz and Les éditions de L'Orient-Le Jour, 2013, p. 44.
107 JOREIGE, KHALIL, in MÉVEL, *Le cinéma de Joana Hadjithomas & Khalil Joreige*, op. cit., p. 28.

PERIPHERAL USES OF INFORMAL SETTLEMENTS

Informal settlements have had a multitude of peripheral activities associated with them. Often a shopkeeper would set up their stall in a room, a corridor or on a landing of the "building-village." Carpentry workshops, studios, storage facilities, garages and car parks were also established in individual residences and in blocks. After 1977, the owners of boats moored in Saint George Bay took to parking them in the Phoenicia Hotel when the situation worsened, to save them from being sent up in smoke during a bombardment, as had happened in 1975.[108]

A MANSION CRAMMED WITH RECLAIMED FURNITURE

FIG.105 *Gregory Buchakjian, Tannir-Bokja atelier inside el-Khouri mansion, 2010. Photograph.*

Iconic for its vertiginous mannerist double staircase set either side of a grotto and its galleried façade framed by two corner towers, the El Khoury mansion (bf501, Zokak el-Blatt) belongs to a family that made its fortune in the cotton business in Egypt. In the late 1960s, when the building became too expensive to maintain, the family used the central hall for dealing in furniture and antiques.[109] One room was made available to Mr Tannir, a cabinetmaker, whose job was to restore the pieces before they went on display. From the late 1960s through to 1975, these three functions coexisted in the same space: the home of the El Khourys, a retail showroom and a furniture workshop. From 1978 onwards, refugees lived in the second-floor apartment while Marie el-Khoury still lived alongside Mr Tannir, whose workshop – now a small family business – was flourishing. Since Marie el-Khoury's death in 1994, the Tannir workshop has expanded to fill the whole of the building (FIG.105).

In the 2000s, Marya Bazzi and Huda Baroudi made contact with Mahmoud and Hussein Tannir.[110] Bazzi and Baroudi had recently created Bokja, a brand that reclaims objects and furniture of various styles, giving them a new lease of life by covering them with fabrics and patchwork. Since then, the Tannirs have been part of the Bokja team and Bokja products are made on the Tannir premises – where the Tannirs still don't seem entirely at home. Recovered items of furniture, awaiting transformation, exist alongside remnants of the original décor. Cluttered with boards, equipment and all kinds of materials, with work surfaces and even a wooden room constructed within one interior, the palace is in danger of collapsing from damage which was never repaired, caused by two shell impacts. Along with the house where the singer Fairuz was born (bf565-567), "now reduced to a dilapidated structure deprived of its original meaning",[111] the palace was designated as a site of public importance in the official gazette.[112] Not that anything actually happened.

108 The Buchakjian family owned a motor boat moored in Saint George Bay and made use of this arrangement. When the family left the west sector of Beirut in 1986, the boat was abandoned where it was garaged and they never found out what happened to it.

109 Bodenstein, Ralph, "The Bechara el-Khoury Mansion" in Gebhardt, Hans et al., *History, Space and Social Conflict in Beirut: The Quarter of Zokak El-Blat*, Beirut, Orient-Institut, 2005, pp. 96–97.

110 Huda Baroudi, interview with the author, 24 July 2015.

111 Haidar, Mazen and Rayess, Akram, "Public Sounds, Private Spaces: Towards a Fairouz Museum in Zokak el-Blat" in *Divercities: Competing Narratives and Urban Practices in Beirut, Cairo and Tehran*, Beirut, Orient-Institut, 2013.

112 Abboud Abi Akl, May, "The campaign conducted by An-Nahar, the municipality of Beirut and the Lebanese heritage foundation to expropriate the house of Fairuz and create a museum dedicated to her work finally bears fruit", *An-Nahar*, 14 January 2015.

THE ALCAZAR WORKSHOP

The Alcazar Hotel (bf364, Minet Hosn) was established by the Tarazis, a family known from 1862 onwards for dealing in antiques and creating oriental décors featuring painted wood panels and inlaid mother-of-pearl. After the Battle of the Hotels, the Tarazi family converted the lounges of the hotel, now closed, into a production workshop for furniture and panelling, where "bosses and staff worked in the same room, without any distinction of class or hierarchy"[113] (FIG.106). In 1987, the deteriorating situation forced the Tarazis to dissolve their company, Alfred et Émile Tarazi & Successeurs, and to leave the Alcazar.[114] Émile decided to continue the business with his son Michel, and then with Michel's son Camille. Meanwhile, Alfred's branch of the family piled up its share of the stock in warehouses. In 2015, Alfred's grandson, also called Alfred, transported this merchandise to the exhibition space at Beirut's Institut Français. His installation *Monument to Dust* is an accumulation of broken-down furniture, letters, photos, audio tapes of extracts from radio programmes (FIG.107). Alfred Tarazi's work fulfils a cathartic function with respect to his own personal history, but also, as Laure Ghorayeb emphasises, with respect to the history of the country as a whole. Ghorayeb suggests that this work should be considered on a par with the Martyrs' Monument.[115]

FIG.106 *Michel Tarazi, Construction of the Oriental Decoration for the Tarazi villa inside the Alcazar Hotel, 1997. Photograph.*

FIG.107 *Alfred Tarazi, Monument to Dust, 2015. Installation.*

OF ANIMALS AND MEN

Triggered by the arrival of migrants and then refugees, the ruralisation of the urban space was manifested in sights as surreal as a pigeon loft on the roof of the Phoenicia[116] and goats in the Heneiné Mansion, both in reality[117] and on film.[118] In informal dwellings, some families kept sheep in the courtyards[119] and, on the demarcation line, a member of the militia had between 1500 and 2000 chicks "playing loud music so that the din of nearby battles wouldn't upset the unfortunate birds."[120] In building-villages, families raised poultry or rabbits, valued for providing a quick and effective source of meat.[121] Rabbits could be seen hopping around in the Abboud Abdel Razzak residence (bf1787, Minet Hosn), in a scene worthy of Lewis Carroll or David Lynch. The two squatters who kept them had converted the southern *liwan* of the central hall into a farm, with an enclosure formed of consoles, tables, cabinets and jerrycans. The rabbits could get out into the garden through holes in the wall; plastic piping and containers

113 Tarazi, *Vitrine de l'Orient*, op. cit., p. 219.
114 *Ibid.*, p. 233.
115 Ghorayeb, Laure, "Monument to Dust: an installation by Alfred Tarazi that should be set alongside Martyrs' Monument", *An-Nahar*, 17 November 2015.
116 Hadjithomas Mehanna, Tania, *Le Phoenicia, un hôtel dans l'Histoire*, Beirut, Tamyras, 2012, p. 89.
117 Bodenstein, "Qasr Heneiné", op. cit., p. 151.
118 Jocelyne Saab, interview of 2 November 2015.
119 Baalbaki and Baalbaki, interview of 19 September 2014.
120 Oliver Saidi, "La ligne verte de Beyrouth 1975-1991", op. cit., p. 49.
121 Baalbaki and Baalbaki, interview of 19 September 2014.

acted as water troughs and boxes with holes in were used for giving birth (female rabbits entered via the hole to have their litter inside). Nonetheless, this facility hardly met the standards of enlightened livestock keepers: the arrangements were insalubrious and not good for the animals, who were basically left to fend for themselves.[122]

PLACES OF WORSHIP

With the arrival of migrants from the south and the rise of the Amal Movement and Hezbollah, *husseiniyas* – Shia mosques – were improvised. On Michel Ange Street, a *mousalla* – prayer room – dedicated to Imam Baqir, the fifth Shia imam, was set up in a room adjacent to the hall of a building which still bears the sign "centre sportif Saadé" (Saadé sports centre) (bf2880, Ras Beyrouth). The sign shows a picture of a man and a woman wearing swimsuits and holding hands: a curious conjunction of a pagan image and a monotheistic place of worship. On the façade of another modern building, (bf386, Minet Hosn), the new use was signalled by means of calligraphy showing the names of Muhammad, Ali, Fatima, Allah (in the middle), Hassan, Hussein and Zeinab, along with verse 33 of the 33rd surah, *Al-Ahzab* (The Clans) of the Quran.

After the church of Saint-Nicolas was destroyed in a bombardment, the parish decided to consecrate the Trad residence (bf1125, Achrafieh), which had been abandoned and then occupied by the Lebanese forces. The Maronite militia was part of the movement that had "invaded districts traditionally occupied by the middle and upper Greek Orthodox bourgeoisie."[123] Here, the orthodox community of Achrafieh was able to kill two birds with one stone: they secured a temporary place of worship and, at the same time, rid themselves of an unwanted partisan presence that was defiling "their" neighbourhood.

No less unusual was the temporary conversion of a residential block (bf1784, Minet Hosn) into a synagogue, during the Israeli occupation.[124] In a curious reversal of functions the Maghen Abraham synagogue had itself become a refuge, a few weeks earlier, until, "during a fierce Israeli assault, a shell blew a hole in the roof of the cream-colored stucco synagogue, sending about 60 Jewish and Moslem refugees sleeping there fleeing into the street."[125]

MEDICAL CARE

At times of crisis emergency centres were created for the provision of medicines and medical services. During the 1982 Israeli invasion, the Bristol Hotel became a centre of operations for the International Committee of the Red Cross (ICRC),[126] while Massabki Hotel in Chtaura[127] and the Near East School of Theology were converted into field hospitals. Of the latter, it was reported that "the conference hall where ecclesiastical nuances were once the topic of discussion now contains two operating tables for assembly line amputations and a bin for severed limbs."[128] In 1978, when Achrafieh came under heavy fire, ICRC manager Nayla Hachem set up a hospital in the half-built structure of an abandoned building site. "We created space for an operating room in this setting of reinforced concrete. . . using the steel wires protruding from the pillars for hanging up serum bags, shirts, linen, towels soaked in blood."[129] The ministry of social affairs provided 200 beds which had been donated by Sweden – "children's beds, less than 1.70 metres long" – but they said, "Well, it doesn't matter, their feet will just have to stick out."[130]

122 Maya Kharrat, interview with the author, 3 September 2014.
123 Davie, "Les marqueurs de territoires idéologiques", Groupe Eidos et Maison des Sciences de la Ville, Tours, 1992.
124 Nigol Bezjian, interview with the author, 25 May 2015.
125 Associated Press, "Beirut's only Synagogue is Casualty of the Israelis", *New York Times*, 12 August 1982.
126 *L'Orient-Le Jour*, 19 August 1982, p. 4.
127 "L'hôtel Massabki à Chtaura transformé en antenne médicale", *L'Orient-Le Jour*, 12 June 1982, p. 2.
128 Cahill, Kevin M., "Beirut's Smell of Death", *New York Times*, 24 July 1982.
129 Hachem, Nayla, *Beyrouth, comme si l'oubli* , Lunay, Zellige, 2012, pp. 256–60.
130 *Ibid.*

CRIME SCENES

FIG.108 *Fouad Elkoury, At Takieddin el-Solh's, Civil War series, 1984. Photograph.*

FIG.109 *Gregory Buchakjian, Abboud Abdel Razzak Mansion, where Takieddine el-Solh resided, 2012. Photograph.*

In 2015, the Internal Security Forces discovered terrorists engaged in plotting an attack in a dilapidated building (bf3766, Achrafieh).[131] As well as providing a base for criminal activities, abandoned buildings are also potential crime scenes. In June 2014, a reality TV documentary followed a police investigation into a taxi driver's disappearance. Traced telephone calls led the detectives to the Abdel Razzak residence (bf 1787, Minet Hosn). "As soon as we entered the building and began to search a terrible smell assailed us. The smell of a corpse," recounts an officer. The police arrested a suspect who confessed to the crime. He had kidnapped the victim, thinking – wrongly – that he was wealthy, and had imprisoned and then killed him, disposing of the body in a ground-floor room. The police exhumed the body, buried in the sand 1.5 metres below the surface.[132] It remains unclear whether the killer and his accomplice were also the owners of the rabbit farm described on p. 197.

This tragedy is a grim episode in the turbulent history of a building which, after being chosen as the Ottoman governor's residence,[133] fell into the possession of the Naamani family, whose fortune vanished when an uninsured ship was wrecked at sea.[134] Occupied by Daoud Ammoun, and by his son Charles (parliamentary deputy and then representative of Lebanon at UNESCO),[135] it was acquired by Abboud al-Merabi Abdel Razzak, an eminent figure and member of parliament originally from Akkar, and passed to his son, Mohammad al-Abboud al-Merabi Abdel Razzak, also a politician, who was married to Fadwa el-Barazi. Mohammad Abdel Razzak was assassinated on the steps of the presidential palace in Kantari, 50 metres away, on 14 July 1953.[136] His widow stayed on in the building and married her second husband, Takieddin el-Solh, a politician and prime minister who was famous for wearing the tarboosh at a time when this custom was dying out. The Abdel Razzaks filed a lawsuit against the Barazi el-Solhs, claiming that the property should be returned to them. The two parties engaged the country's most eminent lawyers, granting them shares in the property by way of payment. These lawyers are now long since dead – currently leaving no fewer than 40 claimants on the property among their heirs.[137] Despite having a front-row view of the battle of Kantari, in October 1975, the building survived the ravages of war. It appears "opulently occupied" in a photograph taken by Fouad Elkoury in 1984.[138] The situation remained the same until 1986, when Takieddin el-Solh left Lebanon. The building was listed in the 1990s, yet in 2002 it was reported that marbles were being ripped out, as a prelude to demolition.[139] Fadwa el-Barazi explains that "despite the lawsuit between us we reached agreement on dividing the

131 "In pictures: the terrorists' apartment in Achrafieh", *Lebanon 24*, 16 November 2015.
132 Fawaz, Maroun, "Bel Jerm El Machhoud", MTV Lebanon, season 2, episode 28, 4 June 2014.
133 Touma Arida's words, recounted by his daughter May, interview with the author, 25 August 2012.
134 Fadwa el-Barazi, interview with the author, 7 September 2012.
135 Abboud Abi Akl, May, "Who is going to protect the memory of Beirut and compensate the rights holders?" *An-Nahar*, 10 May 2002, p. 22.
136 "Les différentes étapes historiques de l'armée durant le mandat de Camille Chamoun (1952-1958)", *Histoire de l'armée libanaise*, 30 September 2008.
137 Touma Arida, op. cit.
138 Fouad Elkoury, email to the author, 2 August 2012.
139 Abboud Abi Akl, "A property where Takieddin el-Solh lived under threat in Kantari", *An Nahar*, 2 May 2002, p.1.

property",[140] planning to demolish it and sell up. The process of dismantling the building was already under way when "a journalist published an article and Walid Bey [Jumblatt] protested, saying that we didn't have the right to demolish a historic monument."[141] Minister of culture, Ghassan Salamé, intervened to stop the demolition. The widow of the two statesmen adds that "the municipal authorities stopped us from laying a finger on the building. All that's left inside is sand and stones"[142] (PL.22, 47, 48).

RUINS AS A PERFORMANCE SPACE

"It was all desolate, magnificent. No door. A hole in the façade, pierced by a rocket attack. The sign was hanging above the ground, held there by electricity wires. Just three walls. The fourth had been blown away." [143] The novel *Le quatrième mur* (*The Fourth Wall*) is based on the narrator's promise to stage Anouilh's *Antigone* in an imaginary film theatre in the Sodeco neighbourhood, in the middle of the demarcation line, with actors of various origins from either side of the line. In the 1980s, the idea of using a city-centre performance space was implemented in *A Suspended Life*, which was partly filmed in the interior of the Grand Théâtre de Beyrouth (bf891, Bachoura). After 1990, as the city was gutted, the interest in ruins grew proportionally. In 1993, Greta Naufal, Imad Issa, Barbara Kassir and Majid Kassir gathered at St George Maronite Cathedral where they gave an entirely unauthorised performance of *In the Ruins*, witnessed by an audience exclusively comprised of stray dogs. When the performers learned that the Syrian *Mukhabarat* – intelligence officers – were on their way, they took fright and left.[144] In the following year, in this same field of ruins that was once the city centre, Catherine Cattaruzza appropriated parts of the public space as locations for ephemeral micro-installations.

In the Ruins and Cattaruzza's *No Man's Land* happened at a pivotal time, shortly before the city centre was placed under Solidere's supervision. Soon after that, what had been a wild area became a controlled, policed territory where any subversive activity was impossible. Closed off by the war, opened up in the post-war period, access to this area, now under reconstruction, became controlled. In the autumn of 1997, the Grand Théâtre opened for a performance. "A rescued fragment in the middle of the vast building site of what is called the city centre, it gives a sense of what existed before the tabula rasa: in it we can read our past in its entirety – and this authenticity, this transparency, is absolute."[145] *Hommage au Grand Théâtre de Beyrouth* (*Homage to the Grand Théâtre de Beyrouth*) was devised by the company Théâtre Écarlate, with partners including Atelier de Recherche ALBA.[146] As Pierre Hage-Boutros noted, "It is paradoxical that Gilles Zaepffel, who managed to get the venue opened again, is himself a foreigner in our city. The new territory where the Grand Théâtre de Beyrouth lingers on no longer belongs to us."[147]

In 1998, in the ghostly ruins of St Elias Greek Catholic Cathedral, *Silence bien plus tard* combined an installation by Catherine Cattaruzza comprising Polaroids, blue pigment, rock salt, graphite, gold leaf, light bulbs and electric wires with piano improvisations on Éric Satie performed by Cynthia Zaven. In the same year, the Ayloul Festival featured a six-hour theatrical performance staged in the basement of the Ezzeddine building.[148] Outside the Solidere zone, the Imprimerie Catholique premises, near the front line, became a cultural venue – La Fabrika. It was operated by Agenda Culturel through to the 2000s, when the owners brought the venture to an end and partially demolished the building – in order to declare it unsafe,

140 ABBOUD ABI AKL, "Who will protect the memory of Beirut and compensate the rights holders?", op. cit.
141 EL-BARAZI, interview of 7 September 2012.
142 *Ibid.*
143 CHALANDON, SORJ, *Le quatrième mur*, Paris, Grasset & Fasquelle, 2013, pp. 178–9.
144 BARBARA KASSIR, interview with the author, 31 August 2009.
145 HAGE-BOUTROS, PIERRE, "L'oubli de l'oubli. Réflexions suite à l'Hommage au Grand Théâtre de Beyrouth", Atelier de Recherche ALBA website, October 1997.
146 "Hommage au Grand Théâtre de Beyrouth", Atelier de Recherche ALBA website, 1997.
147 HAGE-BOUTROS, PIERRE, "L'oubli de l'oubli", op. cit.
148 KHOURY, ELIAS, "'Quizoola!' Programme Note by Elias Khoury, co-director of the Ayloul Festival", *Forced Entertainment*, 2000.

so that they could tear it down completely.[149] In 2000, Ashkal Alwan organised Hamra Street Project, an arts and cultural platform located across several disused cinemas on Hamra Street. At the Colisée cinema, reduced to a skeletal remnant of its former self, Lamia Joreige showed *Replay*, a video installation based on two photographs from the Lebanese Civil War, re-enacted by two performers: "A man never stops falling, never stops dying (right screen). A woman never stops running, never stops escaping (left screen). Two bodies separated by the immutable sea (middle screen), are perpetuating a vain act."[150] Other events took place in the remains of industrial buildings, exploring issues around public space rather than housing – part of a period of cultural renewal in which the actors involved had neither the requisite funds nor appropriate venues available to them.[151]

Initiatives in the 2010s gave new life – for the long term, more or less – to some abandoned buildings. In 2012, Ghassan Maasri created Mansion, a cultural centre and arts incubator, in a building (bf1856, Mousseitbé) that had been abandoned in its original condition.[152] In 2013, the painter Tom Young, who had previously staged an exhibition in a dilapidated house, met Fayza el-Khazen, the last occupant of the iconic Maison Rose (bf585, Ras Beyrouth), who was about to pack up and leave. He set up a studio in the apartment and became part of the building's final days as a residence. Taking a different angle again, Zeina el-Khalil appropriated derelict locations with traumatic histories in order to undertake healing rituals there.[153]

EROS AND THANATOS: ILLICIT ACTIVITIES, SECRET PLEASURES

"Am I the woman of your life?"
"You are the woman of my – death."[154]

FIG.110 *Seta Manoukian, La fête rose, 1981. Acrylic on canvas, 125 × 175 cm.*

FIG.111 *A Suspended Life, film by Jocelyne Saab, 1985.*

149 Émile Nasr, interview with the author, 19 October 2015.
150 "Replay", Lamia Joreige website.
151 Wilson-Goldie, Kaelen, "On the Politics of Art and Space in Beirut", *Nafas*, August 2009.
152 Ghassan Maasri, interview with the author, 29 September 2015.
153 El Khalil, Zena, "Sacred Catastrophe: Healing Lebanon", Zena el-Khalil website, 2017.
154 Toufic, Jalal, *Jouissance in Postwar Beirut*, 2014.

Abandoned sites provide ideal hideaways for illicit activities. Numerous buildings, like the one that became Mansion, served as hideouts for the production and consumption of narcotics: so how many acts of violence, how many rapes were perpetrated in these labyrinthine interiors? Residents in Khandaq el-Ghamik hinted darkly of one house that "there are shady characters hanging out there", but the exact nature of the "things" that happened there remained unspoken (PL.9).

In the 1990s, it became fashionable to organise raves in factories, warehouses and other ruins. The City Center cinema (bf1523, Bachoura) became an "alternative" venue for arts events and techno club nights.[155] Variously nicknamed the Bubble, the Dome and the Egg, it symbolised this attempt to appropriate the city by young people in the grip of both euphoria and despair, aware of the raves happening in Goa and Ibiza and the post-apocalyptic ambience following the fall of the Berlin Wall and the war in the former Yugoslavia.[156] Historically or symbolically linked with death, these spaces took on an erotic aspect through the movements of bodies being flaunted, watching each other, touching and caressing. This encounter of Eros and Thanatos had one of its most outlandish manifestations in the nightclub BO18, Bernard Khoury's bunker sunk into the ground on the site of the Karantina massacre.

This conjunction of pleasure and death was also manifested in vampire-themed artistic productions, such as the films of Ghassan Salhab and the writings of Jalal Toufic.[157] During the war years, the link between the body and the city had already been highlighted both in film and painting. In *La Fête Rose*, Seta Manoukian merges her own flesh with the deserted streets of the Lazariyeh district (FIG.110). The eroticisation of the ruin brings this relationship into its sharpest focus, notably in the scenes of *A Suspended Life* where two adolescent girls discuss their sexual desires against the apocalyptic backdrop of the Cité Sportive (FIG.111). Two contemporary photographic projects explore the body and sexuality in the landscape: *The Reeds* by Lara Tabet and *Breaking Out* by Myriam Boulos. The former infiltrates a world of sexual encounters taking place in a hazy, shadowy setting amid vegetation, while the latter shows people who are partly or entirely naked walking in the public space. In reality, making love in unusual locations is partly a function of a sociological situation – most young people live with their parents, and all but the wealthiest, whose families own "chalets" in ski resorts or by the sea, lack access to a place where they can explore their sexuality – and partly driven by a sense of adventure.

> *We met on top of an abandoned building [bf1236, Achrafieh]. The whole of Beirut was spread out below us. We started to kiss. Then we made love. Suddenly there was an enormous firework display. It was ecstasy, like in* Les amants du Pont Neuf.[158] *I repeated the experience after that, in different places, with other partners. I was especially fond of a dilapidated building in Gemmayzeh, moments away from the crowds wandering from one bar to the next.*[159]

The above account expresses this desire to appropriate the city erotically – a city the people of Beirut felt was escaping them. Some went so far as to create a love nest in a deserted villa (bf26, Saïfi).

> *We took occupation of a mezzanine, accessed by a ladder. When we weren't there we hid the ladder and when we were in our nest we pulled it up out of sight. I cleaned the place and decorated it with fabrics, cushions, candles, knick-knacks. We went there regularly until one day, from our hideout, we heard some thugs coming in and going about their shady business. We were absolutely petrified and stayed holed up there until they went. We never set foot in the place again.*[160]

One illicit activity – criminality – had chased away another: lovemaking.

155 SPRINGER, DANIEL, "The Value of a War-Scarred Ruin in Beirut", *Failed Architecture*, 9 December 2013.
156 BUCHAKJIAN, "Beirut by Night", op. cit., pp. 271–2.
157 TOUFIC, JALAL, *Vampires: An Uneasy Essay on the Undead in Film*, Sausalito, Post-Apollo Press, 2003.
158 Film by Leos Carax, 1991.
159 H. C., interview with the author, 20 August 2010.
160 N. I., interview with the author, 8 September 2010.

SELF-APPOINTED GUARDIANS OF ABANDONED BUILDINGS

FIG.112 *Gregory Buchakjian, Dismantled Musical Scores pulled apart in Victoria K.'s Apartment, 2012. Photograph.*

Resplendent opposite the Bibliothèque Orientale is the neoclassical façade of an abandoned building known for having been the home of Pierre Gemayel (bf285, Saïfi). From 2011 onwards, Valérie Cachard and I regularly visited the first-floor apartment that was formerly the home of Victoria. During these visits, we retrieved a number of documents and objects that had belonged to her.

In March 2013, Valérie Cachard met a man aged around sixty who, so he said, had been a bodyguard of "Sheikh Pierre" and had grown up with "Sheikh Bashir", Pierre Gemayel's son. He promised to take us to visit the Kateb Party leader's apartment, which had been locked up for decades. When we met, instead of following the staircase up to the residence in question, he took us through a window, in Victoria's kitchen, which was separated from the rest of the accommodation by a locked door. The former bodyguard launched himself at the door to break it down. The situation was absurd, because what was on the other side of the door was easily accessible. Valérie, feeling that he was "killing Victoria all over again", pleaded with him to stop these theatricals.

Four years previously, I had approached a crumbling residence (bf471, Zokak el-Blatt). A man in his seventies who said he was the guardian of the building refused to allow me in. He was originally from South Lebanon. I asked him if he had come to Beirut with the waves of refugees and he answered:

> *"Certainly not! I've been here for more than fifty years! I'm a pharmacist. I was assistant to the sheikh!"*
> *"Which sheikh?"*
> *"Sheikh Pierre!"*

In 2013, Camille Tarazi and I managed to gain access to the building and we realised that this former right-hand man to the Maronite "Sheikh" had, in fact, been guarding a memorial dedicated to "Hajj" Zuheir Shehadeh of the "Islamic resistance" (FIG.75). While we were contemplating the stucco work, the curtains and the fresco dedicated to this commander, a man followed us in. He crossed the room, went into a corner and relieved himself, not at all bothered by our presence. A building that had been an inviolable sanctuary on one day became a public latrine on another.

My third encounter with a self-appointed guardian took place at Victoria's home (PL.45). The door was open; the central hall was empty. In a bedroom, a young man was sleeping on a mattress on the floor; next to him were two pairs of shoes, a water bottle and a few belongings. Waking up, he explained that he was guarding the place to protect it from thieves, tramps, drug addicts, thugs and people who do "bad things." This was "Sheikh Pierre's house", he said, adding that it was still his property. He ignored that the Gemayels who were tenants had terminated their contract many years ago. Moreover, he spoke of the political leader, who had died thirty years previously, as if he might return at any moment. A well-presented individual, with a sense of a mission entrusted to him, he was planning to undertake repairs in a property whose owners he knew nothing of – and who knew nothing of him. He added that we had been lucky, because he had forgotten to lock the door before going to sleep. When I advised him to keep an eye out for dangers that might lie in wait for him, he replied: "But the building's protecting me!"

APPENDICES

FORCES INVOLVED IN THE LEBANESE CIVIL WAR (1975–90)

LEFT FORCES

The "Joint Forces" or "Left Forces", sometimes called the Palestinian–Progressive or Leftist–Muslim forces, were the armed wing of the Lebanese left, represented by the Lebanese National Movement under Kamal Jumblatt on the one hand and the Palestinian organisations on the other. The largest Left parties or organisations were the Independent Nasserists or *Murabitun* of Ibrahim Koleilat, the Popular Nasserist Organisation of Maarouf Saad, the Lebanese Communist Party (LCP), the Communist Action Organisation in Lebanon (CAOL), the Progressive Socialist Party of Kamal Jumblatt and the Syrian Social Nationalist Party (SSNP). The most important Palestinian organisations were the Palestine Liberation Organisation (PLO) of Yasser Arafat, the Popular Front for the Liberation of Palestine (PFLP) of George Habash, the Popular Front for the Liberation of Palestine – General Command (PFLP–GC) of Ahmed Jibril, the Democratic Front for the Liberation of Palestine (DFLP) of Nayef Hawatmeh and Zuheir Mohsen's Al Sa'iqa.

Essentially a political mass movement at the start of the war, by the early 1980s the Shia Amal had developed into a substantial militia under the leadership of Nabih Berri. The same period also saw the emergence of Hezbollah, which, since 1990, has been the only organisation to dispose of an arsenal in Lebanon, and later in neighbouring countries.

CHRISTIAN, RIGHT-WING FORCES

The conservative Christian political forces, sometimes called the Lebanese Resistance,[1] formed the Lebanese Front, whose most important component was the Kataeb or Phalangist Party of Pierre Gemayel. Among its allies were the National Liberal Party (NLP) of Camille Chamoun, with its militia, the *Numur* (Tigers), the Marada Movement of Suleiman Franjieh, the Guardians of the Cedars of Étienne Sakr, and al-Tanzim. In 1978, the Marada Movement left the Lebanese Front.

In the early 1980s, Bashir Gemayel "unified the rifles" under the flag of the Lebanese Forces (not to be confused with the official Lebanese Armed Forces), which became the armed wing of the Phalange. Later, following his death, the Lebanese Forces separated from the Phalange to become a militia and party in their own right.

FOREIGN FORCES

The first phase of the war (1975–6) ended with the deployment of the Arab Deterrent Force (ADF), a multinational peacekeeping force with contingents from Saudi Arabia, the United Arab Emirates, Sudan, Libya, North and South Yemen and Syria, the largest by far being from Syria. By 1979, with the departure of the other contingents, the Syrian Army was left alone in Lebanon, where it would remain until 2005.

In 1978, the Israeli Army invaded South Lebanon, creating a buffer zone under the control of a proxy militia known as the Free Lebanon Army and later as the South Lebanon Army (SLA). In 1982, Israel launched a large-scale invasion that took it as far as Beirut before its army gradually withdrew to the "security zone" in the south. Israel's withdrawal to within its own borders in 2000 would see the collapse of the SLA.

Following the Israeli invasion of 1978, the UN created a peacekeeping force, the United Nations Interim Force in Lebanon (UNIFIL). After the war of 2006, UNIFIL's strength was increased and its mandate expanded.

On the occasion of the Siege of Beirut in 1982, a Multinational Force (MNF) was established by the USA, France and Italy to ensure the safe departure of Palestinian fighters from the country. This was then withdrawn; however, following Israel's entry into the city and the Sabra and Shatila massacres, it returned, reinforced by a contingent from the United Kingdom, to remain in Beirut until 1984.

1 Not to be confused with the Lebanese Resistance Detachments (the official title of Amal) or the Lebanese National Resistance Front formed to fight Israeli occupation by the Lebanese/Palestinian Left in 1978.

SOURCES

1. FIELD RESEARCH

Seven hundred and forty-four abandoned residential buildings were identified in the different administrative divisions of Beirut. Others were inspected in the suburbs and elsewhere in the country.

1.a. Abandoned buildings in the city of Beirut identified between November 2009 and February 2016.

District	Sector	Number
Ashrafieh	Achrafieh	9
	Adlieh (palais de justice)	2
	Furn el-Hayek	35
	Ghabi	20
	Hôtel-Dieu	10
	Mar Mitr (Saint-Dimitri)	17
	Nasra (Nazareth)	33
	Sioufi	7
TOTAL ASHRAFIEH		133
Ain el-Mreisseh	Ain el-Mreisseh	33
	Jamia (AUB)	1
TOTAL AIN EL-MREISSEH		34
Bachoura	Bachoura	23
	Basta Tahta	34
TOTAL BACHOURA		57
Mazraa	Abi Haidar	3
	Aamlieh	8
	Basta Faouka	13
	Horsh	3
	Malaab	4
	Mazraa	7
	Parc	10
	Ras el-Nabeh	19
TOTAL MAZRAA		67
Medawar	Khodr	10
	Mar Mikhael	25
	Remeil	18
TOTAL MEDAWAR		53
Minet Hosn	Bab Idriss	4
	Kantari	21
	Minet Hosn	13
TOTAL MINET HOSN		38

District	Sector	Number
Mousseitbeh	Dar el-Fatwa	5
	Mar Elias	3
	Mousseitbeh	22
	Sanayeh	14
	Tallet Khayat	1
	Unesco	6
	Wata	4
	Zarif	15
TOTAL MOUSSEITBÉ		70
Ras Beirut	Ain el-Tineh	6
	Hamra	55
	Jumblatt	14
	Manara	22
	Koraitem	1
	Raouché	2
	Ras Beirut	5
	Snoubra	4
TOTAL RAS BEIRUT		109
Remeil	Geitaoui	12
	Hekmeh	39
	Orthodox Hospital	19
	Qobaiyat	10
	Saint-Nicolas	22
TOTAL REMEIL		102
Saifi	Gemmayzé	17
	Mar Maroun	16
	Yassouieh (Saint Joseph University)	19
TOTAL SAIFI		52
Zokak el-Blatt	Serail	16
	Batrakieh (Patriarcate)	13
TOTAL ZOKAK EL-BLATT		29
GRAND TOTAL		744

1.b. Other abandoned buildings visited in the suburbs or provinces

Governorate / District	Locality	Description
North		
Batroun	Tannourine	Houses
Mount Lebanon		
Aley	Aley	Grand Hôtel Gebeily
	Bhamdoun	Synagogue
		Hotels
		Residential buildings and villas
	Shemlan	Villas
	Shuwayfat	Houses
	Qmatiyeh	Houses and villas
	Sofar	Grand Hôtel and Casino
		Villa Donna Maria Sursock
	Souk el-Gharb	Secondary school
		Houses and villas
Baabda	Bourj el-Barajneh	Houses and villas
	Falougha	Hotel
	Furn el-Chebbak	Villa Catafago
	Kfar Selwan	Group of houses
	Tarshish	Military installations
Chouf	Ain Zhalta	Houses
	Jiyeh	Houses
	Maaser Beiteddine	Silkworm farm
	Maaser el-Chouf	Houses
Keserwan	Jounieh	Houses
	Kfardebian	Chalet
Metn	Ain Aar	Silkworm farm
	Aoukar	Sports club
		Villa
	Bauchrieh	Silkworm farm
	Beit Chabeb	Spinning mill
		Houses
	Bickfaya	Hôtel Cesar Amer
		Houses
	Bois de Boulogne	Restaurant du Bois
		Villa Jabre
	Brummana	Rabbit enclosure (Fatté family)
	Dahr el-Sawan	Seraglio
		Houses
	Dhour Shweir	Grand Hôtel Kassouf
		Villas
Nabatieh		
Hasbaya	Hasbaya	Shehab Palace
Marjeyoun	Khiam	Prison camp

1.c. Maps and plans

Date	Title	Creator / Source
1876	Plan de Beyrouth dédié à S.M.I. le Sultan Abdul Hamid II/par Julius Löytved... ; levé et dessiné par Stuckly Aug	Julius Löytved
1922	Beyrouth/dessiné au Bureau topographique de l'Armée française du Levant	Service géographique du Levant, Bibliothèque nationale de France
1926	Aerial photograph of Beirut	Armée française du Levant
1943	Aerial photograph of Beirut	Armée française du Levant
1966	Cadastral plan, Beirut	Dar Kabess
1977	Hotel district and city centre	Wathiqat Harb Lubnân, Beyrouth, Dar Assayad, 1977, vol. 1. p. 227.
1983	Aerial photograph of Beirut city centre	Lebanese Army, Directorate of Geographic Affairs
2004	Cadastral plan of Beirut	Municipalité de Beyrouth, topographe Kozhaya Sfeir
2009	Beirut Mapping Security	Mona Fawaz, Ahmad Gharbieh, Mona Harb

2. WRITTEN SOURCES

The press has been a very important source for facts about the war, especially for the years 1975–6 and 1982. Recourse was also had to blogs and websites, i.e. news organisations, image libraries and sites related to art and culture.

2.a. Press reports and articles

Title	Period searched
Al-Akhbar	2010-2018
An-Nahar	1975-1990
	1994-2018
As-Safir	1975-1976, 1994-1996
	2010-2017
La Revue du Liban	1936-1990
Le Monde	1975-2018

Title	Period searched
Magazine Hebdo	1982
L'Orient-Le Jour	1975-1976, 1978, 1982
	2009-2018
The Guardian	2010-2018
The New York Times	1975-1990, 2000-2018
The Washington Post	1975-1990, 2000-2018
Time	1975-1976, 1982

2.b. Websites and blogs

Name	URL
111101 [Artworks, writings and References in Lebanon]	*http://111101.net*
L'Agenda culturel	*http://agendaculturel.com*
Agial Art Gallery & Saleh Barakat Gallery	*http://agialart.com*
Akershus Kunstsenter	*http://akershuskunstsenter.no*
Al Mashriq	*http://almashriq.hiof.no*
Al-Monitor	*http://al-monitor.com*
Arab Center for Architecture	*http://arab-architecture.org*
Arab Image Foundation	*http://arabimagefoundation.org*
Ashkal Alwan	*http://ashkalalwan.org*
Atelier de recherche ALBA	*http://alba.edu.lb/ar*
Atlas Group Archive	*http:// theatlasgroup.org*
BBC	*http://bbc.com*
Beirut Art Center	*http://beirutartcenter.org*
Beirut.com	*http://beirut.com*
Beirut State of Mind	*http://beirutstateofmind.blogspot.com*
Beit Beirut Museum and Cultural Center	*http://beitbeirut.org*
Bokja Design	*http://bokjadesign.com*
Caroline Tabet	*http://carolinetabet.com*
Centre Pompidou	*https://www.centrepompidou.fr*
Christo et Jeanne-Claude	*http://christojeanneclaude.net*
CNN	*http://cnn.com*
Corbis	*http://corbisimages.com*
Dahesh Museum of Art	*http://daheshmuseum.org*
Darat al Funun – The Khalil Shoman Foundation	*http://daratalfunun.org*
Dictaphone Group	*http://dictaphonegroup.com*
Étapes	*http://etapes.com*
Failed Architecture	*http://failedarchitecture.com*
Fouad Elkoury	*http://fouadelkoury.com*
Galerie Imane Fares	*http://imanefares.com*
Galerie Janine Rubeiz	*http://www.galeriejaninerubeiz.com*
Gregory Buchakjian	*http://buchakjian.net*
Guggenheim Museum	*http:// guggenheim.org*
Hospitalitynet	*http://www.hospitalitynet.org*
Images d'armée	*http://imagesdarmee.com*

Name	URL
Jadaliyya	*http://jadaliyya.com*
Joana Hadjithomas et Khalil Joreige	*http://hadjithomasjoreige.com*
L'œil de la photographie	*http://loeildelaphotographie.com*
Lamia Joreige	*http://lamiajoreige.com*
Lawrence Abu Hamdan	*http://lawrenceabuhamdan.com*
Lebanon 24	*http://lebanon24.com*
Lotus Edde Khouri	*http://lotuseddekhouri.com*
MACVAL Musée d'art contemporain du Val-de-Marne	*http://macval.fr*
Magnum	*http://magnumphotos.com*
Marfa' Projects	*http://marfaprojects.com*
Memorial Museums	*http://memorialmuseums.org*
Messy Nessy Chic	*http://messynessychic.com*
Middle-East Eye	*http://www.middleeasteye.net*
Nabil Gholam Architects	*http://nabilgholam.com*
Nada Sehnaoui	*http://nadasehnaoui.com*
Nadour	*http://nadour.org*
Naharnet	*http:// naharnet.com*
National Museum of Beirut	*http://beirutnationalmuseum.org*
Noorderlicht	*http://noorderlicht.com*
Now.	*https://now.mmedia.me*
Orient XXI	*https://orientxxi.info*
Palais de la Porte dorée, musée de l'Histoire de l'immigration	*http://histoire-immigration.fr*
Phoenicia Beirut	*http://phoeniciabeirut.com*
Saatchi Gallery	*http://saatchigallery.com*
Saint-Georges Beirut	*http://saintgeorgebeirut.com*
Saradar Collection	*http://saradar.com/saradar-collection*
Sfeir Semler Gallery	*http://sfeir-semler.com*
Station Museum	*http://stationmuseum.com*
Sursock Museum	*http://sursock.museum*
Tanya Traboulsi	*http://tanyatraboulsi.com*
The Beirut Report	*http://www.beirutreport.com*
White Cube	*http://whitecube.com*
World Monuments Fund	*https://www.wmf.org*
Zena el-Khalil	*http://www.zenaelkhalil.com*

2.d. Unpublished sources

Author	Description	Date
Aftimus, Youssef	Speeches of Youssef Aftimus, in Arabic and in English, some handwritten, some typewritten	1920-1950
	"Status of the Lebanese-Syrian Association of Engineers and Architects"	n.c.
	Letters to Youssef Aftimus	1926, 27, 34, 47
Buchakjian, Gregory and Raad, Walid	Correspondence	2017
Cottard, Eugène	"Carnets du Dr Eugène Cottard [6 novembre 1914-2 décembre 1914]." transcribed by Françoise and Jean Raab, 13 pp.	1914
	"Journal de voyage et de séjour en Syrie [Fin septembre à fin décembre 1908]." 1908. transcribed by Françoise and Jean Raab, 51 pp.	1908
Beirut Alcazar Hotel	Hotel register for the year 1975	1975
Tarazi, Émile	Typewritten memoirs	1975-1987

See also s. 6 below: *"Documents discovered in Beirut's abandoned dwellings"*

3. AUDIOVISUAL SOURCES

Fiction and documentary films are also abundantly cited, notably for the war years and the period immediately afterwards. Cinema is one of the visual and artistic practices that are among the concerns of this research.

3.a. Full-length fiction films

Title (original language / English)	Date	Director
'71	2014	Yann Demange
Al Aasar / The Tornado	1992	Samir Habchi
Al Bayt al zahr / Around the Pink House	1999	Joana Hadjithomas et Khalil Joreige
Ashbah Bayrut / Phantom Beirut	1998	Ghassan Salhab
Atlal / The Last Man	2006	Ghassan Salhab
Beyroutou el Lika / [Beirut the Encounter]	1981	Borhane Alaouié
Civilisées/Civilized People	1999	Randa Chahal Sabbag
Bayrout ya Bayrout / Beirut Oh Beirut	1975	Maroun Bagdadi
Die Fälschung/ Circle of Deceit	1980	Volker Schlöndorff

Title (original language / English)	Date	Director
Ghazl banet / A Suspended Life	1987	Jocelyne Saab
Héritages / Heritages	2014	Philippe Aractingi
Hors la vie / Out of Life	1991	Maroun Bagdadi
Houroub saghira / Little Wars	1982	Maroun Bagdadi
Je veux voir / I Want to See	2008	Joana Hadjithomas et Khalil Joreige
Liban le pays du miel et d'encens / Lebanon, Land of Honey and Incense	1988	Maroun Bagdadi
Paris, Texas	1984	Wim Wenders
Roma città aperta / Rome, Open City	1945	Roberto Rossellini
West Beyrouth / West Beirut	1998	Ziad Doueiri

3.b. Short films

Title (original language / English)	Date	Director
Après le silence / After the Silence	1995	Ghassan Kotait
B Mitl Beirut	2004	Roy Dib
Beau Rivage	2004	Claude el-Khal
Le Beau Rivage	2007	Nina Francis Najjar
Été 91 / Summer 91	2014	Nadim Tabet et Karine Wehbé

3.c. Documentary films

Title (original language / English)	Date	Director
Beyrouth de pierre et de mémoire / Beirut of Stone and Memory	1992	Philippe Aractingi
Beyrouth, ma ville / Beirut, My City	1982	Jocelyne Saab
Chemins de femmes / Women's Journeys	1994	Philippe Aractingi
Hamasât/Whispers	1980	Maroun Bagdadi
Havanna – Die neue Kunst, Ruinen zu bauen / Havana: The New Art of Making Ruins	2006	Florian Borchmeyer
Khiam	2000	Joana Hadjithomas et Khalil Joreige
Khiam 2000-2007	2008	Joana Hadjithomas et Khalil Joreige
Koullouna Lil Watan / We Are All for the Fatherland	1979	Maroun Bagdadi
La ligne verte / The Green Line	1988	Bahij Hojeij
Le Liban dans la tourmente / Lebanon in a Whirlwind	1975	Jocelyne Saab
My Architect	2003	Nathaniel Kahn
Seule avec la guerre / Alone with War	2000	Danielle Arbid

3.d. Videos

Title (original language / English)	Date	Director
And the living is easy	2015	Lamia Joreige
Attempt 137 to Map the Drive	2011	Grazielle Rizkallah Toufic et Jalal Toufic
Beirut	2007	Hale Tenger
Beyrouth 2012	2012	Bane Saleh
Eye for an Eye	2009	Sonny Sanjay Vadgama
Houna wa Roubbama Hounak / Here and Perhaps Elsewhere	2003	Lamia Joreige
In this house	2005	Akram Zaatari
Measures of distance	1988	Mona Hatoum
The Bachar tapes	2001	Walid Raad
The disquiet	2013	Ali Cherri
Un cercle autour du soleil / A Circle Around the Sun	2005	Ali Cherri

3.e. Television Reports

Title	Programme title	Journalist / Producer	Date	Broadcaster
18 mois de guerre	Temps présent	Pierre-Pascal Rossi	1976	RTSR
24 Heures à Beyrouth Est	24 Heures	Gilles de Maistre	1989	Canal Plus
Art in Beirut. Photographer Gregory Buchakjian. Abandoned Sensuality	Visual Arts-Features	Eric Gonon	2014	Blouin Artinfo
Au temps des snipers	Beit Beirut/Immeuble Barakat	Anne Ilcinkas	2011	L'Orient-Le Jour
Beau Rivage, Hotel of Tortures		Rami al-Amin	2010	Al Jadeed
Beirut Photographer	Witness	Mariam Shahin	2012	Al Jazeera
Beyrouth. . . La vie quand même	Grands Reportages	Michèle Cotta	1990	TF1
Beyrouth l'heure syrienne	24 Heures	Gilles de Maistre	1990	Canal Plus
Bineyet Barakat. Chahed Samet	Zakirat Makan	Rakan Mayasi	2007	Future TV
Civil War – Lebanon	This Week	Ian Stuttard	1976	Thames Television
Dahesh: The man. The philosophy. The legend. The controversy	Sireh w'infatahit	Zaven Kouyoumdjian	2010	Future TV
Guerre au Liban. Les gardiens du Cèdre	Un jour une heure	n.k.	1976	RTSR
Episode 3	Harb Lubnan	Omar Issaoui	2001	Al Jazeera
Episode 4	Harb Lubnan	Omar Issaoui	2001	Al Jazeera
House of Memory		Maureen Ali	2001	OR-Tv
L'avenir de la maison jaune	Beit Beirut/Immeuble Barakat	Anne Ilcinkas	2011	L'Orient-Le Jour
La vie heureuse	Beit Beirut/Immeuble Barakat	Anne Ilcinkas	2011	L'Orient-Le Jour
Mona's House	n.k.	n.k.	N.c.	SWR
Quotidien de misère : Beyrouth, la rage de vivre	Temps présent	Christian Mottier	1982	RTSR
Saison 2 - Épisode 28	Bel Jerm el Machhoud	Maroun Fawaz	2014	MTV-Lebanon
Shooting in Beirut | Phantom|			2015	UTV Motion Pictures
Une architecture unique	Beit Beirut/Immeuble Barakat	Anne Ilcinkas	2011	L'Orient-Le Jour

3.f. Online archives of video recordings and television news

Name	Period	Source
AP Archive	1975-1977	*http://aparchive.com*
INA	1975-1990	*https://www.ina.fr*
ITN Source	1975-1976	*http://www.itnsource.com/en*
Saradar Collection. Words on Works	2016-2018	*http://www.saradar.com/saradar-collection/english/programes/words-on-works*

3.g. Music videos

Title	Musician / Group	Publisher	Date
When You Came Into My Life	Scorpions	Sony Music Germany	1996
Whoopy	The Wanton Bishops	Beirut Jam Sessions	2012

3.h. Amateur Films

Title	Maker	Date	Source
Greetings from Beirut	David Daniels	n.c.	*https://vimeo.com/9854688*
In Search of Dr Dahesh		2011	*https://www.youtube.com/channel/UClPBvAvjujG4NpCnhZqu7CQ*
Stories of a Beirut House	Helle Egsgaard	2011	*http://vimeo.com/73571642*

3.i. Published audio recordings

Title	Programme title	Journalist / Producer	Date	Origin
Volume 8 N[os] 2 & 3, Side D	Audio Arts	Michael Archer	1987	Tate
Beirut's Holiday Inn: Once Chic, Then Battered, Still Contested	Parallels	Alice Forham	2014	BBC
Gregory Buchakjian in Beirut: A Course of Catastrophe	Radio Open Source	Christopher Lydon	2013	90.9 WBUR
Scratching on Things I Could Disavow. A History of Art in the Arab World		Walid Raad	2012	
The Holiday Inn in Beirut	Witness	William Kremer	2014	BBC

3.j. Non-published audio recordings

Description	Origin	Date	Medium
A hostage's message to his family, explaining how the ransom is to be paid	Recording sent by kidnappers	1986	Audio cassette
A hostage's message to his family, mistreatment of hostage (blows and cries)	Recording sent by kidnappers	1986	Audio cassette

4. IMAGES

Description	Date	No. of images
Photographs taken in Beirut by Gregory Buchakjian or others accompanying him, indexed by geographical origin	2009-2016	16 948
Photographs taken by Gregory Buchakjian in the suburbs or the provinces, indexed by geographical origin	2009-2016	949
Photographs, drawings, lithographs, paintings and screengrabs of sources (artworks, press pictures, amateur photos) representing views and scenes of Beirut life, indexed by geographical origin	1800-2015	6 423

5. ORAL ACCOUNTS, CORRESPONDENCE WITH THE AUTHOR, ETC.

This category covers interviews, correspondence addressed to the author and exchanges on social networks. A number of oral testimonies come from unidentified persons encountered by chance in the field.
The people below are listed under the categories in respect of which they have been quoted. A person may appear under more than one category if their testimony addresses more than one aspect of the research.

5.a. Residents and their heirs and descendants

Name	Occupation
Alexandre Abdeni	Head of Development at Compagnie Immobilière Libanaise, joint owner of the Centre Saint-Charles (Holiday Inn Hotel)
Zeina Abirached	Graphic novelist, formerly resident on the Green Line
Kheireddine el-Ahdab	Former resident of the Ain el Tineh neighbourhood
Me Touma Arida	Magistrate, neighbour of the Abboud Abdel Razzak / Takieddine el-Solh residence (account communicated by his daughter May)
Fadwa Barazi el-Solh	Widow of Mohammad Abdel Razzak and of Takieddine el Solh, living in the Abboud Abdel Razzak residence
Nigol Bezdjian	Artist and filmmaker, resident of the Zarif neighbourhood
Alain Brenas	Advertiser and director of the School of Cinema at the Académie Libanaise des Beaux-Arts. User of an office building on the Green Line
Wassim Chemaitilly	Physician, formerly resident on the Green Line
Joumana Ghandour	Architect, former resident of the Ghandour Building
Nayla Ghandour de Coster	Former resident of the Ghandour Building
Fadi Ghazzaoui	Resident of the Ras el Nabeh neighbourhood
Sawssan Hajj	Former police inspector, resident of the Mazraa quarter
Ayla Hibri	Photographer, resident of the Zokak el-Blat quarter
Zaza et Philippe Jabre	Financier and art collector, owner of the Villa Jabre
Bassam Kahwaji	Artist, former resident of the Gemmayzeh neighbourhood
Fayza el-Khazen	Publisher, former resident of the Maison Rose [Pink House]
Kristine Genevive Khouri	Art historian, former resident of the Kantari neighbourhood
Myrna Majdalani	Resident of the Mazraa quarter
Ginane Makki-Bacho	Artist, resident of Jnah
Mme Medawar	Resident of temporary accommodation
Rayya Morcos	Former resident of a building occupied first by militias and then by the police
Michel Moufarrège	Descendant of the family that owned the "House of the Virgin"
Ibrahim Mounmeh	Pharmacist, resident of the Ras el-Nabeh neighbourhood
Greta Naufal	Artist, former resident of Ras el-Nabeh wounded by a sniper
Wyssem Noshi	Designer, tenant in an abandoned building
Amer Omari	Hairdresser, former tenant in an abandoned building
Hrant Ourgandjian	Physician, author's uncle, last tenant in an abandoned building
Mouhamad Rabah	Managing director of property developers ZRE
Michel Raggi	Former resident on the Green Line
Rosy Raggi	Film director, former resident on the Green Line
Bane Saleh	Videomaker, member of a family that owned a building occupied by a militia
Jocelyne Saab	Filmmaker, former resident of a mansion taken over by refugees
Amal Saadé	Artist, former resident of an abandoned house in the southern suburbs
Georges Schoucair	Film producer, former resident on the Green Line
Laure de Selys	Artist, neighbour of the former Lebanese Forces headquarters
M. Souheil	Last tenant in an abandoned building
Michèle Standjofski	Cartoonist, former resident of a building occupied by refugees
Alfred Tarazi	Artist, descendant of the family that owned the Alcazar Hotel.
Camille Tarazi	Architect and director of Maison Tarazi, a descendant of the family that owned the Alcazar Hotel and the Dimitri Tarazi residence
Raja Tarazi	Former inhabitant and current neighbour of the Dimitri Tarazi residence
Joseph Tarrab	Art critic. Former resident of Wadi Abu Jmil
Saad Wazzan	Real estate developer
Adolphe Youssevitch	Interior designer, relative of former residents on the Green Line
Mme Zeinab	Tenant in a partly abandoned building
Nanette Ziadé	Journalist, former inhabitant of the Ziadé residence

5.b. Former fighters or politicians and people close to them

Name	Occupation
Me Touma Arida	Magistrate, close to Walid Jumblatt (account communicated by his daughter May)
-	Members and former members of political parties who requested anonymity or were encountered in the street
Chahine Fayad	Office holder in the Phalange, responsible for the front on the Green Line in Beirut and its suburbs
Najib Khazzaka	Journalist, close to the Palestinian organisations and then to Walid Jumblatt
Alexandre Medawar	Journalist
Zalfa Rustom	Film producer, daughter of a National Liberal Party politician

5.c. Victims of war and relatives

Name	Occupation
Gerard Ateshian	Director of the Musculoskeletal Biomechanics Laboratory at Columbia University and former detainee
Sarkis Buchakjian	Watchmaker and jeweller, the author's father and a former detainee
Stéphanie Cachard	Jewellery designer, daughter of a former hostage at the Semiramis Hotel, Damascus.
Charles Dantzig	Writer and friend of Charlotte Aillaud, survivor of the Nazi concentration camps
Greta Naufal	Artist and former resident on the Green Line, victim of a sniper
Grégoire Sérof	Architect, former detainee

5.d. Refugees, squatters and various occupants

Name	Occupation
Ayman Baalbaki	Artist, former refugee in the Wadi Abu Jamil neighbourhood
Saïd Baalbaki	Artist, former refugee in the Wadi Abu Jamil neighbourhood
Mahmoud Tannir	Joiner, occupant of the El Khoury mansion

5.e. Researchers, artists, cultural actors

Name	Occupation
Zeina Abirached	Graphic novelist
Anne-Marie Afeiche	Director, National Museum of Beirut
Naji Assi	Architect
Antoine Atallah	Architect
Vartan Avakian	Artist
George Azar	Photographer
Ayman Baalbaki	Artist
Saïd Baalbaki	Artist
Marc Baroud	Designer
Huda Baroudi	Co-founer of Bokja
Zeina Bassil	Illustrator
Patrick Baz	Photographer
André Bekhazi	Architect, dean of the Académie Libanaise des Beaux–Arts
Nicolas Bellevance-Lecomte	Joint founder of the Carwan Gallery
Georges Boustany	Creator of the Facebook page *La guerre du Liban au jour le jour*
Valérie Cachard	Writer
Raed Charaf	Sociologist and illustrator
Patrick Chauvel	War photographer
Marc Chelhot	Collector of visual images
Sandra Dagher	Joint founder, Beirut Art Center
Gabriel Daher	Expert in Orientalist painting
May Davie	Historian, Université de Tours
Michael Davie	Geographer, Université de Tours
Marc Dibeh	Designer
Fouad Elkoury	Photographer
Lina Ezzeddine	Author of a book on the names of the streets of Beirut
Omar Fakhoury	Artist
Fadi Ghazzaoui	Urban explorer
Nabil Gholam	Architect
Jad Ghostine	Architect
Mazen Haidar	Architect and writer
Youssef Haïdar	Architect
Mona Hallak	Architect, member of the Expert Advisory Committee of Beit Beirut
Barbara Kassir	Former librarian of the Goethe Institute, Beirut
Maya Kharrat	Director of the School of Agronomy, Saint Joseph University, Beirut

Name	Occupation
Ghassan Kotait	Filmmaker and assistant director of the School of Cinema at the Académie Libanaise des Beaux–Arts
Imad Kozem	Author of *Pure Nostalgia* and founder of the eponymous Facebook group
Diala Lteif	Designer
Ghassan Maasri	Architect, founder of Mansion
Fadi Maassarani	Collector of visual images
Ginane Makki-Bacho	Artist
Aline Manoukian	Picture researcher, former war photographer
Carla Mardini	Museologist, member of the Expert Advisory Committee of Beit Beirut
Carlo Massoud	Designer
Alexandre Medawar	Journalist
Nina Francis Najjar	Filmmaker responsible for a film on the Beau Rivage
Émile Nasr	Director of Agenda Culturel
Greta Naufal	Artist
Levon Nordiguian	Historian, director of the photographic collection at the Bibliothèque Orientale
Lea Pavlikevitch	Collector of visual images
Walid Raad	Artist
Tania Rayes-Ingea	Author of *Beyrouth, le centre-ville de mon père*
Joseph Rustom	Lecturer in cultural heritage studies in the School of Architecture at the Académie Libanaise des Beaux–Arts
Jocelyne Saab	Filmmaker
Walid Sadek	Artist and thinker
Bane Saleh	Videomaker
Ghassan Salhab	Filmmaker
Alfred Tarazi	Artist
Camille Tarazi	Architect, director of Maison Tarazi
Giorgio Tarraf	Political scientist
Hale Tenger	Artist
Lyna Yared	Collector of visual images
Serge Yared	Musician and urban explorer
Paola Yacoub	Artist
Jean-Pierre Zahar	Architect
Serge Yazigi	Urbanist
Tom Young	Artist
Akram Zaatari	Artist
Lamia Ziadé	Artist, illustrator and writer

6. DOCUMENTS DISCOVERED IN BEIRUT'S ABANDONED DWELLINGS

While little use has been made of individual documents as sources, the collection as a whole retains its importance as a complement to the written or oral accounts in documenting the life of former residents.

The names of those whose connection with these dwellings is not already a matter of public knowledge have been disguised in order to safeguard their privacy.

Location Found	Natural or legal person concerned	Date	Description
Bf294, Ashrafieh	Unknown	n.d.	Arabic language course
		1999	Residence permit
		1998	Letter in Singhalese
Bf1083, Ashrafieh	Family A	n.d.	6 perspective drawings of interior designs
		1962	2 passports
		n.d.	2 Air France coach tickets
Bf1237, Ashrafieh	Barakat Family	n.d.	Photographs
		1965	Letter from Mary (. . .) to M. & Mme Barakat
		n.d.	Photographs
	Dr Nagib Schemali	1932	Letter addressed to Patriarch Arida
		n.d.	Dental care booklet for children
	Photo Mario	c. 1975	Stock of photographs
	Unknown	c. 1958	Middle East Airlines leaflet
		c. 1970	Magazine page with advert for Patek Philippe / Sarkis Buchakjian
Bf1512, Ashrafieh	Nada el-Khoury	n.d.	Folder with fashion magazine cuttings, annotations in Arabic, fashion drawings, samples
		c. 1990	Address book
		n.d.	Samples of embroidery and crochet work
Bf4229, Ashrafieh	Etienne Sakr, Guardians of the Cedars	c. 1983	Diners Club International card in the name of Étienne Sacre
		n.d.	Blank prisoner detention forms
Bf74, Ain el-Mreisseh	Restaurant Quo Vadis	n.d.	Headed notepaper
		1975	Carte Blanche credit card statement
		1975	Food price list
		n.d.	Sick note in the name of AS
		1959	Schedule of redundancy payments
Bf335, Ain el-Mreisseh	Mme B	n.d.	Pan American Airways ticket wallet
		1962-1968	3 account books
	Mme C	1995	Payslip (American University of Beirut, Jaffet Library)
		1994	Tenancy agreement
		1969	Typescript "La orientación de la mujer libanesa"
		1960	Academic transcript (Beirut College for Women)
		1971	*Aramco World* magazine, special issue on "The Arab Woman"
		1994	Letter from Syracuse University
	M. D.	1990	Birth certificate
		1974	Interim certification of doctorate in medicine, Université d'Angers
	Family M	1997	Certificates of birth, marriage etc.
		1996	Application for rent allowance from the American University of Beirut
		1995	Deposition to the prosecuting authorities alleging theft by a domestic servant
		1970	Grocery bill
		1985	Passes issued by the Progressive Socialist Party and by Amal
		2000	Banker's reference from the Banque Libano–Française
		1992	Letter from FH
			Video cassette boxes for *La maison du plaisir* and *Sex and Stars*
			Class list from the Collège Louise Wegmann
		1988-1995	Letters and greetings cards
		1989	7 letters from N to GM
		1989-1992	6 letters from SJ to GM
		N.c.	6 telexes from SJ to GM
		1988-1995	Documents issued by Middle East Airlines

Location found	Natural or legal person concerned	Date	Description
Bf142, Medawar	Family P	1977	Passport
		n.d.	Photographs
		n.d.	Letters and greetings cards in French and Armenian
		n.d.	Photographs
		1964	Documentation from "Club Sculpture humaine"
		1969	Cover of *Playboy* magazine
		1983	Page from *Oui* magazine
		n.d.	Album of photographs annotated in Armenian on the back
		n.d.	Programme for show "Paris Nu York"
		1965-1968	Exercise book including draft letters, a Turkish lesson, accounts, mathematics lessons, descriptions of space missions, German phrases, drawings of a woman, trees, business studies lesson
	Lebanese Forces	n.d.	Photo album devoted to Bashir Gemayel
		n.d.	Ammunition belt
		n.d.	Fragment of calendar
Bf364, Minet Hosn	Hôtel Alacazar	1975	Hotel register of the Alcazar
Bf1787, Minet Hosn	Takieddine el Solh and Fadwa Barazi el Solh	n.d.	Photographs
		1984-1986	Payroll register
		1982	Accounts book
		1968	Election campaign press pack
		1972	Cadastral plan of a property
		1983	Letter from the Debbané company about fertiliser
		n.d.	Water receipts
		n.d.	Electricity receipts
		n.d.	Books
		n.d.	Electoral register
Bf335, Ras Beirut	Palestine Liberation Organisation	1979	Issue form for a sub-machine gun
		1979	Diary for 1979 with handwritten manual on the art of regular and guerrilla warfare
		1977	Book *Vietnam: Destruction, War Damage*
	M. K.	1970	Car insurance agreement
	Unknown	1970, 1986	Newspapers dated 3 October 1970 (death of Nasser) and 19 June 1986
		n.d.	Fragment of Palestinian driving licence
		n.d.	6 postcards of the Hermitage Museum
		n.d.	2 postcards of forests in the USSR
		n.d.	5 stereo slides of Leningrad
Bf2652, Ras Beirut	M. Z.	n.d.	Letter to May ____, from M. Z.
		1979	Student card (Manchester University)
		1978	British Rail card
		n.d.	Manchester–London train ticket
		n.d.	Vaccination certificate
Bf2880, Ras Beirut	Various	1972-1982	Documents issued by the military tribunal, statements
Bf701 ou 702, Remeil	M. A.	1975	Letter from Dublin (in Italian)
	H. E.	1957	Reference from the Hôtel Riviera in the name of H. E., "apprentice waiter"
		1965	Redundancy notice issued by the Lucullus restaurant following its expropriation
		1965	Reference from the Lucullus restaurant in the name of H. E., "waiter."
Bf285, Saifi	Victoria K.	1969	Songbook, Class 11C, Collège Protestant Français
		1970	Recitation book, Class 11C, Collège Protestant Français
		1959	National lottery ticket
		1952-1967	2 letters to Victoria from her sister Mary
		1979-1980	2 letters to Victoria from Bouchra
		1958	Letters to Victoria from Galal
		n.d.	Letter to Victoria from Denise
		1949	Letter to Victoria from M. Homsi
			Letters to Victoria from Marie O.
		1977	Letter from Victoria to Mme Louise Wegmann
		1958	Diary for the year 1958
		n.d.	Address book
		n.d.	Greetings cards
		n.d.	Photographs

BIBLIOGRAPHY

1. THEORY, IDEAS

1.a. Works

Agamben, Giorgio, *Homo sacer: Sovereign Power and Bare Life*, Trans. Daniel Heller-Roazen, California, Stanford University Press, 1998

Bachelard, Gaston, *The Poetics of Space*, Trans. Maria Jolas, 4th edition, Boston, Beacon, 1994

Barthes, Roland, *A Lover's Discourse, Fragments*, London, Vintage, 1993
———, *Camera Lucida, Reflections on Photography*, Trans. Richard Howard, New York, Vintage Classics , 1980

Baudrillard, Jean, *The System of Objects*, Trans. James Benedict, London and New York, Verso Books, 2005
———, *Simulacra and simulation*, Trans. Sheila Glaser, Michigan, University of Michigan Press, 1994

Benjamin, Walter, *Œuvres*, vol. III, Trans. Maurice de Gandillac, revised by Pierre Rusch, Paris, Gallimard, 2000 (Folio Essais)
———, "Paris – Capital of the Nineteenth Century", *New Left Review*, no. 48, 1968, pp. 77–88

Blanchot, Maurice, *L'espace littéraire*, Paris, Gallimard, 2012 [1955] (Folio Essais)

Borges, Jorge-Luis, *A Universal History of Infamy*, New York, E.P. Dutton, 1972
———, *Collected Fictions*, Trans. Andrew Hurley, London / New York, Penguin Publishing Group, 1999

Bourdieu, Pierre, *Sociology in Question*, Trans. Richard Nice, London, Sage, 1993

Certeau, Michel de, *The Writing of History*, Trans. Tom Conleyn, New York, Columbia University Press, 1993

Certeau, Michel de, Giard, Luce and Mayol, Pierre, *L'invention du quotidien, I: Arts de faire*, Paris, Gallimard, 1990 (Folio essais no. 146)
———, *L'Invention du quotidien, II : Habiter, cuisiner*, Paris, Gallimard, 1994 (Folio essais no. 238)

Deleuze, Gilles, *Cinéma 2: L'image-temps*, Paris, Les éditions de Minuit, 1985

Deleuze, Gilles and Guattari, Felix, *A Thousand Plateaus: Capitalism and Schizophrenia*, Trans. Brian Massumi, London, Athlone Press, 1987

Derrida, Jacques, *Archive Fever: A Freudian Impression*, Trans. Eric Prenowitz, Chicago, University of Chicago Press, 1998

Didi-Huberman, Georges, *Génie du non-lieu: Air, poussière, empreinte, hantise (Claude Parmiggiani)*, Paris, Les éditions de Minuit, 2001 (Fable du lieu)
———, *Images malgré tout*, Paris, Les éditions de Minuit, 2003 (Paradoxe)
———, *L'image survivante: Histoire de l'art et temps des fantômes selon Aby Warburg*, Paris, éditions de Minuit, 2002 (Paradoxe)
———, *L'œil de l'histoire: Tome 1, Quand les images prennent position*, Paris, Les éditions de Minuit, 2009 (Paradoxe)

Dillon, Brian, *Ruins*, London, Cambridge, Massachusetts, Whitechapel Gallery, The MIT Press, 2011 (Documents of Contemporary Art)

Eco, Umberto, *La guerre du faux*, Paris, Grasset et Fasquelle, 1985

Foucault, Michel, *The Archaeology of Knowledge and The Discourse on Language*, Trans. A.M. Sheridan Smith, New York, Pantheon Books, 1972
———, *Discipline and Punish*, Trans. Alan Sheridan, London, Vintage, 1979

Halbwachs, Maurice, *The Collective Memory*, Trans. F. J. Ditter and V. Y. Ditter, New York, Harper & Row, 1980 [1950]

Le Goff, Jacques, *History and Memory*, Trans. Steven Rendall and Elizabeth Claman, New York, Columbia University Press, 1996

Lefebvre, Henri, *The Production of Space*, Trans. Donald Nicholson-Smith, New York, Wiley-Blackwell, 1992

Nora, Pierre and Ageron, Charles-Robert, *Les Lieux de mémoire, tome 1: La république*, Paris, Gallimard, 1997 [1984]

Perec, Georges, *Life: A User's Manual*, Trans. David Bellos, Boston, David R. Godine, 2009

Rancière, Jacques, *Le destin des images*, Paris, La Fabrique, 2003
———, *The Politics of Aesthetics. The Distribution of the Sensible*, Trans. Gabriel Rockhill, London / New York, Continuum, 2007

Ricœur, Paul, *History and Truth*, Trans. Charles A. Kelbley, Evanston, Northwestern University Press, 1965
———, *Memory, History, Forgetting*, Trans. Kathleen Blamey and David Pellauer, Chicago, University of Chicago Press, 2004
———, *Temps et récit: Tome 3, Le temps raconté*, Paris, Seuil, 1991 (Points Essais)

Sebald, Winfried Georg, *De la destruction comme élément de l'histoire naturelle*, Arles, Actes Sud, 2004

Simmel, Georg, *Essays on Sociology, Philosophy and Aesthetics*, Trans. David Kettler, New York, Harper & Row, 1965

Toufic, Jalal, *The Withdrawal of Tradition Past a Surpassing Disaster*, Beirut, Forthcoming Books, 2009

Virilio, Paul, *A Landscape of Events*, Cambridge, Massachusetts, MIT Press, 2000 (Writing Architecture Series)
———, *The Vision Machine*, Bloomington, Indianapolis, Indiana University Press, 1994

Volney, Constantin-François, *A New Translation of Volney's Ruins*, New York, Garland Publishing, 1979

1.b. Articles, book chapters, conference papers

BATAILLE, GEORGES, "Poussière", *Documents*, vol. 1, no. 5, 1929

DEBORD, GUY, "Theory of the Dérive", *Les lèvres nues*, no. 9 (December 1956), pp. 10-13, Trans. Ken Knabb

DEMOS, T.J., "Sites of Collective Counter-Memory", *Animate Projects*, 2012

DIDI-HUBERMAN, GEORGES, "Aby Warburg et l'archive des intensités", Études photographiques, no. 10, La ressemblance du visible / Mémoire de l'art, 2001, pp. 144–68

NORA, PIERRE, "General Introduction: Between Memory and History", Ed. Pierre Nora, *Realms of Memory*, Trans. Arthur Goldhammer, New York, Columbia University Press, vol. 1, 1996, pp. 1–20

SAID, EDWARD, "Reflections on Exile", *Granta*, no. 13, 1984, pp. 159–72 (After the Revolution. Essays & Memoir)

VIRILIO, PAUL, "De la géopolitique à la métropolitique", Ed. Antoine Picon, *La ville et la guerre*, Besançon, Éditions de l'Imprimeur, 1996, pp. 200-229. (Tranches de villes)
———, "The Imbalance of Terror", Ed. Paul Virilio, *A Landscape of Events*, Cambridge, Massachusetts, The MIT Press, 2000, pp. 23–30 (Writing Architecture Series)

2. HISTORY, GEOGRAPHY AND SOCIETY

2.a. Works

ARNAUD, JEAN-LUC, *Beyrouth, Grand Beyrouth*, Beirut, Presses de l'Ifpo 1997, pp. 209–27

ASHWORTH, GREGORY JOHN, *War and the City*, London / New York, Routledge, 1991

BEYHUM, NABIL, SALAM, ASSEM and TABET, JADE (Eds.), *Beyrouth: Construire l'avenir, reconstruire le passé ?*, Beirut, Dossiers de l'Urban Research Institute, 1995 (Proceedings of the symposium organised by the Urban Research Institute in April 1992)

BOUTROS, ANTOINE (Ed.), *Wathiqat Harb Lubnân (Documentation of the Lebanese War)*, vol. 1, Beirut, Dar Assayad, 1977 Clerc-Huybrechts, Valérie, *Les quartiers irréguliers de Beyrouth*, Beirut, Presses de l'Ifpo, 2008 (Contemporain publications 24)

COURBAGE, YOUSSEF, et FARGUES, PHILIPPE, *La situation démographique au Liban*, Beirut, Publications de l'Université Libanaise, 1974

DAVIE, MICHAEL F (Ed.), *Beyrouth : Regards croisés*, Tours, Centre de Recherches et d'Études sur l'Urbanisation du Monde Arabe (URBAMA), 1997

EDDÉ, CARLA, *Beyrouth, naissance d'une capitale : 1918-1924*, Arles, ACTES SUD / Sindbad, 2009 (La bibliothèque arabe, Hommes et sociétés)

EL-KHAZEN, FARID, *The Breakdown of the State in Lebanon*, Cambridge, Massachusetts, Harvard University Press, 2000

EVANS, JENNIFER V.V., *Life Among the Ruins: Cityscape and Sexuality in Cold War Berlin*, Basingstoke, Palgrave Macmillan, 2011

FREIHA, ASMA and GHANEM, VIVIANE, *Les Libanais et la vie au Liban : De l'indépendance à la guerre, 1943-1975*, Beirut, Dar Assayad, 1992

GEBHARDT, HANS, SACK, DOROTHÉE, BODENSTEIN, RALPH, FRITZ, ANDREAS, HANSSEN, JENS, HILLENKAMP, BERNHARD, KÖGLER, OLIVER, MOLLENHAUSER, ANNE and STOLLEIS, FRIEDERIKE, *History, Space and Social Conflict in Beirut: The Quarter of Zokak El-Blat*, Beirut, Orient-Institut, 2005

GLASS, CHARLES, *Tribes with Flags: A Dangerous Passage Through the Chaos of the Middle East*, New York, Atlantic Monthly Press, 1990

FRIEDMAN, THOMAS L, *From Beirut to Jerusalem*, New York, Anchor, 1990

HALEY, EDWARD P., and SNIDER, LEWIS W., *Lebanon in Crisis: Participants and Issues*, Syracuse, Syracuse University Press, 1979

HALL, PETER, and PFEIFFER, ULRICH, *Urban Future 21: A Global Agenda for Twenty-First Century Cities*, London / New York, Routledge, 2000

HANNOYER, JEAN (Ed.), *Guerres civiles. Économie de la violence, dimensions de la civilité*, Paris, Karthala, 1999 (Hommes et sociétés)

HANSSEN, JENS, *Fin de Siècle Beirut. The Making of an Ottoman Provincial Capital*, Oxford, Clarendon Press, 2005

HAUGBOLLE, SUNE, *War and Memory in Lebanon*, Cambridge, Cambridge University Press, 2012

KALAWOUN, NASSER, *The Struggle For Lebanon. A Modern History of Lebanese-Egyptian Relations*, London, I.B. Tauris, 2000

KASSIR, SAMIR, *La guerre du Liban: De la dissension nationale au conflit régional, 1975-1982*, Paris / Beirut: Karthala – Centre d'études et de recherches sur le Moyen-Orient contemporain, 1994 (Hommes et sociétés)
———, *Beirut*, Oakland, University of California Press, 2011
———, *Being Arab*, Trans. Will Hobson, London / New York, Verso Books, 2013

Katz, Samuel, *Armies in Lebanon 1982-84*, Oxford, Osprey Publishing, 2012 (Men at Arms Series no. 165)

Kevorkian, Raymond, Nordiguian, Levon, and Tachjian, Vahé, *Les Arméniens 1917-1939 : La quête d'un refuge*, Beirut: Presses de l'Université Saint-Joseph, 2006

Khalaf, Samir, *Civil and Uncivil Violence in Lebanon: A History of the Internationalization of Communal Conflict*, New York, Columbia University Press, 2002

Khoueiry, Antoine, *Al Harb fi Lubnan, 1976*, Jounieh, Dar Al Abjadiya, 1977 (Hawadeth Lubnan no. 2)

Khouri, Robert, *Liban 1860, Chronique des événements*, Bouar, Daccache, 2003

Kiwan, Fadia (Ed.), *Le Liban aujourd'hui*, Paris / Beirut, CNRS Éditions, 1994

Labaki, Boutros, and Abou Rjeily, Khalil, *Bilan des guerres du Liban, 1975-1990*, Paris, L'Harmattan, 2000

Ménargues, Alain, *Les Secrets de la guerre du Liban : 1, Du coup d'état de Béchir Gémayel aux massacres des camps palestiniens*, Paris, Albin Michel, 2004

———, *Les Secrets de la guerre du Liban : 2, Des massacres de Sabra et Chatila au voyage d'Amine Gemayel à Damas*, Beirut: Librairie Internationale, 2012

Menassa, Bechara, *Anatomie d'une guerre et d'une occupation : événements du Liban de 1975 à 1978*, Paris, Galilée, 1978

Mermier, Franck, *Récits de villes : d'Aden à Beyrouth*, Arles, Actes Sud / Sindbad, 2015 (La bibliothèque arabe, Hommes et sociétés)

Mermier, Franck, and Varin, Christophe (Ed.), *Mémoires de guerres au Liban, 1975-1990*, Arles, Actes Sud / Sindbad, 2010 (La bibliothèque arabe, Hommes et sociétés)

Naeff, Judith, *Precarious Imaginaries of Beirut: A City's Suspended Now*, Basingstoke, Palgrave Macmillan, 2018

Nordiguian, Levon (Ed.), *Les "petites écoles" du Mont-Liban, Joseph Delore, s.j. (1873-1944)*, Beirut, Presses de l'Université Saint-Joseph, 2003

Philipp, Thomas, Hanssen, Jens and Weber, Stefan, *The Empire and the City. Arab Provincial Capitals in the Late Ottoman Empire*, Beirut / Würzburg, Orient Institut Beirut, Ergon, 2002 (Beiruter Texte un Studien no.88)

Roguet, Christophe-Michel, *Insurrections et guerre des barricades dans les grandes villes / par le général de brigade Roguet*, Paris, J. Dumaine, 1850.

Salam, Nawaf and Sassine, Fares, *Liban: Le siècle en images*, Beirut, Dar An-Nahar, 1999

Salibi, Kamal, *A House of Many Mansions: The History of Lebanon Reconsidered*, 4th edition, London / New York, I.B. Tauris, 2003

Sawalha, Aseel, *Reconstructing Beirut: Memory and Space in a Postwar Arab City*, Austin, University of Texas Press, 2011

Sehnaoui, Nada, *L'occidentalisation de la vie quotidienne à Beyrouth : 1860-1914*, Beirut, Dar An-Nahar, 2002

Rustum Shehadeh, Lamia (Ed.), *Women & War in Lebanon*, Gainesville, University Press of Florida, 1999

Tarazi Fawaz, Leila, *Merchants and Migrants in 19th Century Beirut*, Cambridge, Massachusetts, Harvard University Press, 1983 (Harvard Middle Eastern Studies n° 18)

Taoûtel, Christian and Wittouck, Pierre, *Le Peuple libanais dans la tourmente de la Grande Guerre 1914-1918, d'après les archives des Pères jésuites au Liban*, Beirut, Presses de l'Université Saint-Joseph, 2015

Tabet, Jade (Ed.), *Beyrouth, La brûlure des rêves*, Paris, Autrement, 2001 (Monde n° 127)

Ter Minassian, Taline, *Erevan, la construction d'une capitale à l'époque soviétique*, Rennes, Presses Universitaires de Rennes, 2007 (Art & Société)

Yawmiyat al harb al lubnaniyya (Calendar of the Civil War in Lebanon), Beirut, Palestine Liberation Organisation (PLO), 1977

Traboulsi, Fawwaz, *A History of Modern Lebanon*, London, Pluto Press, 2007

Traugott, Mark, *The Insurgent Barricade*, Berkeley, University of California Press, 2010

Tuéni, Gebran, and Trad, Georges, *Beyrouth : Souvenirs, réalité*, Paris / Beirut, Hachette / An-Nahar Arab and international, 1982

Tueni, Ghassan and Sassine, Fares (Eds.), *El Bourj, Place de la liberté et porte du levant*, Beirut, Dar An-Nahar, 2000

2.b. Articles, book chapters, Conference papers

Abou Zaki, Hala Caroline, "Guerres ignorées, guerres oubliées ? Mémoires de guerres dans le camp de Chatila", Eds. Franck Mermier and Christophe Varin, *Mémoires de guerres au Liban, 1975-1990*, Arles, Actes Sud / Sindbad, 2010, pp. 313–32 (La bibliothèque arabe)

Ajay, Nicholas Z, Jr., "Political Intrigue and Suppression in Lebanon during World War I", *International Journal of Middle East Studies*, vol. 5, no. 2, 1974, pp. 140–60

Almaani, M.S.S., "Lebanese Housing Sector, 1970–1985", *Cities*, vol. 10, no. 1, 1993, pp. 67–80

Anastasiou, Harry, "Communication across Conflict Lines: the Case of Ethnically Divided Cyprus", *Journal of Peace Research*, vol. 39, no. 5, 2002, pp. 581–96

Arnaud, Jean-Luc, "Trop grand Beyrouth?", Ed. Jean-Luc Arnaud, *Beyrouth, Grand Beyrouth*, 1997, Beirut, Centre d'études et de recherches sur le Moyen-Orient contemporain , pp. 209–27 (Les Cahiers du CERMOC no. 16)

Babikian, Christine, "Développement du port de Beyrouth et hinterland", Ed. Jean-Luc Arnaud, *Beyrouth, Grand Beyrouth*, Beirut, Centre d'études et de recherches sur le Moyen-Orient contemporain, 1997, pp. 25–34 (Les Cahiers du CERMOC no. 16),

BADIE, BERTRAND, "Les impasses de la 'politique du ghetto'", Ed. Jean Hannoyer, *Guerres civiles: Économie de la violence – Dimensions de la civilité*, Paris, Karthala, 1999, pp. 153–62 (Hommes et sociétés)

BARAKAT, LILIANE, "Le centre-ville de Beyrouth, Pratiques et perceptions", Eds. Nabil Beyhum, Assem Salam and Jade Tabet, *Beyrouth: Construire l'avenir, reconstruire le passé ?*, Beirut, Dossiers de l'Urban Research Institute, 1995, pp. 192–206 (Proceedings of the symposium organised by the Urban Research Institute in April 1992)

BECKER, ANNETTE, "Religion et ferveur", Eds. Claire Garnier and Laurent Le Bon, *1917*, Metz, Centre Pompidou-Metz, 2014, pp. 247–48

BEYHUM, NABIL, "Beyrouth histoire de deux villes où tuer est une pulsion qui se répète", Ed. Jean Hannoyer, *Guerres civiles: Économie de la violence – Dimensions de la civilité*, Paris, Karthala, 1999, pp. 123–36 (Hommes et sociétés)
———, "Les Démarcations au Liban d'hier à aujourd'hui", Ed. Fadia Kiwan, *Le Liban aujourd'hui*, Paris, 1994, pp. 276–77 (CNRS Éditions)
———, "La place des Canons et la guerre", Eds. Ghassan Tueni and Fares Sassine, *El Bourj, Place de la liberté et porte du levant*, Beirut, Dar An-Nahar, 2000, pp. 94–5
———, "Population Displacement in the Metropolitan District of Beirut. Are the Displacements Over?", *Center for Migration Studies Special Issues*, vol. 11, no. 4, 1994, pp. 11–23

BOU AKAR, HIBA, "Contesting Beirut's frontiers", *City & Society*, vol. 24, no. 2, 2012, pp. 150–72

BOUDISSEAU, GUILLAUME, "Hamra: Nouveau centre ancien", Ed. Jean-Luc Arnaud, *Beyrouth, Grand Beyrouth*, Beirut, Centre d'études et de recherches sur le Moyen-Orient contemporain, 1997, pp. 67–80, (Les Cahiers du CERMOC no. 16)

BOUSTANY, OMAR, "J'irai danser sur vos tombes", Ed. Jade Tabet, *Beyrouth, La brûlure des rêves*, Paris, Autrement, 2001, pp. 186–90 (Monde no. 127)

BRONES, SOPHIE, "Al-Khandaq al-Ghamik ou la mémoire en ruine", Eds. Franck Mermier and Christophe Varin, *Mémoires de guerres au Liban, 1975-1990*, Arles, Actes Sud / Sindbad, 2010, pp. 441–58 (La bibliothèque arabe)

BROUILLET, ALAIN, "La seconde force multinationale à Beyrouth (24 septembre 1982-31 mars 1984)", *Annuaire français de droit international*, vol. 31, no. 1, 1985, pp. 115–66

BUCHAKJIAN, GREGORY, "Dernières nuits au Holiday Inn", Ed. Nayla Tamraz, *Proceedings of the symposium organised by the Department of French Literature and the Masters in Art Criticism and Curatorial Studies of Saint Joseph University of Beirut on 16 and 17 May 2014*, Beirut, Presses de l'Université Saint-Joseph, 2015, pp. 21–32

CHAIB, KINDA, "Une figure de martyr au Sud-Liban", Ed. Franck Mermier and Christophe Varin, *Mémoires de guerres au Liban, 1975-1990*, Arles, Actes Sud / Sindbad, 2010, pp. 246–63 (La bibliothèque arabe)

CLARK, GILLIAN, COSTANTINI, LORENZO, FINETTI, ANGELO, GIORGI, JOHN, JONES, ANDREW, REESE DAVID, SUTHERLAND, SHEILA and WHITEHOUSE DAVID, "The Food Refuse of an Affluent Urban Household in the Late Fourteenth Century: Faunal and Botanical Remains from the Palazzo Vitelleschi, Tarquinia (Viterbo)", *Papers of the British School at Rome*, vol. 57, 1989, pp. 200–32

CORM, GEORGES, "La reconstruction du centre de Beyrouth: Un exemple de fièvre immobilière au Moyen-Orient", *Revue d'économie financière*, vol. 3, no. 1, 1993, pp. 323–35

COULLON, GÉNÉRAL JEAN-CLAUDE, "Beyrouth: Mission de paix, La 31ème Brigade – juin à septembre 1983", *Objectif Doctrine*, Les cahiers du retex, no. 27, 2001, pp. 1–8

DAVIE, MAY, "La formation historique de la place des Canons", Eds. Ghassan Tueni and Fares Sassine, *El Bourj, Place de la liberté et porte du levant*, Beirut, Dar An-Nahar, 2000, pp. 12–17
———, "Pouvoir rural, pouvoir urbain, L'échec de l'État au Liban", *Cahiers de la Méditerranée*, no. 80, 2010, pp. 211–23 (Dynamiques des ports méditerranéens)

DAVIE, MICHAEL F., "A Post-War Urban Geography of Beirut", *1993 Eurames Conference*, Warwick, 1993
———, "'Beyrouth-Est' et 'Beyrouth-Ouest': Territoires confessionnels ou espaces de guerre? Essai d'interprétation", Ed. Michael Davie, *Beyrouth: Regards croisés*, Tours, Centre de Recherches et d'Études sur l'Urbanisation du Monde Arabe (URBAMA), 1997, pp. 17–49
———, "Comment fait-on la guerre à Beyrouth?", *Hérodote*, no. 29/30, 1983, pp. 17–54
———, "La gestion des espaces urbains en temps de guerre, Circuits parallèles à Beyrouth", *Reconstruire Beyrouth, Les paris sur le possible*, Lyon, Maison de l'Orient Méditerranéen, 1991, pp. 157-193 (Études sur le Monde Arabe)
———, "Les marqueurs de territoires idéologiques", Tours, Groupe Eidos et Maison des Sciences de la Ville, 1992
———, "Quelles limites géographiques pour Beyrouth?", Eds. Nabil Beyhum, Assem Salam and Jade Tabet, *Beyrouth: Construire l'avenir, reconstruire le passé?*, Beirut, Dossiers de l'Urban Research Institute, 1995, pp. 30–41 (Proceedings of the symposium organised by the Urban Research Institute in April 1992)

DEBOULET, AGNÈS and HILY, MARIE-ANTOINETTE, "Les migrants de Beyrouth, Emplois à bon marché et zones refuges", *EchoGéo*, no. 8, 2009

DEREZ, MARK, "The Burning of Leuven", Eds. Jo Tollebeek and Eline van Assche, *Ravaged: Art and Culture in Times of Conflict*, Leuven / Brussels, M - Museum Leuven, Mercatorfonds, 2014, pp. 81–5

DESCIMON, ROBERT, "Les barricades de la Fronde parisienne, Une lecture sociologique", *Annales, Histoire, Sciences Sociales* 45e année, no. 2, 1990, pp. 397–422

DIKOMITIS, LISA, "Three Readings of a Border: Greek Cypriots Crossing the Green Line in Cyprus", *Anthropology Today*, vol. 121, no. 5, 2005, pp. 7–12

EDDÉ, CARLA, "Beyrouth, le Mont-Liban et ses environs au XIXe siècle: Pratiques de l'espace, Le cas de la communauté maronite", Ed. Jean-Luc Arnaud, *Beyrouth, Grand Beyrouth*, Beirut, Centre d'études et de recherches sur le Moyen-Orient contemporain, 1997, pp. 35–49 (Les Cahiers du CERMOC no. 16)
———, "La Première Guerre mondiale: Une catastrophe sans précédent au 'Liban'", Ed. Levon NORDIGUIAN, *Les "petites écoles" du Mont-Liban, Joseph Delore, s.j (1873-1944)*, Beirut, Presses de l'Université Saint-Joseph, 2003, pp. 93–100

EL-MASRI, SOUHEIL, "Displacements and Reconstruction: The Case of West Beirut – Lebanon", *Disasters*, vol. 13, no. 4, 1989, pp. 334–44

FAOUR, ALI, "War and Displacement in Lebanon", *Al Mustaqbal Al Arabi*, no. 114, 1988

FATTORE, MARIE-CLAIRE, "Recompositions socio-spatiales avant et après la guerre: Le quartier Mousaytbé", Ed. Jean-Luc Arnaud, *Beyrouth, Grand Beyrouth*, Beirut, Centre d'études et de recherches sur le Moyen-Orient contemporain, 1997, pp. 89–99 (Les Cahiers du CERMOC no. 16)

FAWAZ, MONA, HARB, MONA and GHARBIEH, AHMAD, "Living Beirut's Security Zones: An Investigation of the Modalities and Practice of Urban Security", *City & Society*, vol. 24, no. 2, 2012, pp. 173–95

FITCHETT, JOSEPH, "From Khans to Khiltons", *Saudi Aramco World*, vol. 24, no. 6, 1973, pp. 16–29

FREGONESE, SARA, "Between a Refuge and a Battleground: Beirut's Discrepant Cosmopolitanisms", *Geographical Review*, vol. 102, no. 3, 2012, pp. 316–36

GEBRANE-BADLISSI, ELIANE, "Réfugiés et résidents anciens dans deux quartiers de Beyrouth: Ramlet el-Baïda et Raouché", Ed. Michael Davie, *Beyrouth: regards croisés*, Tours, Centre de Recherches et d'Études sur l'Urbanisation du Monde Arabe (URBAMA), 1997, pp. 127–51

HANSSEN, JENS, "'Malhamé–Malfamé': Levantine Elites and Transimperial Networks on the Eve of the Young Turk Revolution", *International Journal of Middle East Studies*, vol. 43, no. 1, 2011, pp. 25–48

HARRIS, WILLIAM, "Syria in Lebanon", *Middle East Research and Information Project (MERIP) Reports*, no. 134, 1985, pp. 9–14 (Asad's Syria)

KANAFANI-ZAHAR, AÏDA, "La réconciliation du Mont-Liban: La raison d'État et la légalisation communautaire au détriment de la mémoire", Eds. Franck Mermier and Christophe Varin *Mémoires de guerres au Liban, 1975-1990*, Arles, Actes Sud / Sindbad, 2010, pp. 285–312 (La bibliothèque arabe)
———, "Le musée national de Beyrouth: Mémoire des contraires, frontière et passage, échafaud et liberté", Eds. Franck Mermier and Christophe Varin *Mémoires de guerres au Liban, 1975-1990*, Arles, Actes Sud / Sindbad, 2010, pp. 127–33 (La bibliothèque arabe)

KARAMÉ, KARI H., "Maman Aida, a Lebanese Godmother of the Combattants: Fighting Without Arms", Ed. Lamia Rustum Shehade, *Women and War in Lebanon*, Gainesville, University of Florida Press, 1999, pp. 195–208

KEMP, PERCY, "La cité État, Beyrouth entre deux formes de résistance", *Esprit*, vol. 50, no. 5-6, May 1983, pp. 53–67
———, "La stratégie de Bachir Gemayel", *Hérodote*, no. 29/30, 1983, pp. 55–82

KFOURY, LILIANE, "Mémoires de guerre des habitants d'un quartier de Beyrouth, Ras Al-Nabaa", Eds. Franck Mermier and Christophe Varin *Mémoires de guerres au Liban, 1975-1990*, Arles, Actes Sud / Sindbad, 2010, pp. 478–84 (La bibliothèque arabe)

KHATER, AKRAM FOUAD, "'House' to 'Goddess of the House': Gender, Class, and Silk in Nineteenth Century Mount Lebanon", *International Journal of Middle East Studies*, vol. 28, no. 3, 1996, pp. 325–48

KOCACHE, MOUKHTAR, "Up in the Air", *Home Works II: A forum of cultural practices*, Beirut, Ashkal Alwan, 2003, pp. 110–20

LAMLOUM, OLFA, "Retour sur les traces d'un conflit: Amal vs Hezbollah (1988-1990)", Eds. Franck Mermier and Christophe Varin, *Mémoires de guerres au Liban, 1975-1990*, Arles, Actes Sud / Sindbad, 2010, pp. 205–225 (La bibliothèque arabe)

LARKIN, CRAIG, "Remaking Beirut: Contesting Memory, Space, and the Urban Imaginary of Lebanese Youth", *City & Community*, vol. 9, no. 4, 2010, pp. 414–42

LAVIE, AVIV, "Never, Never Land: On Khiam Prison in Southern Lebanon", *Middle East Report*, no. 203, 1997, pp. 34–37 (Lebanon and Syria: The Geopolitics of Change)

"Lebanon a Year Later: The Crisis Deepens", *Middle East Research and Information Project (MERIP) Reports*, no. 30, 1974, pp. 26–8

MAALOUF, LYNN, "Les disparitions forcées au Liban: L'héritage immuable d'une nation", Eds. Franck Mermier and Christophe Varin, *Mémoires de guerres au Liban, 1975-1990*, Arles, Actes Sud / Sindbad, 2010, pp. 265–84 (La bibliothèque arabe)

MOUAOUAD, YOUSSEF, "1914-1918 ou la guerre de la famine", Ed. Levon Nordiguian, *Les "petites écoles" du Mont-Liban, Joseph Delore, s.j (1873-1944)*, Beirut, Presses de l'Université Saint-Joseph, 2003, pp. 100–107

MARTHELOT, P., "Une ville remplit son site: Beyrouth", *Méditerranée*, vol. 4, no. 3, 1963, pp. 37–56

MØYSTAD, OLE, "Morphogenesis of the Beirut Green-Line", *Cahiers de géographie du Québec*, vol. 42, no. 117, 1998, pp. 421–435

NASR, SALIM, "Backdrop to Civil War: The Crisis of Lebanese Capitalism", *Middle East Research and Information Project (MERIP) Reports*, no. 73, 1978, pp. 3–13

NIVET, PHILIPPE, "Tourisme de guerre", Eds. Claire Garnier and Laurent Le Bon, *1917*, Metz, Centre Pompidou-Metz, 2012, pp. 276–77

OLIVER SAIDI, MARIE-THÉRÈSE, "La ligne verte de Beyrouth 1975-1991", *Guerres mondiales et conflits contemporains*, no. 190, 1998, pp. 43–60

PAPASTAMKOU, SOFIA, "De la crise au Liban au mémorandum du 17 septembre 1958: La politique étrangère de la France entre deux Républiques et une guerre", *Matériaux pour l'histoire de notre temps*, vol. 99, no. 3, 2010, pp. 76–83

PERETZ, DON, "The Arab Refugee Dilemma", *Foreign Affairs; an American Quarterly Review*, vol. 33, no. 1, 1954, pp. 134–47

PHARÈS, JOSEPH and BOURGEY, ANDRÉ, "Les bidonvilles de l'agglomération de Beyrouth", *Revue de géographie de Lyon*, vol. 48, no. 2, 1973, pp. 107–39

RICHARD, THIBAULT, "Les batteries fixes d'artillerie côtière allemande pendant la seconde guerre mondiale dans le cotentin: Principes de construction et choix des sites", *Guerres mondiales et conflits contemporains*, no. 165, 1992, pp. 43–51

RICHET, DENIS, et LAPEYRE, MARIE-CLAUDE, "Les barricades à Paris, le 12 mai 1588", *Annales, Histoire, Sciences Sociales* 45e année, no. 2, 1990, pp. 383–95

Rustum Shehadeh, Lamia, "Women in the Public Sphere", Ed. Lamia Rustum Shehadeh, *Women & War in Lebanon*, Gainesville, University Press of Florida, 1999, pp. 45–70

Saab, Édouard, "L'appel du vide", *L'Orient-Le Jour*, 8 May 1975, p. 1
———, "Le Liban face à lui-même, I- Ces camps qui ceinturent les villes", *L'Orient-Le Jour*, 7 June 1975, pp. 1, 6

Sassine, Fares, "Modernisme et folklore, Les cinémas du Bourj", Eds. Ghassan Tueni and Fares Sassine, *El Bourj, Place de la liberté et porte du levant*, Beirut, Dar An-Nahar, 2000, pp. 28–45

Sfeir-Khayat, Jihane, "Beyrouth au milieu du XIXe siècle: Naissance d'un centre", Ed. Jean-Luc Arnaud, *Beyrouth, Grand Beyrouth*, Beirut, Centre d'études et de recherches sur le Moyen-Orient contemporain, 1997, pp. 51–62

Shiblak, Abbas, "Residency Status and Civil Rights of Palestinian Refugees in Arab Countries", *Journal of Palestine Studies*, vol. 25, no. 3, 1996, pp. 36-45

Slaiby, Ghassan, "Les actions collectives de résistance civile à la guerre", Ed. Fadia Kiwan, *Le Liban aujourd'hui*, Paris, CNRS Éditions, 1994, pp. 119–36

St, Aubin, W., de, "Peace and Refugees in the Middle East", *Middle East Journal*, vol. 3, no. 3, 1949, pp. 249–59

Soliman, Ahmed M, "Diversity of Ethnicity and State Involvement on Urban Informality in Beirut", *Theoretical and Empirical Researches in Urban Management*, vol. 3, no. 9, 2008, pp. 15–32

Théry, Marc de La Gorce, Paul-Marie, Dabezies, Pierre, Thobie, Jacques and Coullon, Général Jean-Claude, "La force multilatérale d'interposition (FMI, 1982) puis de sécurité (FMSB, 1983-1984) à Beyrouth", *Guerres mondiales et conflits contemporains*, no. 168, 1992, pp. 101–11

Toubi, Jamal, "Social Dynamics in War Torn Lebanon", *The Jerusalem Quarterly*, no. 17, 1980, pp. 83–109

Traboulsi, Fawwaz, "Société violente ou système de guerre?" Ed. Jean Hannoyer, *Guerres civiles:* Économie de la violence - Dimensions de la civilité, Paris, Karthala, 1999, pp. 139–152 (Hommes et sociétés)

Traugott, Mark, "Barricades as Repertoire: Continuities and Discontinuities in the History of French Contention", *Social Science History*, vol. 17, no. 2, 1993, pp. 309–23

Van de Sompel, Ronald, "Out of the Libraries Emerge the Butchers", Ed. Ronald Van de Sompel *Arts and Culture in Times of Conflict, Contemporary Reflections*, Leuven, Mousse Publishing, Museum Leuven, 2014, pp. 12–35

Weizman, Eyal, "The Art of War", *Frieze*, no. 99, 2006

Žižek, Slavoj, "The Non-Existence of Norway, Slavoj Žižek on the refugee crisis", *London Review of Books*, 9 September 2015

2.c. Dissertations and theses

Brones, Sophie, "Beyrouth et ses ruines (1990-2010), Une approche anthropologique", doctoral thesis, Paris, Université Paris X, 2010

Davie, May, "La millat grecque-orthodoxe de Beyrouth 1800-1940", doctoral thesis, Paris, Université Paris IV Sorbonne, 1993

Halabi, Mohamad-Bassim, "Illegitimate Settlements in West Beirut: A Manipulation of Tenure Policies and Class Struggle over Land", Masters dissertation, Cambridge, Massachusetts, Massachusetts Institute of Technology, 1988

3. ARCHITECTURE AND TOWN PLANNING

3.a. Works

ABOUSSOUAN, CAMILLE, *Architecture Libanaise du XVe au XIXe siècle*, Beirut, Cahiers de l'Est, 1985

AKL, ZIAD and BEYHUM, NABIL (Eds.), *Conquérir et reconquérir la ville, L'aménagement urbain comme positionnement des pouvoirs et contre-pouvoirs*, Beirut, Académie Libanaise des Beaux-Arts, 2009

AKL, ZIAD and DAVIE, MICHAEL (Eds.), *Questions sur le patrimoine architectural et urbain au Liban*, Tours, Centre de Recherches et d'Études sur l'Urbanisation du Monde Arabe (URBAMA), 1997 (Villes du Monde Arabe no. 2)

ALMARCEGUI, LARA, *Vacant Buildings in the Hotel District, Beirut*, Genève, Attitudes, 2012

ANDRIEUX, JEAN-YVES (Ed.), *Patrimoine: Sources et paradoxes de la modernité*, Rennes, Presses Universitaires de Rennes, 2011, (Art & Société)

ARBID, GEORGES (Ed.), *Fundamentalists and Other Arab Modernisms, Kingdom of Bahrain National Participation, 14th International Architecture Exhibition, la Biennale di Venezia*, Venice, Ministry of Culture, Kingdom of Bahrain, 2014

BODENSTEIN, RALPH, *Villen in Beirut, Wohnkultur und sozialer Wandel 1860–1930*, Petersberg, Imhof Verlag, 2012

CHING, FRANCIS D., JARZOMBEK, MARK M. and PRAKASH, VIKRAMADITYA, *A Global History of Architecture*, New York, John Wiley & Sons, 2007

COHEN, JEAN-LOUIS, *Architecture in Uniform: Designing and Building for the Second World War*, New Haven, Yale University Press, 2011

DAVIE, MAY, *Beyrouth 1825-1975: Un siècle et demi d'urbanisme*, Beirut, Ordre des Ingénieurs et Architectes de Beyrouth, 2001
———, *Beyrouth et ses faubourgs (1840-1940), une intégration inachevée*, Beirut, Centre d'études et de recherches sur le Moyen-Orient contemporain, 1996 (Les Cahiers du CERMOC: Études Urbaines no. 15)

DAVIE, MICHAEL (Ed.), *La maison beyrouthine aux trois arcs: Une architecture bourgeoise du Levant*, Beirut / Tours, Académie Libanaise des Beaux-Arts (ALBA), Institut d'Urbanisme, Centre de Recherches et d'Études sur l'Urbanisation du Monde Arabe (URBAMA), 2003

DEBRAY, RÉGIS (Ed.), *L'abus monumental? Actes des entretiens du patrimoine: Théâtre national de Chaillot, Paris, 23, 24 et 25 novembre 1998*, Paris, Fayard, 1999

ETTINGHAUSEN, RICHARD and GRABAR, OLEG, *The Art and Architecture of Islam 650–-1250*, The Pelican History of Art, London, Penguin Books, 1987

FISCHFISCH, ANTOINE, *Formes urbaines et architecturales de Beyrouth (depuis le XIXe siècle jusqu'à nos jours)*, Beirut, Académie Libanaise des Beaux-Arts (ALBA), 2011

FOURNIÉ, PIERRE and AMMOUN, DENISE, *La Résidence des Pins, Beyrouth*, ACR Édition, Paris, Courbevoie, 1999

GINSBERG, ROBERT, *The Aesthetics of Ruins*, Amsterdam / New York, Rodopi, 2004

GRAHAM, STEPHEN, *Cities Under Siege: The New Military Urbanism*, New York, Verso, 2011

GUMPERT, MATTHEW and TOUFIC, JALAL (Eds.) *Thinking: The Ruin*, Istanbul, Istanbul Studies Center, 2010

HADJITHOMAS MEHANNA, TANIA, *Le Phoenicia, un hôtel dans l'Histoire*, Beirut, Tamyras, 2012

HARBISON, ROBERT, *The Built, the Unbuilt and the Unbuildable: In pursuit of Architectural Meaning*, 3rd edition, Cambridge, Massachusetts, MIT Press, 1991

KFOURY, SEMAAN, *Maisons Libanaises*, 1st edition, Beirut, Académie Libanaise des Beaux-Arts (ALBA), 1999

KHALAF, SAMIR and KHOURY, PHILIP SHUKRY, *Recovering Beirut: Urban Design and Post-War Reconstruction*, Leiden, Brill, 1993

KHOURY, BERNARD, *Bernard Khoury: Local Heroes*, Milan, Skira, 2015

KOZAH, FOUAD KAMAL, *Chroniques du Levant: Mémoires d'un architecte libanais*, Paris, L'Harmattan, 2010

PICON, ANTOINE (Ed.), *La ville et la guerre*, Besançon, Éditions de l'Imprimeur, 1996 (Tranches de villes)

SALIBA, ROBERT, *Beirut 1920-1940. Domestic Architecture Between Tradition and Modernity*, Beirut, The Order of Engineers and Architects, 1998

SEYRIG, HENRI, AMY, ROBERT and WILL, ERNEST, *Le temple de Bel à Palmyre*, vol. 2, Paris, Librairie Orientaliste Paul Geuthner, 1975 (Institut Français d'Archéologie de Beyrouth, Bibliothèque archéologique et historique, LXXXIII)

TABET, JADE, GHORAYEB, MARLÈNE, HUYBRECHTS, ÉRIC and VERDEIL, ÉRIC, *Beyrouth*, Paris, Institut Français d'Architecture, 2001 (Portrait de ville)

TER MINASSIAN, TALINE (Ed.), *Patrimoine & Architecture dans les États Post-Soviétiques*, Rennes, Presses Universitaires de Rennes, 2013 (Art & Société)

VIRILIO, PAUL, *Bunker Archaeology*, Trans. George Collins, New York, Princeton Architechtural Press, 1994

YACOUB, GEBRAN, *Dictionnaire de l'Architecture au Liban au XXe siècle*, Beirut, Alphamedia, 2003

YOUNES, HALA (ed.), *The Place That Remains. Recounting the Unbuilt Territory*, Milan, Skira, 2018

ZUMTHOR, PETER, *Penser l'architecture*, 2nd edition, Basel, Birkhaüser, 2010

3.b. Articles, book chapters, Conference papers

Abou-Hodeib, Toufoul, "Taste and Class in Late Ottoman Beirut", *International Journal of Middle East Studies*, vol. 43, no. 3, 2011, pp. 475–92

Aftimus, Youssef, "Le nouvel art de la construction est un art économique", *Télégraphe Bayrout*, no. 1086, 25–26 November 1948

Amaya-Akkermans, Arie, "Beirut: Reinventing or Destroying the Public Space?", *Hannah Arendt Center for Politics and Humanities*, 23 May 2012

Andrieux, Jean-Yves, "Patrimoine: La dialectique de la nation et du monde, de l'universel et du local", Ed. Jean-Yves ANDRIEUX, *Patrimoine, Sources et paradoxes de la modernité*, Rennes Presses Universitaires de Rennes, 2011, pp. 7–10

Ballard, J., G., "A Handful of Dust", *The Guardian*, 20 March 2006

Beyhum, Nabil, "Le désert au cœur de la ville, ou les nouvelles conceptions dans l'urbanisme du Moyen-Orient", Eds. Nabil Beyhum, Assem Salam and Jade Tabet, *Beyrouth: Construire l'avenir, reconstruire le passé ?*, Beirut, Dossiers de l'Urban Research Institute, 1995, pp. 59–68 (Proceedings of the symposium organised by the Urban Research Institute in April 1992)
———, "Le rôle du symbolisme dans la planification urbaine: Le cas de la place des Canons", Eds. Ziad Akl and Nabil Beyhum, *Conquérir et reconquérir la ville: L'aménagement urbain comme positionnement des pouvoirs et contre-pouvoirs*, Beirut, Académie Libanaise des Beaux-Arts, 2009, pp. 145–62

Bodenstein, Ralph, "Housing the Foreign, A European's Exotic Home in Late Nineteenth-Century Beirut", *Beiruter Texte und Studien*, no. 88, 2002, pp. 105–27

Brones, Sophie, "Ruines en attente", Eds. Franck Mermier and Christophe Varin, *Mémoires de guerres au Liban, 1975-1990*, Arles, Actes Sud / Sindbad, 2010, pp. 457–77 (La bibliothèque arabe)

Chakar, Tony, "The Suburbs and the Vocabulary of Urbanization: Violence as an Architectural Language", Ed. Catherine David, *Tamáss, Contemporary Arab Representations: Beirut / Lebanon 1*, Barcelona, Fundació Antoni Tàpies, 2002, pp. 40–55

Davie, May, "Aperçu historique", Eds. Joanna Andraos and Caroline Tabet, *290 rue du Liban*, Beirut, Engram, 2010, pp. 62–3
———, "Bayrut Al-Qadimat: Une ville arabe et sa banlieue, à la fin du XVIIIe siècle", *National Museum News*, no. 3, 1996
———, "La construction nationale et l'héritage ottoman au Liban", Maison de l'Orient et de la Méditerranée, Lyon, Université Lumière 2, Lyon et CNRS, 2009
———, "Les peintres et l'habitat à Beyrouth entre 1800 et 1900", Ed. Sylvia Agémian, *Regards sur Beyrouth, 160 ans d'images 1800-1960*, Beirut, Sursock Museum, 2013, pp. 35–38

Debray, Régis, "Trace, forme ou message ?", Ed. Regis Debray, *L'abus monumental? Actes des entretiens du patrimoine: Théâtre national de Chaillot, Paris, 23, 24 et 25 novembre 1998*, Paris, Fayard, 1999, pp. 27–44

Dillon, Brian, "Decline and Fall, Tracing the History of Ruins in Art, from 18th-century painting to 21st-century film", *Frieze*, 2000

du Mesnil du Buisson, Robert, "Les anciennes défenses de Beyrouth", *Syria*, vol. 2, no. Section 4, 1921, pp. 317–27

Erlanger, Steven, "Nuremberg Journal: The Architect Who Speared His Own Nazi Demon", *The New York Times*, 8 November 2001

Gebrane-Badlissi, Eliane, "Patrimoine urbain à Beyrouth après la guerre: Entre modernité et tradition", *Confluences Méditerranée*, no. 24, 1997, pp. 139–52

Hage-Boutros, Pierre, "L'oubli de l'oubli, Réflexions suite à l''Hommage au Grand Théâtre de Beyrouth'", Atelier de Recherche ALBA, 1997

Haidar, Mazen and Rayess, Akram, "Public Sounds, Private Spaces: Towards a Fairouz Museum in Zokak el-Blat", Eds. Nadia von Maltzahn and Monique Bellan, *Divercities: Competing Narratives and Urban Practices in Beirut, Cairo and Tehran*, Beirut, Orient-Institut Beirut, 2015

Hertweck, Florian, "Le problème de la reconstruction à l'identique, Le cas de Berlin", Paris, Sorbonne, Abu Dhabi, 2008 (Les héritages culturels dans l'architecture et l'urbanisme au XXIe siècle)

Hild, Theodore W., "The Demolition of the Garrick Theater and the Birth of the Preservation Movement in Chicago", *Illinois Historical Journal*, vol. 88, no. 2, 1995, pp. 79–100

Leary, John Patrick, "Detroitism", *Guernica*, 15 January 2011

Lteif, Diala, "Framing Barakat", *Transblog / Parsons*, 15 December 2011

Makdisi, Saree, "Laying Claim to Beirut: Urban Narrative and Spatial Identity in the Age of Solidere", *Critical Inquiry*, vol. 23, no. 3, 1997, pp. 660–705 (Front Lines / Border Posts)
———, "Reconstructing History in Central Beirut", *Middle East Report*, no. 203, Lebanon and Syria: The Geopolitics of Change, 1997, pp. 23–5 & 30

Medawar, Alexandre, "290 rue du Liban", Ed. Joanna ANDRAOS and Caroline TABET, *290 rue du Liban*, Beirut, Engram, 2010, pp. 6–7

Naeff, Judith, "Disposable Architecture Reinterpreting Ruins in the Age of Globalization: the Case of Beirut", Eds. Christoph Lindner, Miriam Meissner, *Global Garbage: Urban Imaginaries of Waste, Excess, and Abandonment*, Londres/New York, Routledge, 2016, p. 220-260

Papini, Massimiliano, "Construire du neuf, conserver l'ancien: Les destructions dans la Rome antique", Eds. Monica Preti and Salvatore Settis, *Villes en ruine: Images, mémoires, métamorphoses*, Paris, Hazan / Musée du Louvre, 2015, pp. 150–67

Picq, Anne, "Beyrouth, L'immeuble palimpseste", *Beaux-Arts Magazine*, no. 236, 2004, p. 54

Prost, Philippe, "La ville et la guerre de Vauban à Napoléon Ier", Ed. Antoine Picon, *La ville et la guerre*, Besançon, Éditions de l'Imprimeur, 1996, pp. 89–121 (Tranches de villes)

Rustom, Joseph, "The White Pavilions of Interwar Beirut", *Bauhaus Now*, no. 1, November 2017, p. 106-109.

Saito, Hiro, "Reiterated Commemoration: Hiroshima as National Trauma", *Sociological Theory*, vol. 24, no. 4, 2006, pp. 353-376

Shulman, Robin, "Postwar Beirut Debates How Much to Remember, City Acquires Symbol of Its Culture, Its Warfare", *Washington Post*, 23 October 2004, sect. A, p. 14

Stoughton, India, "The Scars of War on Lebanon's Holiday Inn", *Al Jazeera*, 30 December 2015

Tabet, Jade, "Des pierres dans la mémoire", Ed. Jade TABET, *Beyrouth: La brûlure des rêves*, Paris, Autrement, 2001, pp. 65–73 (Monde no. 127)

Ter Minassian, Taline, "La restauration soviétique du temple antique de Garni (Arménie): Un paradigme patrimonial?", *Patrimoine & Architecture dans les États Post-Soviétiques*, Rennes, Presses Universitaires de Rennes, 2013, pp. 25–43

Toufic, Jalal, "Ruins", Ed. Catherine David, *Tamáss, Contemporary Arab Representations: Beirut / Lebanon 1*, Barcelona: Fundació Antoni Tàpies, 2002, pp. 19–25

Verdeil, Éric, "Reconstructions et politiques du patrimoine urbain au Liban", Ed. Philippe Boulanger and Cécile Hullo-Pouyat, *Espaces urbains à l'aube du XXIe siècle: Patrimoine et héritages culturels*, Paris, Presses de l'Université Paris-Sorbonne, 2010, pp. 65–73
———, "Reconstructions manquées à Beyrouth", *Les annales de la recherche urbaine*, no. 91, 2001, pp. 65–73 (Villes et guerres)

Zada, John, "Hallak on 'Beit Beirut'", *The Planisphere*, 8 December 2012

3.c. Dissertations and theses

Bodenstein, Ralph, "Qasr Heneiné, Memories and History of a Late Ottoman Mansion in Beirut", Masters dissertatior, Bonn, Rheinischen Friedrich Wilhelms-Universität, 1999

Jallad, Mayssa, "Beirut's Civil War Hotel District: Preserving the World's First High-Rise Urban Battlefield", Masters dissertatior, New York, Columbia University, 2017

Verdeil, Éric, "Une ville et ses urbanistes: Beyrouth en reconstruction", doctoral thesis, Paris, Université Panthéon-Sorbonne – Paris I, 2002

4. ARTISTIC AND VISUAL PRATICES

4.a. Works and exhibition catalogues

Agémian, Sylvia, Daher, Gabriel, Davie, May, Davie, Michael F., Hallak, Hassan, Khoury, Gérard D. and Moubarak, Samir, *Regards sur Beyrouth, 160 ans d'images 1800-1960*, Beirut, Sursock Museum, 2013

Al-Qasimi, Hoor (Ed.), *Two Suns in a Sunset / Se souvenir de la lumière*, London / Sharjah, Koenig Books, Sharjah Art Foundation, 2016

Amaya-Akkermans, Arie, *Samar Mogharbel, Without Traces*, Beirut, Agial Art Gallery, 2015

Andraos, Joanna and Tabet, Caroline, *290 rue du Liban*, Beirut, Engram, 2010

Arzoumanian, Chaghig, *On Fools and Lands*, Beirut, 2017

Baassiri, Dalia, *Wiped Off*, Beirut, Galerie Janine Rubeiz, 2017

Barakat, Saleh and Sadek, Walid, *The Road to Peace: Painting in Times of War 1975–1991*, Beirut, Beirut Art Center, Alarm, 2009

Basilico, Gabriele, *Beirut 1991 (2003)*, Milan, Baldini Castoldi Dalai Editore, 2008

Basilico, Gabriele and Elkoury, Fouad, *Beirut in Ruins: A Flashback*, Beirut, Solidere, s.d.

Beauvais, Lydia and Méjanès, Jean-François, *Le Brun à Versailles*, Paris, Réunion des Musées Nationaux, 1985 (Expositions du Cabinet des dessins no. 85)

Buchakjian, Gregory, *War and Other (Impossible) Possibilities, Thoughts on Arab History and Contemporary Art*, Beirut, Alarm, 2012

Buchakjian, Gregory, Cottard Hachem, Clemence (ed.), *Traversées photographiques. Le journal du Docteur Cottard*, Beirut, Arab Image Foundation, 2017

Buchakjian, Gregory, Elkoury, Fouad and Khader, Manal, *Passing Time*, Beirut, Kaph, 2017

Buchakjian, Gregory and Tadros, Sary, *Hanibal Srouji: Peindre le feu, l'eau, la terre, la mer*, Beirut, Galerie Janine Rubeiz and Les éditions de L'Orient-Le Jour, 2013

Campany, David, *Dust: Histoires de poussière d'après Man Ray et Marcel Duchamp*, Paris, Le Bal / MACK Books, 2015
———, *Jeff Wall: Picture for Women*, London: Afterall Books, 2011

Cardinal, Philippe and Makram-Ebeid, Hoda (Eds.), *Le corps découvert*, Paris, Hazan, Institut du Monde Arabe, 2012

Chakhtoura, Maria, *Liban 1975-1978: La guerre des graffiti*, Beirut, Dar An-Nahar, 1978

Chevrier, Jean-François, *Jeff Wall*, Paris, Hazan, 2006

Cheval, François (Ed.), "Les heures immobiles - Saida - Bab el-Saray - Photographies anciennes du Moyen-Orient & documents de Jean-Luc Moulène", Chalon-sur-Saône, Nicéphore Niepce Museum, 2002

Cottard-Hachem, Clemence, Salame, Nour (ed.), *On Photography in Lebanon. Essays & Stories.* Beirut, Kaph Books, 2018

Cotter, Suzanne (Ed.), *Out of Beirut*, Oxford, JRP|Ringier, Modern Art Oxford, 2007

Criqui, Jean-Pierre (Ed.), *L'image déjà là: Usages de l'objet trouvé, photographie et cinéma*, Paris, Le Bal, Images en manœuvres, 2011 (Les carnets du Bal no. 2)

David, Catherine (Ed.), *Documenta X - the book*, Kassel, Documenta, Museum Fridericianum Veranstaltung, 1997
———, *Tamáss, Contemporary Arab Representations: Beirut / Lebanon 1*, Barcelona, Fundació Antoni Tàpies, 2002

Debbas, Fouad, *Beyrouth, notre mémoire : Promenade guidée à travers une collection de cartes postales anciennes*, Paris, Henri Berger, 1994

Depardon, Raymond, *Beyrouth centre-ville*, Paris, Points, 2010

Dirié, Clément and Thériault, Michèle, *Joana Hadjithomas & Khalil Joreige*, Zurich, JRP|Ringier, 2013

Demos, T.J., *The Migrant Image: The Art and Politics of Documentary During Global Crisis*, Durham, N.C., Duke University Press, 2013

Eddé, Dominique (Ed.), *Beyrouth Centre Ville/Beirut City Centre*, Paris, Éditions du Cyprès, 1992

Elkoury, Fouad, *Be...Longing*, Göttingen, Steidl, 2011
———, *La Sagesse du Photographe*, Le Vesinet, L'œil neuf éditions, 2004 (Sagesse d'un métier)
———, *Liban Provisoire*, Paris, Hazan, 1998

Enwezor, Okwui (Ed.), *All the World's Futures: 56 International Art Exhibition, La Biennale di Venezia*, Venice, Marislio Editori, 2015

Ferrari, Jérôme and Rohe, Oliver, À fendre le cœur le plus dur, Paris, Inculte, 2015 (Dernière image)

Frank, Robert, *Come Again*, Göttingen, Steidl, 2006

Fontcuberta, Joan, *Le baiser de Judas, Photographie et vérité*, Arles, Actes Sud, 2005

Fortini, Marcel, *L'esthétique des ruines dans la photographie de guerre: Beyrouth centre-ville, une commande exemplaire*, Paris, L'Harmattan, 2014 (Retina)

Garnier, Claire and Le Bon, Laurent (Eds.), *1917*, Metz, Centre Pompidou-Metz, 2014

Hadjithomas, Joana and Joreige, Khalil, Ed. Karl Bassil, *Beyrouth: Fictions Urbaines*, Beirut, Mind the Gap Editions, 1997

Hage, Gilbert and Toufic, Jalal, *Toufican Ruins?* Beirut, Underexposed, 2010

Hajj Ali, Hanane, *Tiyâtr Bayrut (Le Théâtre de Beyrouth)*, Beirut, Amers, 2010

Issa, Rose (Ed.), *Ayman Baalbaki: Beirut Again and Again*, London, Rose Issa Projects, 2011

Joreige, Lamia, *Under-Writing Beirut - Mathaf*, Beirut, Sharjah Art Foundation, 2013
——— (ed.), *Lamia Joreige. Works 1994-2017*. Beirut, Kaph Books, 2018

Jousse, Thierry and Paquot, Thierry, *La ville au cinéma : Encyclopédie*, Paris, Les Cahiers du Cinéma, 2005

Kassatly, Houda, *De pierre et de couleur, vie et mort des maisons du vieux Beyrouth*, Beirut, Layali, 1999
____. *Beyrouth : l'iconographie d'une absence*, Beirut, Al Ayn, 2010

Khatib, Lina, *Lebanese Cinema: Imagining the Civil War and Beyond*, London / New York, I.B. Tauris, 2008 (Tauris World Cinema Series)

Maasri, Zeina, *Off the Wall: Political Posters of the Lebanese Civil War*, London / New York, I.B. Tauris, 2009

Makarius, Michael, *Ruines*, Paris, Flammarion, 2004

Manoukian, Aline (éd.), *Seta Manoukian. Painting in Levitation.* Beirut, Kaph Books, Saradar Collection

Marks, Laura U., *Hanan al-Cinema, Affections for the Moving Image*, Cambridge, Massachusetts, MIT Press, 2015

Mejcher-Atassi, Sonja and Schwartz, John Pedro (Eds.), *Archives, Museums and Collecting Practices in the Modern Arab World*, Farnham, Ashgate, 2012

Mével, Quentin, *Le cinéma de Joana Hadjithomas & Khalil Joreige*, Paris, Independencia, 2013 (Les Petits Entretiens)

Mirza, Randa, *Parallel Universes and Beirutopia*, London, Oodee, 2015 (POV Female / Beirut)

Moure, Gloria, *Gordon Matta-Clark: Works and Collected Writings*, Barcelona, Ediciones Polígrafa, 2006 (20_21)

Munro, John, *Giesen's Lebanon*, Beirut, The Rihani House, 1984

Pamuk, Orhan, *The Innocence of Objects*, New York, Harry N. Abrams, 2012

Polidori, Robert, *Some Points in Between ... Up Till Now*, Göttingen, Steidl, 2010

Preti, Monica and Settis, Salvatore (Eds.), *Villes en ruine : Images, mémoires, métamorphoses*, Paris, Hazan, Musée du Louvre, 2015

Raad, Walid, *The Truth Will be Known When the Last Witness is Dead: Documents from the Fakhouri File in the Atlas Group Archive*, vol. 1, Noisy-le-Sec, Aubervilliers, Cologne, La Galerie de Noisy-le-Sec, Les Laboratoires d'Aubervilliers, Verlag der Buchhandlung Walther König, 2004

Rechmaoui, Marwan, *Metropolis*, Beirut, Kaph Books, 2017

Respini, Eva, *Walid Raad*, New York, The Museum of Modern Art, 2015

Rieffel, Véronique, *Islamania, de l'Alhambra à la burqa, histoire d'une fascination artistique*, Issy-les-Moulineaux, Beaux Arts Éditions, 2011

Ristelhueber, Sophie, *Beyrouth photographies*, Paris, Hazan, 1984

Rouxel, Mathilde, *Jocelyne Saab, La mémoire indomptée*, Beirut, Dar An-Nahar, 2015

Sadek, Walid, *The Ruin to Come*, Taipei, Motto Books and Taipei Biennale, 2016

Salamé, Nour and Tomb, Marie, *L'art au Liban : Artistes Modernes et Contemporains, 1880-1975*, Beirut, Wonderful Éditions, 2012

Salti, Rasha and Antar, Ziad, *Beirut Bereft: The architecture of the Forsaken and Map of the Derelict*, Sharjah, Sharjah Art Foundation, 2010

Sargologo, François, *Beyrouth Empire: Sunduq al-aja'ib*, Beirut, Galerie Janine Rubeiz, 2018

Tabet, Caroline, *Disintegrated Objects*, London, Oodee, 2015 (POV Female / Beirut)

Tabet, Lara, *The Reeds*, London, Oodee, 2015 (POV Female / Beirut)

Tamraz, Nayla (Ed.), "Littérature, art et monde contemporain: Récits, histoire, mémoire", *Proceedings of the symposium organised by the Department of French Literature and the Masters in Art Criticism and Curatorial Studies of Saint Joseph University of Beirut on 16 and 17 May 2014*, 290, Beirut, Presses de l'Université Saint-Joseph, 2015

Tarazi, Camille, *Vitrine de l'Orient, Maison Tarazi, fondée à Beyrouth en 1862*, Beirut, Éditions de la Revue Phénicienne, 2015

Tollebeek, Jo and van Assche, Eline (Ed.), *RavagEd: Art and Culture in Times of Conflict*, Leuven, Brussels, M - Museum Leuven, Mercatorfonds, 2014

Traboulsi, Katya (Ed.), *Generation War*, Beirut, Tamyras, 2013

Van de Sompel, Ronald (Ed.), *Arts and Culture in Times of Conflict: Contemporary Reflections*, Louven, Mousse Publishing, Museum Leuven, 2014

Varnedoe, Kirk and Gopnik, Adam, *High and Low: Modern Art and Popular Culture*, New York, The Museum of Modern Art, 1990

Wehbe, Karine (Ed.), *Stop Here for Happy Holidays: An Investigation into the Beach Resorts of the North Littoral in Lebanon*, Beirut, Sharjah Art Foundation, 2017

Yacoub, Paola and Lasserre, Michel, *Beyrouth est une ville magnifique: Tableaux synoptiques*, Barcelona, Fundació Antoni Tàpies, 2002

Young, Tom and Tarrab, Joseph, *At the Rose House*, Beirut, 2014

Zaatari, Akram (ed.), *Against Photography, an annotated history of the Arab Image Foundation*, Barcelona / Beirut, MACBA, Kaph Books, 2018
____. *Akram Zaatari: Earth of Endless Secrets*, Beirut / Frankfurt, Beirut Art Center, Portikus, 2009

4.b. Articles, book chapters, conference papers

Abi Khalil, Amanda, "Mémoire individuelle, mémoire collective et historique dans les pratiques artistiques contemporaines au Liban", Ed. Nayla Tamraz, *Proceedings of the symposium organised by the Department of French Literature and the Masters in Art Criticism and Curatorial Studies of Saint Joseph University of Beirut on 16 and 17 May 2014*, Beirut, Presses de l'Université Saint-Joseph, 2015, pp. 111–20

Abouzeid, Rania, "Violence, Camouflaged: Portraits of Lebanese Women", *The New Yorker*, 7 May 2015

Amaya-Akkermans, Arie, "No Longer and Not Yet", *The Mantle*, 26 August 2013

Baumann, Stefanie, "Archiver ce qui aurait pu avoir lieu", *Conserveries mémorielles*, no. 6, La Part de fiction dans les images documentaires, 2009

Ben-Ghiat, Ruth, "Un cinéma d'après-guerre: Le néoréalisme italien et la transition démocratique", *Annales, Histoire, Sciences Sociales*, vol. 63, no. 6, 2008, pp. 1215–48

Bertho, Raphaelle, "Beyrouth par Basilico, ou la possibilité d'une ville", *Territoire des images*, 8 April 2015

Buchakjian, Gregory, "Beirut by Night: A Century of Nightlife Photography", *Middle East Journal for Culture and Communication*, vol. 8, no. 2–3, 2015, pp. 256–81
———, "Une Venus et un tas de chiffons", *Michelangelo Pistoletto in Beirut*, Beirut, Beirut Exhibition Center, Galerie Tanit, Galleria Continua and Citadellarte-Fondazione Pistoletto, 2014, pp. 16–17
———, "The Lives and Deaths of Inhabitants in Abandoned Houses", *OAR: The Oxford Artistic and Practice Based Research Platform*, no. 2, 2017 (Validity)

Buchloh, Benjamin, Chevrier, Jean-François and David, Catherine, "1960–1997, The Political Potential of Art", Ed. Catherine David, *Documenta X - the book*, Kassel, Documenta, Museum Fridericianum Veranstaltung, 1997, pp. 374–403, 624–43

Colberg, Jörg, "A Conversation with Dalia Khamissy", *Conscentious ExtendEd*. 18 May 2010

Cornet, Laurence, "Collapsing Clouds of Gas and Dust Vartan Avakian at Marfa'", *Ibraaz*, n0009_05, 25 November 2015

Cotter, Suzanne, "Beirut Unbound", Ed. Suzanne Cotter, *Out of Beirut*, Oxford, JRP|Ringier / Modern Art Oxford, 2007, pp. 25–34

Delacampagne, Christian, "À propos de *Machines Célibataires*", Atelier de Recherche ALBA, 22 September 2000

De Font-Réaulx, Dominique, "Photographier la catastrophe: Enregistrement et mise en scène au XIXe siècle", Eds. Monica Preti and Salvatore Settis, *Villes en ruine: Images, mémoires, métamorphoses*, Paris, Hazan / Musée du Louvre, 2015, pp. 260–75

de le Court, Isabelle, "Wounded Places: Architecture and Landscape in the Photographic Work of Paola Yacoub (2000–2001)", *Contemporary French and Francophone Studies*, vol. 18, no. 5, 2014, pp. 568-576

Dobey, Peter and Amaya-Akkermans, Arie, "Gezi Park: One Year Later", *San Francisco Arts Quarterly*, no. 17, 2014, pp. 38-41

Dussaud, René, "Le peintre Montfort en Syrie (1837-1838)", *Syria*, vol. 1, 1920, pp. 58–71

Farhat, May, "A Mediterraneanist's Collection: Henri Pharaon's 'Treasure House of Arab Art'", *Ars Orientalis*, vol. 42, 2012, pp. 103–13

Foster, Hal, "An Archival Impulse", *October*, no. 110, 2004, p. 3–22

Joreige, Lamia, "Here and Perhaps Elsewhere", Ed. Suzanne Cotter, *Out of Beirut*, Oxford, JRP|Ringier / Modern Art Oxford, 2007, pp. 18–21

Hatoum, Mona and Archer, Michael, "Mona Hatoum, Interviewed by Michael Archer, London, 1987", Ed. William Furlong, *Speaking of Art: Four Decades of Art in Conversation*, Side A, pp. 89–92, London / New York, Phaidon, 2010

Lambert-Beatty, Carrie, "Make-Believe: Parafiction and Plausibility", *October*, no. 115, 2009, pp. 51-84

Launchbury, Claire, "Staging Khiam: Documentary, Theater, and Archive in Postwar Lebanon", *Contemporary French and Francophone Studies*, vol. 18, no. 5, 2014, pp. 514–22

Little, Suzanne, "Repeating Repetition", *Performance Research*, vol. 20, no. 5, 2015, pp. 44–50

Lozier, Claire, "Poétique des ruines et traces de l'histoire: Sur 'Quatre heures à Chatila' de Jean Genet", Ed. Nayla Tamraz, *Proceedings of the symposium organised by the Department of French Literature and the Masters in Art Criticism and Curatorial Studies of Saint Joseph University of Beirut on 16 and 17 May 2014*, Beirut, Presses de l'Université Saint-Joseph, 2015, pp. 55–74

Marsaud, Olivia, "Ali Cherri fait frémir le Liban", *Diptyk*, February 2014, p. 26

Moubarak, Samir, "Diffusion de l'image de Beyrouth et configuration de la ville à travers le livre et la presse jusqu'en 1920", Ed. Sylvia AgÉmian, *Regards sur Beyrouth, 160 ans d'images 1800-1960*, Beirut, Musée Sursock, 2013, pp. 39–78

Mourad, Bariaa, "Memory and Identity in Beirut: The (Im) possibilities of Artistic Historiography", Ed. Ronald van de Sompel, *Arts and Culture in Times of Conflict: Contemporary Reflections*, Louven, Mousse Publishing, Museum Leuven, 2014, pp. 44–9

Panero, James, "What is Strange About the Dahesh Museum?" *The New Criterion*, December 2003

Picard, Andréa, "Ali Cherri: Gazing the Catastrophe", *Cinema Scope*, January 2016, pp. 66–9

Polledri, Claudia, "Autopsie de la ville et / ou de l'histoire? Lecture d'une œuvre de Lamia Joreige", Ed. Nayla Tamraz, *Proceedings of the symposium organised by the Department of French Literature and the Masters in Art Criticism and Curatorial Studies of Saint Joseph University of Beirut on 16 and 17 May 2014*, Beirut, Presses de l'Université Saint-Joseph, 2015, pp. 183–200

———, "Photographier la Ville, Interroger L'Histoire", *Contemporary French and Francophone Studies* vol. 18, no. 5, 2014, pp. 542–548

Protzman, Ferdinand, "The Riddle of Dr. Dahesh", *ARTnews*, vol. 95, no. 11, 1996

Renard, Isabelle, "Barthélémy Toguo: Une écriture plastique de l'exil", *Hommes & Migrations*, no. 1301, 2013, pp. 164–66 (Migrations et mondes ruraux)

Richard, Thomas, "Mémoire de guerre et de résistance dans les films libanais", *Contemporary French and Francophone Studies*, vol. 18, no. 5, 2014, pp. 505–13

Rieffel, Véronique, "L'art contemporain arabe: Érotisme ou exotisme?" Eds. Philippe Cardinal and Hoda Makram-Ebeid, *Le corps découvert*, Paris, Hazan / Institut du Monde Arabe, 2012, pp. 122–33

Rogers, Sarah, "Culture '45 and the Rise of Beirut's Contemporary Art Scene", Ed. Apsara DiQuinzio, *Six Lines of Flight: Shifting Geographies in Contemporary Art*, San Francisco, University of California Press, SFMOMA, 2012, pp. 34–43

———, "L'art de l'après-guerre à Beyrouth", *La pensée de midi*, no. 20 - Beyrouth XXIe siècle, 2007, pp. 115–23

———, "Out of History: Postwar Art in Beirut", *Art Journal*, vol. 66, no. 2, 2007, pp. 9–20

———, "The Artist as a Cultural Diplomat: Johnn Ferren in Beirut, 1963–64", *American Art*, vol. 25, no. 1, 2011, pp. 112–23

Sadek, Walid, "Collecting the Uncanny and the Labor of Missing", Eds. Sonja Mejcher-Atassi and John Pedro Schwartz, *Archives, Museums and Collecting Practices in the Modern Arab World*, Farnham, Ashgate, 2012, pp. 211–24

Savatier, Thierry, "Gregory Buchakjian et les immeubles abandonnés de Beyrouth", *Les mauvaises fréquentations*, 27 July 2014

Sayegh, Ghada, "Penser et figurer la guerre comme rupture, Jocelyne Saab et le Nouveau cinéma libanais (1975-1990)", *La Furia Umana*, no. 7, December 2014, pp. 257–70

———, "Devant Les Ruines", *Hors Champ*, November 2017

Scheid, Kirsten, "Necessary Nudes: Hadatha and Mu'asira in the Lives of Modern Lebanese", *International Journal of Middle East Studies*, vol. 42, no. 2, 2010, pp. 203–230

Schneider, Rebecca, "Performance Remains", *Performance Research*, vol. 6, no. 2, 2001, pp. 100–8

Semin, Didier, "Prends garde aux zeppelins… (Notes sur l'exposition 'Partners' à la Haus der Kunst de Munich en 2003)", Ed. Jean-Pierre Criqui, *L'image déjà là, Usages de l'objet trouvé, photographie et cinéma*, Paris, Le Bal, Images en manœuvres, 2011, pp. 150–71 (Les carnets du Bal no. 2)

Silverman, Max, "Entretien avec Joana Hadjithomas et Khalil Joreige: Je veux voir", *Contemporary French and Francophone Studies*, vol. 18, no. 5, 2014, pp. 530–41

Smithson, Robert, "A Tour of the Monuments of Passaic, New Jersey", *Artforum*, December 1967 Republished, Jack Flam (Ed.), *Robert Smithson: The Collected Writings*, Berkeley, Los Angeles, University of California Press, 1996, pp. 68–74

Tamraz, Nayla, "Le Roman Contemporain Libanais et la Guerre : Récit, Histoire, Mémoire", *Contemporary French and Francophone Studies*, vol. 18, no. 5, 2014, pp. 462–9

———, "Pour une lecture de la ruine: Berytus de Rabee Jaber et Attempt 137 to map the drive de Jalal Toufic et Graziella Rizkallah Toufic", Ed. Nayla Tamraz, *Proceedings of the symposium organised by the Department of French Literature and the Masters in Art Criticism and Curatorial Studies of Saint Joseph University of Beirut on 16 and 17 May 2014*, Beirut, Presses de l'Université Saint-Joseph, 2015, pp. 201–21

Tarrab, Joseph, "Le corps du délit", Eds. Philippe Cardinal and Hoda Makram-Ebeid, *Le corps découvert*, Paris, Hazan, Institut du Monde Arabe, 2012, pp. 36–47

Thomas, Kelly Devine, "The Dahesh Enigma", *ARTnews*, vol. 102, no. 9, 2003

Wilson-Goldie, Kaelen, "Always Struggle with the Object, Always Rewrite the World", *South Magazine*, November 2015
———, "City Limits", *The Review*, 23 April 2009
———, "In Focus: Marwa Arsanios", *Frieze*, March 2013
———, "On the Politics of Art and Space in Beirut", *Nafas*, August 2009

Wright, Stephen, "Tel un espion dans l'époque qui naît: La situation de l'artiste à Beyrouth aujourd'hui", *Parachute*, no. 108, 2002, pp. 13–31

Yacoub, Paola, "Holiday Inn Cycle", Eds. Wolfgang Petritsch and Vedran Dzihic, *Conflict and Memory: Bridging Past and Future in [South East] Europe*, Baden Baden, Nomos, 2010, pp. 143–53

Yacoub, Paola and Lasserre, Michel, "A brief Journey towards Scepticism", Ed. Suzanne Cotter, *Out of Beirut*, Oxford, JRP|Ringier, Modern Art Oxford, 2007, pp. 9–10

4.c. Dissertations and theses

Chelala, Mira, "Textile et guerre", Masters dissertation, Paris, École Nationale Supérieure des Arts Appliqués et des Métiers d'Art (ENSAAMA) Olivier de Serres, 2015

de le Court, Isabelle, "A Tale of Two Cities: Post-Traumatic Art in Post-War Sarajevo and Beirut in Cross-Cultural Perspectives", doctoral thesis, Leeds, The University of Leeds School of Fine Art, History of Art and Cultural Studies, 2012

Polledri, Claudia, "Photographier la ville, penser l'histoire : Beyrouth dans la représentation photographique artistique contemporaine", doctoral thesis, Montréal, Université de Montréal, 2015

Sayegh, Ghada, "Images d'après : L'espace-temps de la guerre dans le cinéma au Liban, du 'nouveau cinéma libanais'(1975) aux pratiques artistiques contemporaines (de 1990 à nos jours)", doctoral thesis, Paris, Université Paris Ouest Nanterre la Défense, 2013

Wilson-Goldie, Kaelen, "Digging for Fire: Contemporary Art Practices in Postwar Lebanon", Master's dissertation, Beirut, Center for Arab and Middle Eastern Studies of the Faculty of Art and Sciences at the American University of Beirut, 2005

5. PERSONAL ACCOUNTS, MEMOIRS, BIOGRAPHIES, FICTION

5.a. Works

Abdel Samad, Nada, *Wadi Abou Jamil, Qissas an Yahoud Bayrout*, (Wadi Abou Jmil, Stories of Beirut's Jews) Beirut, Dar An-Nahar, 2009.

Abirached, Zeina, *Beyrouth Catharsis*,,Paris, Cambourakis,22006
———, *Je me souviens, Beyrouth*, Paris, Cambourakis, 200
———, *Mourir partir revenir : Le jeu des hirondelles*, Paris, Cambourakis, 2007

Aburish, Said K., *The St. George Hotel Bar*, London, Bloomsbury, 1989

Accad, Evelyne, *Coquelicot du massacre*, Paris, L'Harmattan, 2000

Alia, Josette, *Quand le soleil était chaud*, Paris, Grasset & Fasquelle, 1992

Al Zaib, Mohammad, *Lawhât al-ghadr, Lawhât al-tha'r*, Beirut, Dar al Farabi, 1986

Arvieux, Laurent d', *Mémoires du chevalier d'Arvieux, envoyé extraordinaire du Roy à la Porte, consul d'Alep, d'Alger, de Tripoli et autres Échelles du Levant: Contenant ses voyages à Constantinople, dans l'Asie, la Syrie, la Palestine, l'Égypte et la Barbarie..., T, 6 / recueillis... de ses Mémoires originaux et mis en ordre par le R. P. Jean-Baptiste Labat...* Paris, C. J. B. Delespine, 1735

Awwad, Tawfiq Yusuf, *Death in Beirut*, Trans. Leslie McLaughlin, Washington, Three Continents Press, 1984

Ballard, J. G.;*High Rise*, London, Jonathan Cape, 1975

Beydoun, Ahmad, *Le Liban: Itinéraires dans une guerre incivile*, Paris / Amman / Beirut, Karthala, Centre d'études et de recherches sur le Moyen-Orient contemporain, 1993 (Hommes et sociétés)

Bustros, Nicolas de, *Je me souviens*, Beirut, Librairie Antoine, 1983

Corm, Charles, *La montagne inspirée*, 3rd edition, 1987, Beirut, Éditions de la Revue Phénicienne, 1934

Chalandon, Sorj, *Le quatrième mur*, Paris, Grasset & Fasquelle, 2013

Duplan, Nathalie and Raulin Valérie, *Le cèdre et la croix: Jocelyne Khoueiry, une femme de combats*, Paris, Presses de la Renaissance, 2005

Farley, James Lewis, *Two Years in Syria*, London, Saunders and Otley, 1858

Golia, Maria, *Cairo, City of Sand*, London, Reaktion Books, 2004

Guys, Henri, *Beyrout le Liban: Relation d'un séjour de plusieurs années dans ce pays*, T. I, Paris, Comon Éditeur, 1850

Hachem, Nayla, *Beyrouth, comme si l'oubli*, Lunay, Zellige, 2012

Henry, Paul-Marc, *Les jardiniers de l'enfer*, Paris, Olivier Orban, 1984

Jaber, Rabee, *Berytus, une ville sous terre*, Paris, Gallimard, 2009

Kessel, Joseph, *En Syrie*, Paris, Gallimard, 2014 [1926] (Folio)

Majdalani, Charif, *Le Dernier Seigneur de Marsad*, Paris, Seuil, 2013
———, *Villa des femmes*, Paris, Seuil, 2015

Massabki, Jacqueline and Porel, François, *La mémoire des cèdres*, Paris, Robert Laffont, 1989

Michaud, Joseph François and Poujoulat, Jean Joseph François, *Correspondance d'Orient: 1830 - 1831*, T. VI, Paris, Ducollet, 1835

Morand, Paul, *Journal d'un attaché d'ambassade (1916-1917)*, New edition, with an introduction and notes by Michel Collomb, 1997, Paris, Gallimard, 1948

Nasr, Gaby, *Guerroyons*, Beirut, FMA, 1985

Pagès, de, Pierre-Marie-François, Monsieur, *Travels Round the World, in the Years 1767, 1768, 1769, 1770, 1771, By Monsieur de Pagés, ... Translated from the French*, London, J. Murray, 1791,

Pamuk, Orhan, *The Museum of Innocence*, trans. Maureen Freely, London, Faber, 2009

Perthuis, Madame de, *Voyages en Orient, 1853-1855, 1860-1862, Journal de la Comtesse de Perthuis, Manuscrit inédit découvert par Fouad Debbas*, Beirut, Dar An-Nahar, 2007

Pringuey, Roland, *Quarante ans de vie au Liban*, Beirut, FMA, 1996

Randal, Jonathan, *The Tragedy of Lebanon*, London, Chattoo & Windus, 198

Rayes, Gabriel and Rayes Ingea, Tania, *Beyrouth, le centre-ville de mon père*, Beirut, Éditions le la Revue Phénicienne, 2011

Rohe, Oliver, *Terrain vague*, Paris, Allia, 2005
———, *Un peuple en petit*, Paris, Gallimard, 2009

Sacco, Joe, *Palestine*, London, Jonathan Cape, 2003

Seurat, Marie, *Un si proche Orient*, Paris, Grasset & Fasquelle, 1991

Tueni, Nadia, *La Prose, œuvres complètes*, Beirut, Dar an-Nahar, 1986

Wallet, Bernard, *Paysage avec palmiers*, Paris, Gallimard, 1992

Ziadé, Lamia, *Bye Bye Babylone: Beyrouth 1975-1979*, Paris, Denoël, 2010 (Graphic)
———, *Ô nuit Ô mes yeux: Le Caire / Beyrouth / Damas / Jérusalem*, Paris, P.O.L., 2015

5.b. Artists' books

Buchakjian, Gregory (text) and Baalbaki, Saïd (lithographs), *Wadi Abou Jmil*, Berlin, printed by Steffen Tschesno , 2015

Cachard, Valérie (text) and Baalbaki, Saïd (lithographs), *Nos* âmes *en chantier*, Berlin, printed by Steffen Tschesno, 2015

5.c. Articles, book chapters, conference paper

Bassil, Zeina and Buchakjian, Gregory, "Les maisons abandonnées de Beyrouth", *Samandal*, no. 17, 2015, pp. 73–85 (Géographie)

Charara, Waddah, "Journal de G. S., "Déplacée de guerre", Eds. Franck Mermier and Christophe Varin, *Mémoires de guerres au Liban, 1975-1990*, Arles, Actes Sud / Sindbad, 2010, pp. 409–40 (La bibliothèque arabe)

Cobban, Helena, "The Rahmeh Building", *New Statesman*, 14 July 1981.

Di Giovanni, Janine, "Give Me Shelter", *Travel + Leisure Magazine*, June 2012

Garfield, Mark, "Beirut Diary", *Middle East Research and Information Project (MERIP) Reports*, no. 108/109, 1982, pp. 8-10 (The Lebanon War)

Kenny, Timothy, "The Siege of Sarajevo, July 1992", *The Kenyon Review* XXXIV, no. 3, 2012

Toufic, Jalal, *Jouissance in Postwar Beirut*, 2014

ACKNOWLEDGEMENTS

Gregory Buchakjian, Valérie Cachard and Nour Salamé would like to thank for their decisive involvement in this project:

Jean-Yves Andrieux
Zeina Arida
Marc Baroud
Zeina Bassil
Stephanie Cachard
Wassim Chemaitilly
Sandra Dagher
Ariane Delacampagne
Raed Charaf
Marc Dibeh
Nada Habis-Assi
Malek Hosni
Karina Helou
Sary Moussa
Camille Tarazi
Serge Yared

In addition to those who shared their stories - and are mentioned on pp. 218-220 - they express their gratitude to Amanda Abi Khalil, Zeina Abirached, Claudine Abdelmassih, Nathalie et Ghazi Abou Jaoudé, Philippe Acar, Joelle Achkar, Yara Lucia Afram-Boustany, Maya Akiki, Carla Aouad, Catherine Ariss, Naji Assi, Tina Azar, Saïd Baalbaki, Kevork Baboyan, Saleh Barakat, Ala Bassil, Romy Bechara, Nabil Beyhum, Alexandra Bitar, Irène Buchakjian, Sarkis Buchakjian, Sandra Bsaibes, Lea Casini, Dalia Chabarek, Joe Chalhoub, Mira Chelala, Dominique Chouchani, Yannick Clément, Krystel Comaty, Clémence Cottard, Catherine David, Michael F. Davie, Karina et Gilles Debs, Amanda Dufour, Fouad Elkoury, Christina Farah, Paola Gemayel, Véronique Gerard-Powell, Gisèle Ghanem, Carla Habib, Elena Habre, Rana Haddad, Joana Hadjithomas, Pierre Hage-Boutros, Youssef Haïdar, Mona Hallak, Sarah Hatem, Nour Hifaoui, Tamara Hosni, Tatiana Hosni Richa, Sarah Huneidi, Mayssa Jallad, Karim Joreige, Khalil Joreige, Georges Karam, Patrick Kassardjian, Maria Katchadourian, Karen Keyrouz, Manal Khader, Lina Kiryakos, Maria Klat, Karen Klink, Ghassan Kotait, Nanar Kradjian, Diala Lteif, Romy Makdessi, Sara Makdessi, Aline Manoukian, Carla Mardini, Carel Marsouanian, Carlo Massoud, Leonardo Matossian, Caroline Moarbes-Asseily, Rayya Morcos, Laetitia Mourad, Karen Murad, Layal Nakhlé, Karen Nassar, Rania Naufal, Anastasia Nysten, Hrant Ourgandjian, Josephine Parenthou, Nora Razian, Louma Salamé, François Sargologo, Thierry Savatier, Ibrahim Suleiman, Caroline Tabet, Nayla Tamraz, Taline Ter Minassian, Josiane Torbey, Sasha Ussef and Sonia Wansa Hanna.

Their thanks are also addressed to the following institutions: the Lebanese Academy of Fine Arts (Académie Libanaise des Beaux-Arts – Alba) – University of Balamand, the Doctoral School 6 at Université Paris IV, the Oriental Library at Saint Joseph University, the Sursock Museum and the Villa Empain - Boghossian Foundation

ABANDONED DWELLINGS
A HISTORY OF BEIRUT

Book edited by:
Valérie Cachard

Design:
-scope Ateliers
Color separations and scans:
-scope Ateliers
Proofreading of texts in English:
Ros Schwartz

Printed and bound in Belgium

First edition, 2018

ISBN 978-614-8035-11-1
(English Edition)

Credits et courtesies:
The Abraaj Group Art Prize, Dubai: FIG. 28
Académie Libanaise des Beaux-Arts (Alba) – University of Balamand: FIG. 63, 66, 93, 104
Agial Art Gallery and Saleh Barakat Gallery, Beirut: FIG. 42, 44, 47, 48, 52, 74, 86, 92
Alexander and Bonin, New York: FIG. 94
An-Nahar: FIG. 35, 51
Archivio Gabriele Basilico, Milan: FIG. 65
Bibliothèque nationale de France, Paris: FIG. 4
Myriam Boulos: FIG. 107
Yannick Clément: FIG. 21
Collection Dr Eugène Cottard. Courtesy of the Arab Image Foundation, Beirut: FIG. 5
Collection Philippe Jabre: FIG. 1, 3
Contact Press Images: FIG. 41
Denoël, Paris: FIG. 25
Directorate General of Antiquities, Beirut: FIG. 67
DW5 Bernard Khoury, Beirut: FIG. 13
École nationale supérieure des arts appliqués et des métiers d'art (Ensaama), Paris: FIG. 97
Éditions Cambourakis, Paris: FIG. 57, 58
Éditions P.O.L., Paris: FIG. 36
Éditions du Cyprès, Paris: FIG. 11
Galeri Nev Istanbul: FIG. 33, 34
Galerie Imane Farès, Paris: FIG. 17
Hugo Glendinning: FIG. 37
Green Art Gallery, Dubai: FIG. 33, 34
Joe Hayeck: FIG. 66
Mohammad El Hasan Jaber: FIG. 13
Agop Kanledjian: FIG. 39, 92, 103
La Revue du Liban: FIG. 61
L'Orient-Le Jour: FIG. 40
Magnum Photos: FIG. 27, 46, 78
Maison Tarazi, Beirut: FIG. 106
Ministère du Tourisme, Beirut: FIG. 30
Mind the Gap, Beirut: FIG. 12
Nadi Lekol Nas: FIG. 6, 20
Paula Cooper Gallery, New York: FIG. 102
Stefan Rohner: FIG. 94
Saradar Collection, Beirut: FIG. 39, 101, 103, 110
Hady Sy: FIG. 95
Eric Tschernow: FIG. 98
Université Saint-Joseph, Bibliothèque orientale, Beirut: FIG. 35, 40, 51, 61
White Cube, Londres: FIG. 37
Jamie Woodley: FIG. 69
Rana Zaher: FIG. 49

Published by:

KAPH
ART BOOKS FROM THE MIDDLE EAST

Park View building
Mina el Hosn
Solidere, Beirut
Lebanon
Tel. +961 3 601 123
Fax. +961 1 999 068
www.kaphbooks.com

Our books are distributed by:

Les Presses du Réel
(France, Belgium, Switzerland and Luxembourg)
www.lespressesdureel.com

Idea Books (rest of the world)
www.ideabooks.nl

This publication benefits the generous support of SGBL and of Marwan T. Assaf

Published under the Publication Assistance Program Georges Schéhadé, it also benefits support from the Ministry of Europe and Foreign Affairs and from the Cooperation and Cultural Action Department of the French Embassy

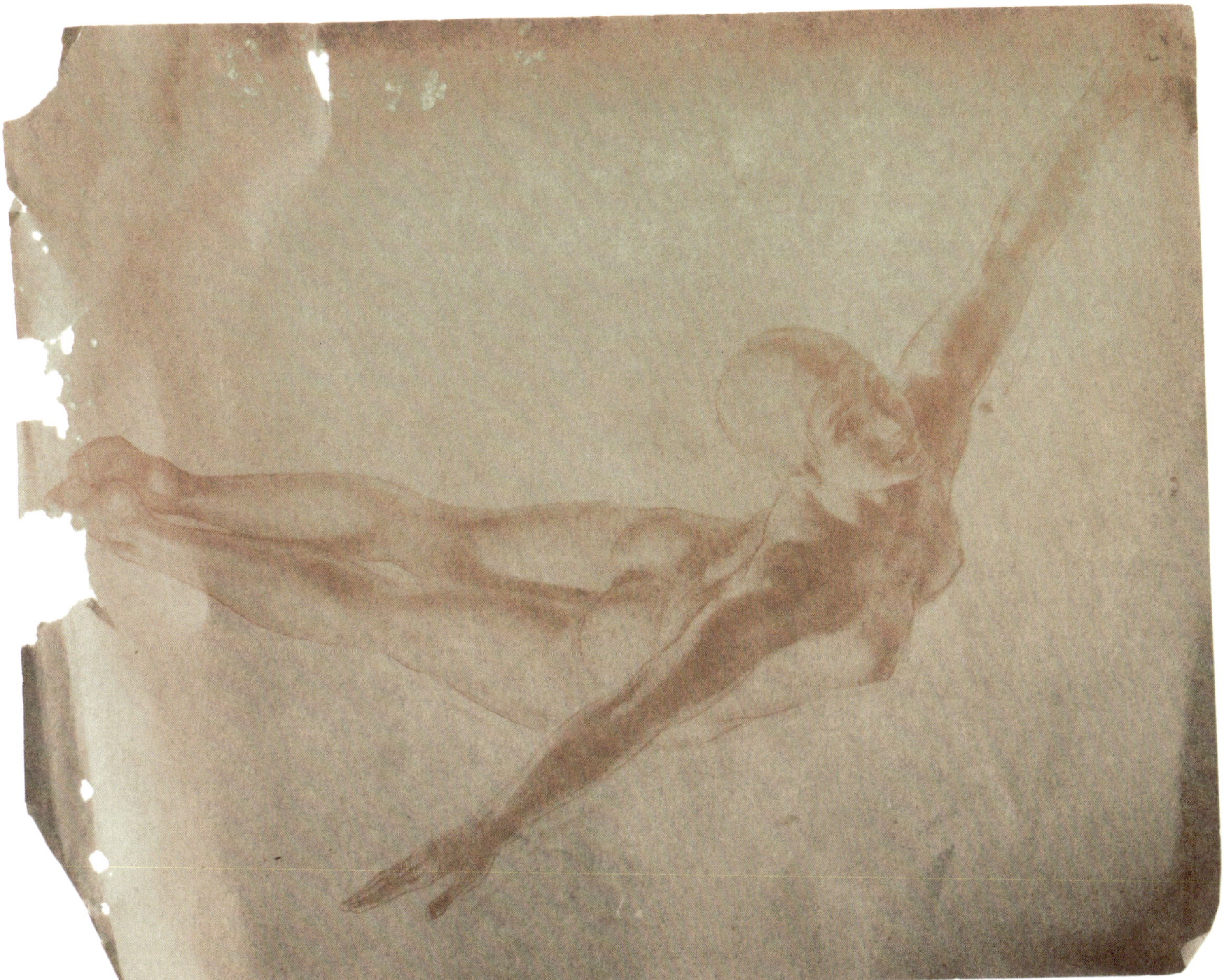

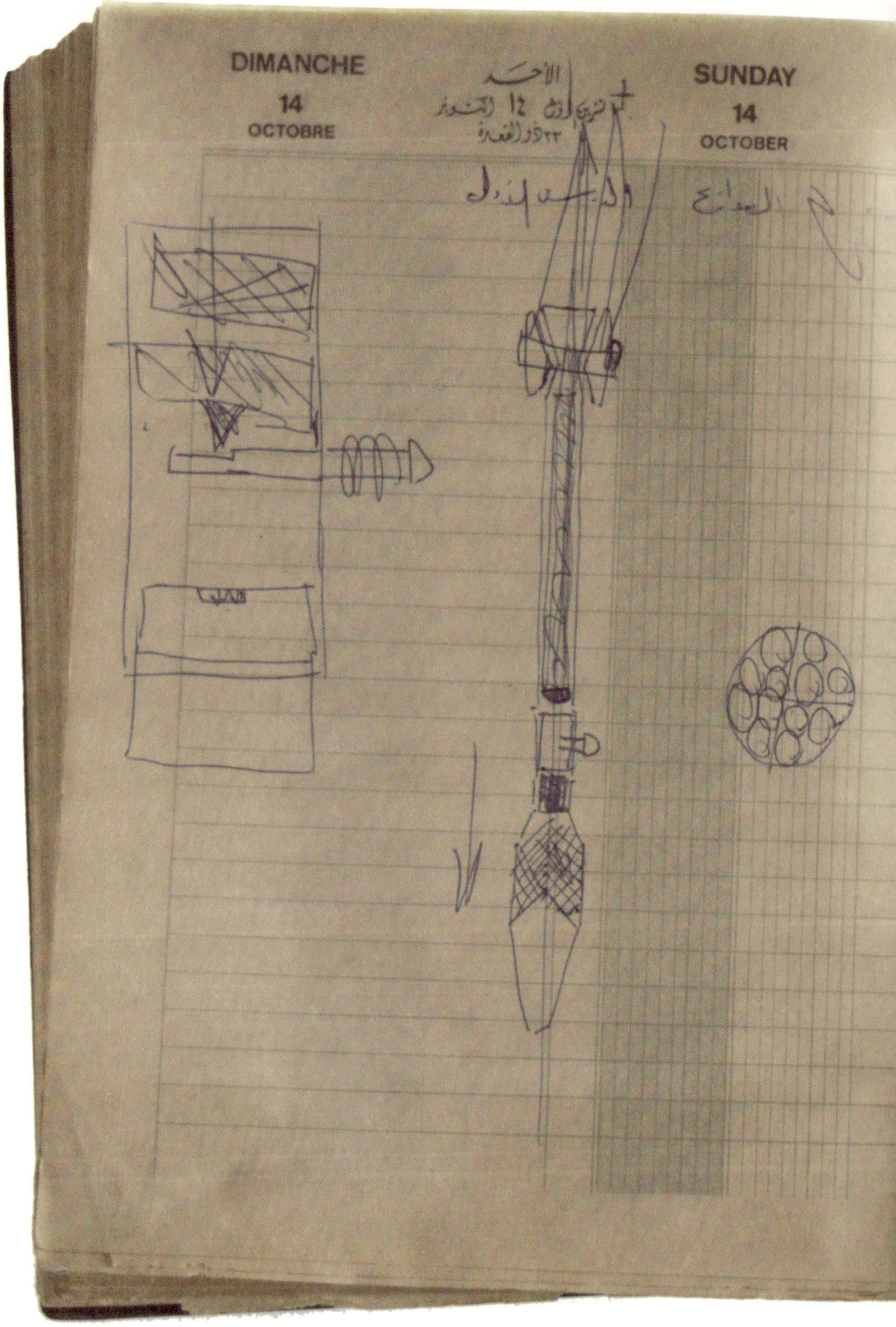
DIMANCHE
14
OCTOBRE
SUNDAY
14
OCTOBER

LUNDI 15 OCTOBRE

الاثنين
تشرين أول ١٥ اكتوبر
٢٤ ذو القعدة

MONDAY 15 OCTOBER

205

LEITZ 4720 (124/o)
DBP